Janette Oke: *A Heart for the Prairie*

Janette Oke:
A Heart for the Prairie

Laurel Oke Logan

The story of one of the most beloved novelists of our time

Published by Bethany House Publishers
A Ministry of Bethany Fellowship International
11400 Hampshire Avenue South
Bloomington, Minnesota 55438

Printed in the United States of America

ISBN 0-7394-1945-5

This book is lovingly dedicated to my mother
for all the things she is to me
that can't be put into words,
and to my father, Edward Oke,
whom I have always respected greatly
and who is also my friend.

LAUREL OKE LOGAN is a wife, mother, and writer. Her most recent effort is the novel *Dana's Valley*, coauthored with her mother. The only daughter and youngest of Janette and Edward, Laurel grew up in a small town on the Canadian prairie with her three brothers. This biography of her mother has its origins in the charming little farmhouse that belonged to Laurel's grandparents. In this country home Laurel learned as a child to treasure the heritage, simple values, and family ties that shaped the life of Janette Oke.

Laurel and her mother spent many hours laughing and crying together as they researched their family roots and checked facts for this biography. Laurel and her husband, Marvin, have four children and make their home in Indiana.

Preface

Have you ever been captivated by an old house? Maybe it peeked out from the front lane, drawing your imagination past the overgrown shrubbery, down a long abandoned path toward the front door as if calling you to follow. And you wondered what it must have been like when the home was young and bustling with family life.

I know about that kind of home. As a child I spent many days visiting my grandparents' farm. The little house had grayed with the years of rain and snow, the porch stooped, and the kitchen floor creaked and bowed with age, but in my mind it still keeps the magical air only childhood can give.

In this little house I learned the importance of simple values and family ties. I watched laughter, tears, and various personalities adjusting to and enjoying one another in very close quarters. I listened to discussions about death, politics, religion, and love—all while the participants, intent on a simple game of Rook, were unaware that young ears took it all in. And I learned the importance of the spirit of community that made life bearable during the lean years on the prairie.

My family is more to me than a list of names, and I treasure the heritage that was carved out by those who came before me. As I grew first to love those in my home and then the members of my extended family, I can say with my whole heart that I am proud to be counted among them.

In doing the research for this book, I have learned even more about the clan. Clearly, the hand of God has been at work through the generations, and it's this discovery that I hope to be able to pass on to my own family and to Janette Oke's readers.

I have also learned a great deal more about her, my mother. I am amazed that someone so close to me could have held so many surprises. I sat talking with her for hours, read many things that she has written about her own life and not published, and also pored over letters she wrote years ago.

One truth about her came as no surprise. The basic desire of my mother is to find God's will and then to do it. Time and time again she has searched for her answer—and always found it.

Now, when I look into the shining, inquisitive eyes of my own children, I am struck by how different their lives would be if my parents and grandparents had not learned to place their trust in God. I may never know the true impact a Christian heritage has made in my life and in the lives of my children. I was taught morals, self-discipline, generosity, and selfless love. And I believe that my family's prayers for us have already had a tremendous effect on our lives, like an umbrella of protection. These treasures far outlast any other family inheritance.

Of course my family is not without its "skeletons in the closet." We don't claim to be perfect, and it's not my purpose here to burden readers with every detail of our lives. But I hope the history contained in these pages will be enjoyable and, if God chooses to use it, an inspiration to continue in the faith—for our own welfare as well as for our children's.

To truly understand ourselves, it often helps to understand our family roots. Due to the efforts of many in my mother's family, particularly those of her sister Sharon Fehr, we have a fairly complete account of family history. It is easy to see how these people and their faith have helped to shape my mother, and it is a great privilege to offer this account of her life to you.

My mother and I know that it is likely that many readers will not have come from a Christian home. And some will know little about their own particular family tree. Even though none of us can go back and change anything that lies behind, we can begin afresh as the ancestors-to-be of our own families. We can choose values and a lifestyle that our children will first observe and then determine whether or not to follow. It is an awesome responsibility and the only truly lasting legacy.

Contents

CHAPTER ONE

The Steeves Family

ON A BRISK FEBRUARY morning, seven-year-old Jean Steeves huddled under the quilts of her shared bed, tucked snugly between her sisters. Fingers of cold searching for exposed skin had roused her. On any other morning, she could have wiggled closer to Betty for warmth and fallen back to sleep, but on this day the crispness of the morning air was broken by a strange cry, and she stirred.

"Betty, wake up," she nudged her sister. "What's that?"

Nine-year-old Betty turned away and mumbled, "It's just an old tomcat."

Jean tried to settle back to sleep, but the weak cry came again.

"That's a baby," she insisted, scrambling over Betty and across the cold floor. "Mom's got a new baby!"

Betty crawled out after her sister, trying not to wake little June, who still slept soundly, oblivious to Jean's excitement. The two girls slipped out of the bedroom to discover that Jean had been right. In the living room they saw that a rocker had been pulled close to the heater-fire, and a small bundle lay cradled in their Aunt Leone's arms.

"Her name is Janette," Leone whispered in answer to their excited questions.

"Can I hold her?" each girl begged.

"Not right now. She's not a very strong baby. And we need to be pretty careful with her for a while," Leone explained, choosing her

STEEVES FAMILY

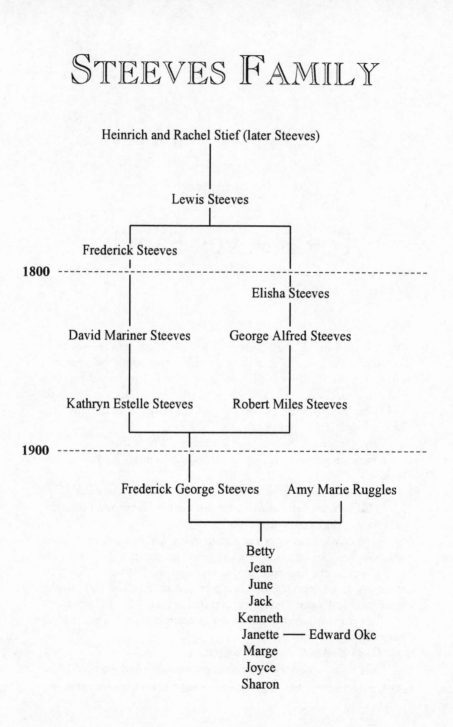

Heinrich and Rachel Stief (later Steeves)

Lewis Steeves

Frederick Steeves

1800 -

Elisha Steeves

David Mariner Steeves   George Alfred Steeves

Kathryn Estelle Steeves   Robert Miles Steeves

1900 -

Frederick George Steeves   Amy Marie Ruggles

Betty
Jean
June
Jack
Kenneth
Janette —— Edward Oke
Marge
Joyce
Sharon

words cautiously. In truth, there were several furrowed brows at the sight of the sickly infant. Even as the older sisters reveled in the discovery of baby Janette, their mother wept alone, struggling with the possibility of losing her new daughter.

Though this young woman had only recently discovered a personal faith in God, scattered across the Canadian prairie that surrounded her stood home after home of those who knew the power of God firsthand.

As the news of the newborn traveled on, aunts, uncles, grandparents, and neighbors were praying fervently for the tiny addition to Fred and Amy Steeves' family. Earnest tears were shed on her behalf, and each prayer reached the attentive ear of the Father.

During the next few months, Janette's little body did gradually gain strength and health, and the prayers for her changed to words of thankfulness.

As she grew, Janette learned by observation that the lives of the family members around her were woven closely together with the values they upheld. Church, faith, and God were a part of her everyday world and conversation.

What Janette did not know was that this family had not always held such strong convictions about the One whom they now considered Lord. Though a thread of faith ran from generation to generation, each member had come to his or her own decision about building upon or rejecting the foundation that had its beginnings hundreds of years before.

Janette's parents, Fred Steeves and Amy Ruggles Steeves, were simple folk—prairie farmers like many of the characters in her stories—and had descended from two long lines of colorful people.

On one side of the family tree, Fred's family had flourished near the shores of the Canadian east coast until his own father had chosen to travel west. Amy had been born in the United States, and over the course of time, her family had also arrived in the wide spaces of the Canadian prairie, searching for productive land and a place to call home.

When Fred moved to Alberta as a young boy, his family left behind an amazing number of relatives. In fact, a remark concerning the

Steeves clan is that "it is more than a family—it's a nation!"

It was in 1766 that the first Steeves family—"Stief" back then—came to settle in Eastern Canada, and their descendants soon numbered in the thousands. In fact, about forty years ago Esther Clark Wright, a family historian, estimated the number to be between fifty and one hundred thousand. And, of course, Mrs. Wright was not including the generations that followed the publication of her work.

The Steeves family emigrated from Germany, seemingly to find freedom of worship. Although the family is uncertain as to when Heinrich and Rachel Stief came to North America, records show that in Pennsylvania on January 27, 1766, Heinrich signed an agreement with John Hughes, an entrepreneur of dubious intent. With the weight of this momentous decision heavy upon him, Heinrich prepared to uphold his end of the bargain. He would sail to what was then Nova Scotia and settle with his family in the Petitcodiac River area.

According to *Samphire Greens*, a book published by Esther Clark Wright about the history of the Steeves family, Mr. Hughes' part of the agreement was to give each settler one lot in a town that was to be built, as well as "two hundred acres of good land for every family of five Protestant persons." Further stipulations were made as to how the land was to be developed and farmed by the settlers, and the payment terms specified.

On June 20, 1766, Heinrich and Rachel stood on deck with their seven sons and watched as the docks of Philadelphia faded from sight. The Delaware River stretched on ahead of them, and as the ship entered the salty waters of Delaware Bay it swayed rhythmically with the waves. Tree-lined hills flattened into broad marshes, and soon, rounding the point of Cape May, the great Atlantic Ocean swelled before them.

Lewis Stief, the youngest son, gazed in awe at the vastness of the rolling waters. He had no memory of his family's voyage across this mighty ocean several years before. The America they left behind burned with the growing fever of revolution, but what lay ahead held dangers of its own—even *his* young mind understood some of that. But a glance toward his father and older brothers, who seemed so tall and strong, filled him with courage. Even the cold wind that cut against his face could not drive the excitement from him.

The ship sailed north to the Bay of Fundy, pointing like a broad, muddy finger out of the Atlantic Ocean, stretching upward past the coast of Maine and separating what is now New Brunswick from Nova Scotia. Famous for its extreme tides, navigation of the bay and the streams that feed it is very difficult. Ships caught in it while the tide is going out are gradually lowered fifty feet, sometimes becoming mired in the muddy floor until the ocean once again washes in to flood the area.

Into this basin sailed the ship carrying young Lewis and his family. They continued on to the northernmost stretch of Chignecto Bay and into the Petitcodiac River mouth. Here the swells churned as the rising tidal waters crashed against the flow of the river, driving it back in the direction from which it had come.

Few settlers had yet entered this wild countryside, but its beauty and natural bounty would cause many to follow. The rolling hills of the coastal areas, covered with pine and spruce, gradually changed, ridge upon ridge, to the inland mountains where oak, maple, ash, and birch sheltered thriving animal life. Deer, rabbits, and game birds were plentiful, and Atlantic salmon could be pulled from most streams and rivers. The land itself offered lumber aplenty, along with spacious areas for cattle to thrive and abundant rainfall for crops and gardens.

Even with the bounty of the land, these new settlers were very uncertain about the impending winter. John Hughes had promised a ship bringing supplies, and they watched the bay intently.

Many nights found Heinrich gazing at the water and praying earnestly in his German mother tongue for God's provision for his family and their new neighbors. He had made the decision to sail to Canada, believing it was God's direction for his family, and now his own faith was being tested. Would God provide?

During the anxious weeks of waiting, turnips and a swamp green called samphire were reportedly their main source of sustenance. Then God provided His own means of help from an unexpected source, proving once again that He is faithful.

The solution actually had its beginnings ten years previously when the area around Monckton township, the land the Steeves family now occupied, had been settled by a group of Frenchmen known as the Acadians. After England claimed the land and expelled these French settlers in 1755, a scattered remnant remained hidden deep in the forests.

The story continues that one day an Acadian named Belliveau appeared cautiously from the woods. Apparently he had recognized that the settlers needed help and, after making certain that they did not speak English and were not a threat, felt he could risk coming to their much needed aid.

This man taught them how to snare rabbits and other game, to make maple syrup, and to kill shad and salmon in the shallow river waters when the tide had ebbed. With the skills needed to survive in their new environment and increasing confidence that they could conquer this land, the settlers began to establish themselves, successfully working the land to meet their families' needs.

Eventually, Heinrich Stief anglicized his name, becoming Henry Steeves. His sons married and spread across the area on farms of their own.

Of these descendants, perhaps the best known is William Henry Steeves, a fourth-generation Steeves and one of the Canadian Fathers of Confederation. There is a famous Canadian painting by Robert Harris of the dark-suited, dignified gentlemen who bound the provinces of Canada into Confederation. Here William stands, on the left, proudly representing his province of New Brunswick. In the community of Hillsborough, where he has been honored, his house stands as a museum. Though we cannot claim his parentage, as he came through the line of Heinrich's son Henry while we descended from Lewis, we appreciate this distant connection to Canadian history.

In the early years of settlement life, while the local population was still small, intermarrying was quite common. Two of Heinrich's great-great-grandchildren married on June 22, 1896. Robert Steeves was the son of farmers, but to this trade Bob added the skills of carpenter, blacksmith, and handyman. His distant cousin Kathryn Steeves was orphaned at the age of eleven and went to live with an older sister who had married a judge. The little sister was given the best that life could offer. She was educated, refined, and lacked nothing. Trained as a teacher, Kathryn spent some years in the occupation.

After their marriage, Bob built a beautiful three-story house that looked out over the gentle slope of fields in Elgin, New Brunswick, and planted fruit trees for Kathryn in the big farmyard. A covered porch opened into the large entry where he worked long hours to build an elegant, wooden stairway. A kitchen, parlor, spare room, and dining room—embellished with a bay window and butler's pantry—completed the main floor. A second covered porch graced the kitchen's entry from the yard.

Six bedrooms were scattered around the second-floor landing and another staircase led to a large, floored attic. It was a home worthy of the woman for whom Bob built it.

Robert and Kathryn's first son, Carl, arrived shortly after their first anniversary. Three years later a beautiful daughter, Julia, became the apple of her father's eye. Horace followed two years after Julia and in the next year, Fred, who would be Janette's father. A second girl, Evelyn, was born in 1905 and was followed in 1906 by their fourth son, Jack, bringing the number to six.

When baby Jack was not yet a year, tragedy struck the Steeves family. In February 1907, whooping cough spread among the children. Kathryn was forced to call a neighbor woman for help in caring for her sick little ones.

The large house echoed with their fevered cries. Kathryn rushed from one child to the next. Soon baby Jack had the added complication of pneumonia, and the tired mother focused her attention on her weak infant. Only little Evelyn seemed untouched.

For this small child, the house seemed to be a foreign place. Rooms once echoing with laughter were now hushed and somber. Evelyn longed to find someone to play with, and wandered through the quiet bedrooms filled with feverish bodies until she discovered Fred.

This four-year-old brother, whom the family had lovingly dubbed "Buster," lay in a cold sweat, his body drained of strength from fighting the illness. Evelyn reached for his exposed arm and patted it gently.

"Poor Ba," she whispered. "Poor Ba."

But soon Evelyn also had fallen ill, and Kathryn was forced to turn over the nursing of her toddler to the capable neighbor lady. It was necessary for her to remain with baby Jack for most of the long hours.

One morning as Kathryn brushed past the other woman who was holding a weakened Evelyn, the chubby arms reached out for her and the tiny eyes searched for her attention. Though Kathryn longed to take the little girl into her arms, she knew she could not take precious time away from her other nursing duties.

It was the last time she saw little Evelyn alive. In the next few moments, the small body succumbed to the illness, and she was gone.

Kathryn struggled with the guilt of that last glimpse and pain of losing her precious little girl. The child was laid in a grave near their wonderful home, but much of the joy it held seemed to have left with tiny Evelyn. Daily routines were empty, laughter less easily achieved, though one by one each of the other children returned to health.

Bob, too, was having great difficulty dealing with the death of Evelyn. Reminders of her were everywhere—the places she had played and the times she had watched him work, filling his ears with her happy chatter. It was as if he were haunted by the joys she had brought to their home.

The following winter, Janette's grandfather Bob escaped those painful reminders by accepting an opportunity to manage a large ranch in Clear Lake, Alberta, which had an absentee owner.

Soon Kathryn received word that Bob wanted the family to follow. The work of packing their household possessions followed, and at last it was time for the final trip down the worn lane, away from the lovely home they'd enjoyed for ten years.

How difficult it must have been for Kathryn as she stood for the last time at little Evelyn's grave to bid her farewell. But she was forced to turn away and join the family she now must see safely to Alberta—hundreds and hundreds of miles away.

Kathryn had many difficult days adapting to her new life. She had left behind her friends, her beautiful home, a lifestyle she loved, and the grave of her fifth child—in exchange for open prairie, isolation, and the hard work of a pioneer woman.

But Kathryn was a determined woman and kept the standards for her family high. She insisted on raising them in cultured style, as a lady and gentlemen, despite the rugged prairie life they endured. Etiquette, education, and many dreams went into the rearing of them. Her greatest hope was that her sons would become fine men, perhaps doctors or lawyers. And to this hope she clung.

Four years of living and farming on the prairie passed slowly, with frequent moves from one ranch to another. As a hired worker, Bob was unable to immediately replace the exceptional home the family had known. But in 1911, when their eldest child, Carl, was fourteen, Bob moved the family to a homestead at Yetwood, Alberta.

The move brought mixed emotions. For Bob it was a wonderful feeling to once again work his own land, but upon surveying the eight-by-fourteen-foot granary that was to be their home until the new house could be completed, Kathryn could not share his enthusiasm. Far removed from the comfortable life she had known, she shuddered at the work that lay ahead of her.

However, in rather short order, Bob had completed a second house. Here the family added two more children, Ralph and Walter. The large home became the Yetwood post office, and the Steeves traveled by team twice weekly into the town of Champion, fifty miles round trip, to pick up and deliver the Yetwood mail.

Bob also established himself with a small community store. But later, when the Depression hit, even the store was lost, and again Kathryn found herself teaching school in order to help support the family.

Days were long and busy for Kathryn. Supper would be needed on the table shortly after she had arrived home from her teaching position, and there were many other household chores that would need her attention. And Walter, her youngest child, was only three years old, far from independence from his mother.

The fact that Julia was quickly approaching womanhood and could carry a woman's share of the work at home was a great help. But on the heels of Julia's achievements in womanly skills, Kathryn knew marriage would soon follow. Then Julia would be leaving to begin a home of her own.

And Kathryn was correct. Julia was courted and won by a young man named Bernard Gray. Kathryn was pleased—but the empty kitchen that greeted her when she returned home haunted her. Her boys rushed in and out of the house, but there was no daughter with whom to share the burden of a woman's work and the pleasure of women's conversation.

When word came months later that Julia had fallen ill, the family was fearful. The flu epidemic of that year had been quite severe, and Julia, especially, was in danger. The life of the child she carried was threatened by a premature birth, and Julia's body had already weakened from her illness.

After fighting many hours, the tiny infant arrived, and died shortly afterward. Dark days followed when Julia also succumbed to the disease. The grief of her young widower punctuated the family's own heartache, and there were few dry eyes at the funeral service. Family members and neighbors alike felt the pain of such bitter loss and wept for the young wife and mother who lay in the coffin, cradling her tiny infant in her arms.

Fred Steeves, who would be Janette's father, was then a young man of nineteen. His broad shoulders sagged as he turned from the crowd of mourners, tears streaming over his cheeks.

A neighbor girl, Amy Ruggles, wished with all her heart she could say something that could bring him comfort. Fred was a good friend to her, and it was so difficult to see him in such pain.

At the time she had no way of knowing that this man would someday be her husband, and that in the many years of their married life, this was one of the few times she would see him cry.

All in all, life on the prairie had been difficult for Bob and Kathryn Steeves' family. Even with his many skills, Bob experienced much bad fortune. Kathryn continued to struggle against the crude lifestyle of the prairie, but she was still determined to do her best for her sons.

Carl, her eldest, chose a life of farming alone on the prairies. By the time Janette was old enough to remember her uncle, he was almost a recluse. Brilliant and creative in technical things, he was also withdrawn and odd, and children who did not know him well were afraid of him. Carl remained a bachelor, though there was at least one sweetheart. A teacher had come to the area from the East but she returned home, so it was assumed she hadn't shared his feelings.

Horace, next in line, eventually became a druggist in a small town in northern Alberta. Over the years his visits with other family members were few and far between. When he did arrive, the country cousins were in awe of him and his family. The shiny automobile that pulled into their farmyard carrying unfamiliar people in fine clothes was somewhat intimidating to the shoeless children who welcomed them.

Janette's father, Fred, was the third son. His younger children knew him as a farmer, fisherman, and hunter, but earlier in his life baseball had been his great interest. And he was good at playing, once even pitching a no-hit, no-run game. His wife, Amy, who attended this game, said, "The only chance for the rest of his teammates to play was when they got up to bat."

Fred himself told an amusing story of a game where in one inning he struck out the first four batters at the plate—and, amazingly, the opposing team still scored. Apparently the catcher simply could not hold on to the ball and each of the batters had run to base on the last strike when the ball had rolled out of the catcher's glove.

A friend of his has said, "I loved to watch Fred play ball. When he got up to bat, he'd look as if he wasn't going to do anything. Then he'd hit that ball and it'd go and go and go—and never touch the ground!"

Fred played on several teams in southern Alberta, often with his younger brother Jack, but his favorite team was the Enchant Nine. He was paid a small amount each game, which, in the early years of his marriage, was counted on by his family as their livelihood. Other teams did not treat him as well, at times even insisting that Amy pay to watch the game.

Many years later, when his daughter Sharon sat with an elderly Fred to choose old family photos for reprints, he picked the picture of the Enchant Nine out of the album and handed it to her. A quiet man, his words often were few, but she knew he was saying, "This shows what was important in my life. You need to include a copy of this."

Jack, in the middle of the family line, became a successful farmer and businessman. For some years he sold International Harvester equipment and at the same time managed a farm east of town. Later he sold both and moved farther north to raise purebred Hereford cattle. He married Amy's sister, Laurine Ruggles, so their children and Janette's siblings referred to themselves as "double cousins," becoming close friends and swapping offspring back and forth between the two homes for various reasons over the years. For Janette, it was like having two sets of parents and two batches of brothers and sisters.

Ralph was the next-to-last of Fred's brothers. He also remained a bachelor, though it did not seem to be for lack of interest. Apparently there simply had not been the right girl at the right time. Janette was sure this uncle would have made a wonderful husband and daddy. He was always patient and loving, spoiling her over the years and looking out for her whenever he could.

Walter was the baby of the family and still a young boy when Kathryn felt she could no longer endure the harsh life she was living. She took Ralph and Walter and moved into a small house in the town of Champion, twenty-five miles away, seemingly confident that Bob would follow. But this did not happen. Family and neighbors who knew them were grieved to see two fine but stubborn people hurt themselves and the family they loved by allowing years of growing resentments to drive them apart. It seemed apparent, though, that neither was willing to take the first step toward compromise.

Later, when Jack married, Ralph and Walter returned to the family home to live with him and his new bride, Laurine. This meant that, young as she was, she began married life with not just the care of a home and new husband, but also of Jack's father, two teen-aged brothers-in-law, and a hired hand.

After watching her youngest son return to farm life, Kathryn gave up hope that things between Bob and her would change, and she moved to the city of Calgary. The rift and separation was hard on all the family members—even those sons who had already married and were on their own, for they had deep love and respect for their mother and yet felt they could not side with either parent.

It was hardest, perhaps, on the younger ones. As soon as World War II broke out, young Walter enlisted in the Canadian Army and was sent out as a telegrapher with the Communications Corp. He spent most of the war years overseas, met and married an English girl, and brought her and their baby girl back to Canada with him after the war. He then used his G.I. Bill to go back to school.

After some difficult years, he realized his dream of becoming a druggist—only to be the first of Janette's uncles to die. Walter was fifty-four when he suffered a heart attack, leaving his wife and four grown children to cope with the sudden and unexpected loss.

It would be wonderful to be able to write that all Janette's family members were believers. Many of the Steeves clan are. Though little is known about the spiritual status of Kathryn, she left behind a well-marked Bible. Her husband, Bob, who used to delight in silly arguments concerning popular religious trivialities such as "How many angels can fit on the head of a pin?" did not make his peace with God until shortly before his death, this due to the urgings of his daughter-in-law Laurine.

Bob and Kathryn's sons grew up with some spiritual training, though morality and proper living were what had been thoroughly stressed. As the boys passed into manhood, they did not seem to feel that a personal commitment to God was important. And for some of the brothers, there followed many years uncommitted to the Lord who had touched the lives of their family all the way back to Heinrich Stief, and no doubt beyond.

CHAPTER TWO

The Ruggles Family

THE RUGGED SHORES of Massachusetts Bay were the first foot-hold in North America for Janette's mother, Amy Ruggles', ancestors. During a time in England when the Puritan movement was seeking church reform, two brothers by the name of Ruggles boarded ship with John Winthrop and began the long and difficult journey that brought them to the New World. Full of hope for religious freedom and a better life, they built crude shelters and settled into colonial life at Charlestown, Massachusetts, in 1630. Later they moved across the river to where the city of Boston was founded.

Because of its excellent location, Boston flourished and streams of Puritan immigrants followed after. Among these were Thomas Ruggles, a third brother, and his young family, who brought with them from England the Ruggles crest and coat of arms.

Here again, the pages of our family's history tell of a young boy and an ocean voyage. It must have been exciting for Thomas' eight-year-old son, Samuel Ruggles, to see the shores of a new land rise before him as if out of the ocean itself. And as the ship glided past the scattered islands, the bay that would soon be named Boston Harbor welcomed them in. Samuel anticipated seeing his new home and the family members who had gone on ahead several years before. The difficulties of the sea voyage soon melted into distant memory.

Thomas Ruggles' family made its home in Roxbury, Massachu-

RUGGLES FAMILY

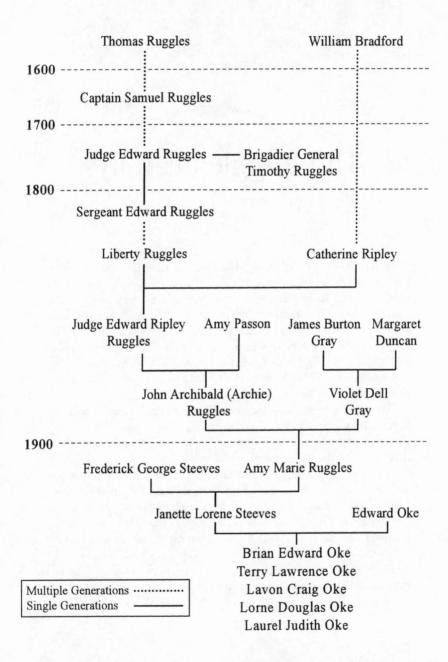

Thomas Ruggles   William Bradford

1600

Captain Samuel Ruggles

1700

Judge Edward Ruggles —— Brigadier General
Timothy Ruggles

1800

Sergeant Edward Ruggles

Liberty Ruggles   Catherine Ripley

Judge Edward Ripley Amy Passon   James Burton Margaret
Ruggles   Gray   Duncan

John Archibald (Archie)   Violet Dell
Ruggles   Gray

1900

Frederick George Steeves Amy Marie Ruggles

Janette Lorene Steeves   Edward Oke

Brian Edward Oke
Terry Lawrence Oke
Lavon Craig Oke
Lorne Douglas Oke
Laurel Judith Oke

Multiple Generations ⋯⋯⋯⋯⋯
Single Generations ——————

setts, where his young son grew to be Captain Samuel Ruggles. As each generation married and fathered sons of its own, a line of soldiers, lawyers, and ministers began to form. Because of this, it has been suggested that the Ruggles seem to like being paid for talking or fighting. Even now, some joke that the saying still holds true, with the possible addendum of payment no longer being necessary.

Brigadier General Timothy Ruggles, one of the descendants of Captain Samuel Ruggles, served "with distinction" in the French and Indian War. After being elected to the First Colonial Congress as president, he began to differ with his colleagues on the role England should play in the Americas. Being a devout loyalist, he sided with England, eventually being forced to leave his estate, his possessions— and his wife, who refused to evacuate with him to Nova Scotia, Canada.

His brother, Honorable Edward Ruggles, remained in Massachusetts and, as seems to have happened painfully often in early American history, raised a son who fought on the side opposite his uncle. Sergeant Edward Ruggles served in George Washington's Continental Army. It is through this son that our branch of the family tree continues.

Two generations later, Edward's grandson, Liberty Ruggles, grew to adulthood in Illinois during the 1840s. It was a time when the excitement of the opening West pulsed through the veins of many young men. The California Gold Rush was drawing those who sought easy fortune, and the golden grasses of the fertile prairies made many a farmer east of the Mississippi yearn for the promising new land. Young Liberty had his eye on the territory of Minnesota.

On February 4, 1851, Liberty Ruggles married Catherine Ripley—a fifth-generation granddaughter of Governor William Bradford, who came to America on the *Mayflower* and played an important role in the first years at Plymouth. He was its second governor and was credited by some as having begun the tradition of observing Thanksgiving.

Seven years after the marriage of Liberty and Catherine, they made the decision to fulfill his long-held dream, leaving family behind and embarking on the journey to Minnesota. It was the same year that the territory became a state. Perhaps they were unaware that this act of Congress also divided the Sioux Reservation in half, causing the discontent of the tribes living in Minnesota to escalate at an alarming rate.

In the summer of 1862, after the payment of annuities to the Sioux in this area was delayed, a sudden surge of their anger exploded in a massacre in the Minnesota Valley. During this time more than 350 settlers lost their lives, and when U. S. General Sibley brought his troops against the bands, 269 more were discovered to be held captive and were freed.

Panic spread across the plains of Minnesota, even though word came that the Sioux were being pursued into the Dakotas and beyond the Missouri River. It was this panic that brought Liberty, Catherine, and their small family back to the shelter of the more largely populated area of Faribault, Minnesota.

Janette's great-grandfather Edward Ripley Ruggles, son of Liberty, was just six years old when his family moved back to the eastern side of the Mississippi. During his childhood he experienced the move from Illinois, witnessed the fear of extreme violence in an unsettled land, and was blinded in one eye by a rock from a slingshot.

Once grown, Edward pushed farther west to South Dakota where, at age twenty-five, he married seventeen-year-old Amy Passon, whose family had also come from Minnesota. Two years later they were living in Webster, South Dakota, a town so newly settled that his second son was the first white child to be born there.

Soon Edward and Amy were raising four sons and one daughter on the windswept plains. What hopes there may have been for a larger family were stilled when, at the early age of twenty-eight, Amy went through "the change" and her fifth child became her last.

Even with the growing family to keep her busy, Amy had a difficult time adjusting to the isolation of frontier life. This loneliness was never more evident than when she happened upon a familiar man from home. While she and Edward were walking down the town's dusty street, the older gentleman rounded a corner and was instantly recognized by Amy. Losing all sense of propriety in her complete shock and excitement, Amy rushed toward the man with such exuberance that Edward was embarrassed and disgusted.

The years were profitable for Edward. He began a rise into political life that he continued to pursue after the family returned to Minnesota in 1894. This was the year that his eldest son, Archie, who was nearing fifteen, ran away from home to find work farther west, being joined shortly after by his younger brother, Sid.

Edward opened a law office in the lakeside town of Osakis in 1898. The family prospered, and after just a few years of "trying their wings," Archie and Sid returned to live with the family in their new home. Edward's stature in the community had grown and his sons enjoyed the hopeful looks from many of the local young ladies who exclaimed at attention from one of the "Honorable Ruggles' " sons.

A favorite community event of the time was a box social. Ladies from around the area brought decorated boxes filled with the best cooking and baking they could offer. Gentlemen then bid for the box of their choice and the money was used for a special cause.

Archie Ruggles stood with a friend, surveying the possibilities and watching as a young man chose the box of Violet Gray, a young teacher at a local school. Though he had known her for some time, Archie could not help but notice how particularly lovely she was on that evening and made up his mind to find time to talk with her. Taking the next opportunity, he offered Vi a ride home and she accepted.

Soon the couple announced that they planned to be wed. Edward and Amy were delighted at the news, but Violet Gray's family had opposing reactions. They had heard the tales of Archie's younger days and considered him to be too wild for their daughter. This may not have been fair to the young Mr. Ruggles, but the Grays' protective feelings toward their daughter and their other three children were understandable. They had experienced great difficulties in raising their family to adulthood.

Violet's father, Burt Gray, was the youngest of thirteen children and the son of Quakers from Maine. During the Civil War, he went south with others from the area to fight for the Confederacy. On July 4, 1865, when peace had just been declared, he married Margaret Duncan and moved with her to Texas. He was twenty-eight at the time and, according to their birth years in the family records, she was fourteen.

Burt and Maggie were able to make a good life for themselves under the hot Texas sun. In just a few years they had a home, land, and family of three. Then, suddenly, their years of fortune seemed to end.

In a quick sweep of death's crooked hand, all three children were stolen from them, leaving Burt and Maggie reeling with grief. For Burt, there were bouts of severe heartache, and on one occasion Maggie entered their room to find her shattered husband clutching the children's clothing and sobbing uncontrollably.

Soon he was even denied the opportunity to grieve when Maggie took sick with the same illness that had claimed their young family. Burt was warned to take her to a climate more favorable for her condition as quickly as possible, or she might be the next to die.

The decision to move was made in haste. As soon as the few possessions that would fit into their covered wagon were loaded, Burt and his sick wife set out. The neighbor who had been given the trust of selling the land, house, and remaining belongings was soon far behind them—and was never heard from again.

Their covered wagon rolled north in search of cooler weather. On one particular evening in Missouri, the story is told that Jesse James spent time with them at their camp. The infamous gunslinger had posed no threat, simply shared their fire and weak coffee, then left as quietly as he had come.

Finally, the Grays' wagon came to a stop on a farm near Osakis, Minnesota, where they settled and began their second family of four children—Lily, Violet, Irving, and Jesse. It was in Osakis that daughter Violet was courted by Archie Ruggles, the "judge's son."

After overcoming her family's protest, Violet and Archie were married under the trees on the Gray family farm near the shore of Lake Osakis in July of 1902. From there they went to live on various local farms where Archie could find work.

It was not until several months after their wedding that Archie and Violet Ruggles were able to have a wedding photograph taken of them, and Vi was somewhat reluctant. When the cameraman instructed them to hold perfectly still, she held her breath and drew in her stomach, trying not to let her tension show in her face.

When the photo arrived, she gazed at it for quite some time, uncertain if her secret was evident or not. Little Royal was, at the time of the photography session, already on the way. Perhaps it had been unwise to go ahead with what they would consider their "wedding picture" when the supposed bride was in such a condition. Vi would be absolutely mortified if anyone incorrectly assumed that the picture was taken on the wedding day and that she had already been with child.

In the year of Archie and Vi's marriage, Judge Edward Ruggles gave up his bench with the encouragement of his wife, because Amy was afraid that he was making too many enemies. Instead, he purchased a local summer resort from a woman named Ida Wilde. Amy, being a creative person, dubbed the resort "Idlewilde," and the couple, then in their forties, threw their efforts into making the posh resort profitable. Their wealthy guests stayed in the hotel and surrounding cabins and ate in one central dining room, enjoying the quiet of country life and a wonderful view of Lake Osakis spreading out before them.

Soon their grandchildren began to arrive. Idlewilde was a place to run and play while parents, aunts, uncles, and grandparents worked to keep the resort in order, the guests happy, and the scurrying children out of their path. Royal was the oldest of Archie and Vi's family. Then followed Burt, named after Vi's father. And, on July 30, 1906, a sweet baby girl, Amy Marie, who would be Janette's mother.

In 1906, Edward was given an opportunity to serve as secretary to Congressman Buchman, and he and his wife soon found themselves preparing for a winter's stay in Washington, D.C.

At the train station, Amy kissed the tiny granddaughter, whose name she shared, and her two growing grandsons good-bye, fighting back tears at the thought of how much they would change before she would see them again. The long winter months in the Capital would seem like an eternity away from these children, and it was difficult for her to turn and walk away.

Archie and Vi gathered the children together and headed for home. There was work to do. Chores waited and laundry had to be washed and ironed; dinner would be needed soon, and then the children would be tucked under the covers of their straw-tick beds.

Vi discovered that her family was to increase again. This time there was a special surprise. Twin girls were born, Laurine and Leone. And, of course, with the two babies came multiplied responsibilities. A kind older neighbor noticed the struggling mother and came often to help Vi hang her laundry. It was a welcome change to have another woman to talk with and the two became close friends.

The neighbor, soon known simply as Grandma Riley, was a solid Christian who prayed regularly for Vi, Archie, and their family. When the next baby was born, Grandma Riley was allowed to name him, and Ross was welcomed to the home.

Not long after the birth, whooping cough spread through the area. To the horror of their parents, the toddling twins both fell ill. Upon the recommendation of a doctor, the family would spend the winter in town. Archie moved them to one of the cabins of his parents' Idlewilde resort, and Vi settled in to nurse the youngsters back to health. To their great relief, both recovered.

Word came that Edward was to spend a second two-year term in

Washington with Senator Clapp. So his sons and their families continued to run Idlewilde during his winter absences. Again, Amy was far from her growing grandchildren.

Then Vi's brother, Irving Gray, announced that he had decided to move to the province of Alberta, in Canada. It was difficult for Vi's parents, Burt and Maggie, to see their son travel so far from them. After they watched him drive away, Maggie hurried back into the house to shed her tears in private, but Burt stood for quite some time watching the dust settle back onto the road. Perhaps, he thought, someday he would follow.

The aging couple decided, instead, to move into town where Maggie took in boarders. Now Vi was able to see her mother often, and there was the added advantage of a baby-sitter whenever the young mother needed to work at the resort.

So when Maggie was in her late fifties and Burt seventy-three, they suddenly found themselves with young children under foot again.

Burt, now "Grandpa Gray," found it easier to leave the youngsters to Maggie's care and meet with his Civil War buddies at the local jail. In the clubroom they played cards and reminisced about the "good old days."

Maggie, alone with all six children, often was forced to muster all the stamina her small stature could offer. She was not above using unexpected means of ensuring that her charges did not take advantage of her. Stories of her eccentricities abounded.

She is said to have wielded a hoe as she chased a neighbor girl away from baby Ross. The girl had whooping cough and Ross was a sickly infant, likely to catch whatever came along, so Maggie defended him with whatever she happened to be holding. On another occasion, she scolded young Leone with the threat of hanging her on a roller towel, and she chased eleven-year-old Amy with a pitchfork after the young girl firmly declared, "I won't do chores for anybody when I'm sixteen, not even my dad!" And when two of the boys climbed up the windmill to escape a spanking from her, she stubbornly sat at the bottom until they came down.

Grandma Gray was clearly not a woman to be trifled with, but there are an equal number of stories told about her total selflessness and generosity. She gave freely of all she had.

Finally, Archie and Vi were able to build their own little house on an acreage that Edward purchased shortly after returning to Osakis in 1912. It was small, with only one room, but Archie was proud of his accomplishment and his own ingenuity. There were built-in beds that folded against the wall during the day—a marvelous space-saving idea—and Archie had soon dubbed it the "dear little shack."

Vi had different feelings toward it, and as much as she appreciated the efforts of her husband, she found it humiliating to bring guests there. She was pleased that winters would still be spent in a cabin at Idlewilde, since the "dear little shack" could not be kept warm enough to live in.

In 1916, Vi's sister Lily and her husband, Jasper Root, decided to follow brother Irv's example, and they struck out for Champion, Alberta, to work with Irv on the Guess Ranch. The ranch was owned by Harry Guess, a millionaire from New York, who had purchased four sections on the Canadian prairie. Vi felt the loss of her sister's company deeply. Even the new three-bedroom home that Archie had recently built did little to ease her sorrow.

Since Archie was also feeling the draw to settle on the Canadian prairies, it was decided that the family would board the train for the new "promised land." Burt Gray decided to go north as well and plans were laid for him to go on ahead while Maggie stayed to help Vi with the children on the train trip. Baby Wayne had now joined the family.

One after the other, the clan was moving into Alberta and leaving Osakis behind. Idlewilde was left in the care of Edward, Amy, and the sons who remained. Then the resort suffered a difficult setback. Edward had hired a young mentally handicapped boy from a needy family in order to provide him with employment. The lad was injured in an accident on the property, and Edward, the lawyer, had let his insurance lapse. The boy's family sued, and Edward was forced to mortgage the property to meet the debt. He was unable to recover, and when he died in 1936, the other sons signed their shares of Idlewilde over to the remaining brother, who continued to work the resort. Soon after Edward's death, his wife, Amy, died as well.

After a three-day train trip, Archie's family arrived in Champion, Alberta, and drove the remainder of the way to Guess Ranch. It was March—and cold—and the roads were so bad that their two loaded cars had to be repeatedly pushed up the hills. When they finally arrived at the ranch, excitement seemed to burst from inside them.

At last Archie and Vi were together again with Jasper and Lil. Cousins, who had missed one another dearly, raced through the small home, shouting greetings and embracing. Jasper and Lil, Archie and Vi hugged and cried, laughed and danced around the small kitchen, the happy noises spilling into the cold night air of the Alberta prairie.

For three years the families worked side by side at the Guess Ranch. Then, the wander bug bit Archie again, and the Ruggles clan moved away from the area. In 1922 they returned to the prairie, having saved enough money to be able, at last, to purchase their own section of land.

Section 35 held a two-bedroom house and a granary. Into these two buildings Archie and Vi's seven children and Jasper and Lil's eight were squeezed. Small bodies lay crosswise on beds at night, some even sleeping in the granary. They came to be known as the "thirty-five kids" after the land's section number —and it must have seemed to a neighbor passing in his wagon as though nearly that many children were swarming over the farmyard.

Living together provided many challenging times, but also plenty of opportunities for laughter. One evening when a child was noticed to have sleepy, drooping eyes, his mother told him to "go sleep with Gordon," a young member of the Root family. After this child had gone, another was sent along in hopes that there was still some room in the bed.

Then it was discovered that both mothers had been sending youngsters to squeeze in with poor little Gordon. When they realized what they had been doing they shared a good laugh, not sure just how many children were now crowded obediently into the small bed. "Go sleep with Gordon" quickly became a family catchphrase, repeated often, and "Gordon" came to mean anyone who had a little room to spare.

The fifteen children from teens to tots soon expanded to twenty-three, but the two families had finally put down roots. Archie took over the manager's position at Guess Ranch and added three more sons—Bob, Dorn, and Harry—making a total of seven sons and three daughters for him and Vi.

As these humble years passed, Janette's mother, Amy, grew from a young girl to an attractive and assertive teen. We are told that she always possessed a cheery attitude and a great compassion for others. And it seems there was more than one young man in the neighborhood who had his eye on her. After due courting, she accepted the proposal from one of her suitors—even though another young gentleman stood shyly on the sideline wishing he had been more courageous. But, for reasons she has not divulged, Amy's first engagement was broken, and she was soon accepting calls from the quieter youth.

Amy Ruggles and Fred Steeves were married on November 26, 1925, in the dining room at the Guess Ranch, and the whole community was invited. Her father, Archie, provided his best turkeys; then Vi and her helpers prepared the dinner.

At the last minute an elderly neighbor lady let it be known that she had no transportation to get to the "gala" affair, and so the wedding was delayed while Vi, big-hearted as always, sent one of her sons over the dusty prairie miles to bring back the woman, while the bride, groom, and all the wedding guests waited patiently. When the son returned, he was alone. It seemed the woman had decided to stay home. So the wedding finally proceeded.

Fred and Amy Steeves were given a fine celebration for the start of their marriage—and also lovely wedding gifts from those who loved them. The Guess Ranch's millionaire owner himself sent Amy and Fred a card with a generous sum of $50 as a wedding gift. In those days it went far toward helping the young couple get started.

Fred and Amy spent the earliest days of their marriage in the community where they had been wed. Family surrounded them, as well as neighbors they had known for years. Among these delightful friends were the McCombs, who knew the Lord and often attempted to share their faith. This family prayed faithfully and diligently for their Ruggles neighbors, and their prayers were eventually answered. Over the years, one by one, the family members made personal prayers of commitment. Archie and Vi, along with their children from Royal to young Harry, at some point made his or her peace with God.

And so it is that even Janette's earliest recollections are of a family where God was honored and served, and individuals were concerned about sharing Him with others. One of her treasured memories is of Archie and Vi, her elderly grandparents, having their daily Bible reading and prayer time together.

Never has she known of anyone who seemed to know, pray for, and host more missionaries than her Grandmother Vi Ruggles. After her passing, a scrapbook filled with the pictures of her many missionary friends was found among her possessions.

As for Janette's parents, Amy realized her own need for a relationship with God while her children were very young, but Fred allowed many precious years to slip by him before he offered his heart to the Savior.

CHAPTER THREE

New Life

IN THE FIRST YEARS of their marriage, Fred and Amy Steeves moved frequently from one prairie location to another. And their family began to grow, first with the birth of Betty, then Jean, followed by June, and finally in 1931, a first son, Jack. Amy was delighted at the arrival of her second son in the fall of 1933, but it soon became evident that Kenneth was not well, and there was an aura of suspended fear in the family home. Grandma Vi and Grandpa Archie, as well as Aunt Lil, arrived to help.

Amy wept with them, fighting the hopeless feeling inside her and the realization that she was powerless to stop her worst fears from occurring. Kenneth was with the family for only eight days before he died. His tiny coffin was buried in the Lomond cemetery and was soon joined by that of great-grandmother Maggie Gray, who died the following month.

Dealing with the death of her infant was a very difficult process for Amy. For many days she struggled with her own emotions, trying to bring her life back into focus and drive away the hopelessness that she could not overcome.

At last, feeling that she could not stand her grief any longer, she climbed the loft ladder of the farmyard barn and threw herself down onto the hay. The weight of her enormous grief had finally taken her to the end of her strength, and, in her desperation, she cried out to

God, whom she had always believed existed but did not personally know.

"Oh, God," she prayed, "if you're really there—do something for me."

God did hear Amy's prayer, and though perhaps she could not have explained her experience at the time, she left the barn loft a new person. The God of creation was now her God, and with His help she was ready to go on—and to begin her growth in the Christian faith.

Two years after this monumental experience, Amy found herself again faced with the possibility of losing a child. Baby Janette brought back to Amy all the trauma and pain she had faced with the loss of Kenneth. As the sun began its morning glow over the snowy fields of the Canadian prairie, Amy wept alone. This time she was certain that the God she had chosen to serve would hear her plea, but she fought with her desire to insist that He save this baby.

Over and over in her mind she wrestled with how to pray. She wanted to demand, but she knew this was not what her Lord wanted from her. Finally she realized that she did not need to be afraid of letting go. Through her sobs she placed herself and then the fragile life of her infant daughter into the hands of a loving God. At last she felt peace and understood afresh that her heavenly Father was in control of the situation and that she could rest and allow Him to accomplish His purposes, whatever they might be.

"Not my will, but thine be done," she whispered in the stillness.

Gradually the condition of the tiny baby improved. With the advice of those around her, Amy took Janette off breast milk and placed her on condensed milk, an expensive commodity and difficult to obtain in those days. But the baby continued to gain in health and strength, and was duly fussed over by three older sisters and a brother.

Amy found herself often murmuring prayers of thankfulness as she watched the cheeks grow round and the little arms and legs fill out. She had learned much about the love of God through these difficult times, and her own desire to continue to grow in faith strengthened. In many ways she felt that she, too, was a child, just beginning life under the watchful eye of her heavenly Father.

Fred and Amy Steeves were now raising five children and busy with the activities of farm life. Though it was the mid-thirties and there was never any extra money, they were always able to provide in some way for their family's needs. The youngsters grew quickly, but not without the occasional near-catastrophe that accompanies childhood. Amy found herself again thanking God for being near her children when she could not. And with the comforting distance of time, the family had many good times of laughter in reminiscing over some of those events.

While Janette was a toddler the Steeves family lived along a winding prairie river. It was normally neither a deep nor wide stream. In fact, during times of drought it was all that the little river could manage just to keep on flowing. But in spring flood time it could be a different story.

During one of these periods, the older children were sent to bring in the milk cows. Unknown to them, their little sister Janette decided that she would go too and toddled along after them, carrying a small red ball.

She hadn't gone far when the ball slipped from her hands and went rolling down the riverbank into the swollen stream. Crying out over her lost toy, she ran after it, sliding down the bank, anxious to retrieve the ball that now bobbed along in the current.

Perhaps there would have been no one to tell what really happened had someone not come upon her shortly after, her clothes hooked securely on a prairie cactus, still crying for the ball that had floated downstream.

Another favorite childhood story involved the farm windmill. Every prairie farm had a windmill—a tall, open structure with a ladder hung precariously on one side. Many mothers worried about those windmills, for farm youngsters couldn't seem to stay away from them.

Bill Meikle, a neighbor, enjoyed repeating the story of a very young Janette coming into the house and imploring the adults, "You come turn Margie 'wound?" When they went to see what she meant, there was baby sister, Margie, barely able to walk, dangerously high on the windmill ladder—unable to go on up or come back down.

On the many occasions when the children were bundled into the farm wagon and taken to visit cousins, aunts and uncles, they could hardly contain their excitement. Equally thrilling was the sound of someone else's wagon pulling into the Steeves' yard. The older children would tumble out of the house or race from the farmyard to find out who had arrived and whether or not anyone young enough to play with had come along.

Family meals at Grandma and Grandpa Ruggles' house were "affairs." The men filled the long table in the "cook car"—a once-portable kitchen that had been attached to the house to give extra room. Children were given plates of food and then lined up on the floor along the wall, where they balanced dinner on their laps. It was a little hard to tell if the women were ever able to sit down with the men or if they ate their dinner after the rest were fed, but no one complained. It was so good to be with family, and the adults mostly smiled indulgently at all the happy commotion from the youngsters.

But Grandpa Archie Ruggles seemed a bit gruff to the young ones. They were careful not to cross him, though they were still drawn to him by his obvious love and dry sense of humor. Staying in his home at the time of the birth of younger sister Margie, Janette had just turned two and jabbered and prattled constantly, trying to get her grandpa's attention.

At last he exclaimed in his wry-humor way, "Awe, go dry up."

In a moment she returned with a towel, busily rubbing it against herself, and declared, "There, Grandpa. Me all dried up." The adults roared with laughter, and Grandpa Ruggles figured he'd been bested by a two-year-old.

On another visit when the day was hot and dusty on the prairie, Janette and a cousin close in age decided the best place to be was in the icehouse. There, large blocks of ice were buried in coal slack to keep them frozen through summer days. Since the black dust was damp and dirty, the two children decided they would be better off setting their clothes aside. They carefully removed the garments and then proceeded to dig in the cool playroom.

When they had tired of their little game, they emerged—much to the shock and consternation of their mothers. Blue eyes shone out from little black bodies covered from head to foot with coal dust.

On another occasion, Janette and cousin Richard Steeves decided to explore his father's newly acquired automobile. Jack went into the house, leaving the toddlers bouncing in the backseat.

As it happened, eggs in cartons were also left on the backseat where they were playing. When the excitement of bouncing wore off, they discovered the eggs and set about cooking up some further fun. By the time they were discovered, they had scrambled eggs all over the seat and couldn't understand why Uncle Jack was so upset.

One of the most ordinary creatures on the prairie is the Richardson ground squirrel—usually called gophers locally. Since they were a plague to all farmers, every attempt was made to preserve the few crops that did grow by controlling these animals whenever possible. Farmers shot them, some were poisoned, but even the children were allowed to help when it was time to drown the gophers. The youngsters ran through the fields carrying pails of water to dump down innumerable holes.

Too young to carry water, Janette hurried to follow her older siblings as they rushed into the dry fields. A hot wind blew across her small face and swept on across the bare brown prairie, snatching the sounds of the children's voices and carrying the words off toward the endless horizon to be lost among the drifting clouds. Amid the hustle and confusion of the moment, one small child hurried after the others, trying to share in their excitement, taking it all in. This gopher hunt is Janette's earliest memory of prairie life.

She does not remember the dust, the need, or the difficulty at times in putting a meal on the table. In her childhood memories she does not see her father struggling to make a farm produce when the wind blew the prairie soil across his path in clouds of dust so thick the ears of the horses he was driving were hidden, nor does she recall her mother feeding the family another meal of cottontail-rabbit stew. She has only heard about her father being reluctant to stand in food lines and, instead, setting off to work on a government project building an irrigation ditch, or her mother shaking the dust from the bed covers before tucking the little ones in at night.

She knew nothing at the time of all those hardships. It was her parents who shouldered the burden to worry and struggle for the family. And Fred and Amy soon realized that something had to be done. The stubborn skies refused to give up moisture. The forlorn fields were unable to sustain growth. Because of those conditions, the government urged farmers to move their families farther north, where it had not forgotten how to rain.

Fred and Amy realized they must make a decision, but it would not be easy. So many members of their family lived nearby on the prairie. On both sides their families had roots that reached deep into the prairie soil.

CHAPTER FOUR

Moving North

WHEN IT CAME TIME for Amy Steeves to register her kids for school in the fall of 1938, the county school inspector sent a note asking the number of students who would be attending from the Steeves' household. Amy wrote back, "If we can find a place up north, none."

Inspector McCullough, who himself was from the north, quickly replied with an offer for Fred to work on the northern farm that the inspector and his father owned. Fred went first—alone. When he was certain that he liked what he found, he sent word for his family to join him near the little town of Hoadley, Alberta.

After loading a boxcar at government expense with household goods, six horses, four cows, and Fred's younger brother Ralph as supervisor, they bid tearful good-bye to their prairie family, packed themselves into Grandpa Ruggles' truck, and headed north. Grandma and Grandpa, Amy, six children, the girl who helped Amy with the children, and Inspector McCullough's wife and small son all made the trip together.

Because the Steeves children were still recovering from whooping cough, it was necessary to separate them from the others. Ronny McCullough rode in the cab of the truck and Amy's children rode in the back, under a hand-built protective covering. It was a long drive, lasting until well after dark.

One-quarter mile away from their destination, their truck became stuck in the mud so they were forced to abandon the vehicle and walk the rest of the way. The children were amazed at the mud—since the prairie had been dry for so long they could not recall what it was like.

Because of their whooping cough, the Steeves children were not allowed to go inside the farmhouse, so they waited outside until they were shown where they would sleep. Meantime, they played in the yard, running up and down the slanted wooden door of the root cellar in the darkness and having a wonderful time.

Amy was very disappointed to discover that they would not be with Fred immediately. He was working at another farm, and the family was to stay on in a bunkhouse at McCulloughs' place. After being away from her husband so long and traveling so far, the news was difficult to bear. The next morning, Amy's father took her over to the field where Fred was haying, and she was grateful to be able to see her husband at last.

The entire family together again, they began adjusting to their new lifestyle and a measure of routine returned. It was the time of year for wild blueberries, and Amy and the girls spent many hours in the berry patches. On one such excursion she and the older children picked while some of the younger ones baby-sat Margie, not yet two, who was still having spells of coughing whenever something provoked it.

As the morning wore on, Margie became hungry. They had brought a simple lunch with them to the berry patch, and Margie had decided that it was time to eat and that she wanted the fried liver from the sandwiches. The baby-sitters had learned that crying would send their little sister into a bout of coughing and did all they could to keep it from happening. So they complied, and when the toddler had finished her piece of meat and decided that she wanted more, they obliged, taking it from the other sandwiches. By the time the berry pickers came for their lunch, there was nothing left but bread and butter.

On a trip to the Hoadley Post Office to mail some blueberries back to their family on the prairie, Fred and Amy spotted a farm that had apparently been for sale for a while. With hopeful hearts they considered the possibility of making the purchase and decided it could be done. Fred stopped to see the man, and arrangements were soon made.

Amy was thrilled. The home on the new farm was a real house, and "almost new" in her thinking. While many neighboring families were living in simpler accommodations, her new house seemed so spacious, and she thanked God many times for providing it.

Fred purchased both the adjoining Hoggarth and Robakowskie quarters. Later he purchased another quarter of land, which he logged and then resold, and then a quarter known to the family as the Nelson quarter, across the road from the Hoggarth place. It was unbroken land and used for running cattle and horses.

The farm purchase took some time to be worked through, so the family unloaded their household belongings at the much smaller Robakowskie house while waiting to take possession of the Hoggarth farm. The family was forced to crowd themselves in, sharing beds with rows of children and often feeling they were stumbling over one another. For some of the children, there was also the eerie feel of dark shadows thrown against the windows by the trees and the sound of wind passing through the branches at night. On the prairie there had been none of these sensations.

Soon the time came for the move to the Hoggarth farm, and the house hummed with activity. Amy called out directions to the older children and Ruth, the family's hired girl, about what to pack and whom to chase out of the way. Finally they were ready to leave.

The Hoggarth house was built of sturdy logs and covered with siding. It had once been the Haverigg Post Office before being moved to its present farm site, and the front door still bore a letter-drop slot. The main floor consisted of five small rooms—a kitchen with eating area and pantry, a living room, and three bedrooms, plus a double porch known as the "shed" because of its slanting roof.

Around the yard young spruce trees had been planted, and a caragana hedge lined a path that led north from the front of the house to the road. There was a picket fence around the front yard and a gate at the front entrance. In the years that the family lived in the house, no one used either the gate or the front door. Family and guests alike entered through the farmyard and came directly to the back door in the shed.

The garden, toward the west, had a row of saskatoon bushes and red currants. For several years, the girls were sent out to pick the saskatoons for pies or canning and the currants for jelly. Unfortunately, the currants were known to be loved by worms as well, and finally Amy had the bushes pulled out. Perhaps it had something to do with Amy's brother Bob who, on one visit, helped himself to the lovely red berries. He enjoyed them tremendously until someone opened a berry and showed him the wiggly worm inside. Uncle Bob looked a little sick—and didn't touch the currants again.

The house also had a second story, an unfinished open room. It became the bedroom for some of the children, though it was not insulated. Summer days were hot and stuffy, while winter nights very cold. The stove chimney ran up through the middle of the room, bringing whatever warmth there was in the winter. But under the heavy quilts the warmth of the other bodies sharing one bed soon made the attic room cozy and secure. Even the dark shadows thrown across the open rafters where the roof hung low were not nearly as frightening when the soft breathing of sisters could be heard nearby.

In the mornings, the children had to slip from the warmth, scurry across the cold floor and rush down the stairs to stand by the heater to get dressed. Even the main floor got very cold at night in spite of the banked fires. Janette can remember her father warming socks and shoes over the stove before they were passed to her to put on.

There was one dormer window upstairs, looking north from the front of the house toward the road. Because the roof sloped away in every direction from the chimney, a very careful child could ease out through the window and onto the roof. Some of the more adventurous members of the house tried this test of skill, but it was discouraged by those who were older and wiser.

The kitchen was an odd narrow room with the cooking stove near the entrance to the living room and the table tucked in along the north wall. It was very crowded for such a large family, but they made do until changes could be made. Fred was busy farming two quarters of land and logging another. Home improvements would have to wait.

At the end of Fred's workday in the field, little Janette would often run to meet her daddy. He was tired, dusty, and hot from the beating sun, but her little legs still had difficulty keeping pace with him through the tall jungle-like grasses. He would hoist her up onto his shoulders and carry her back to the house.

For Janette, the sensations of this memory still live on—the gentle up and down motion with each step that her daddy took; the feeling of being high above all of the world, her small hands wrapped around his sweaty forehead; the heady feeling of being borne homeward by her big, powerful daddy.

When Fred arrived in the evening after a busy day of farm duties, he was met with enthusiasm. As soon as he lowered his tired body into his usual chair, his lap was considered available. There was only one condition: no wet pants. It was great motivation for the young family members to become potty trained. Janette never stopped to consider if he wanted her on his knee or not. She felt the place was rightfully hers and was never turned away.

When Fred's big arms wrapped solidly around Janette as she snuggled up against his chest, she felt loved and protected. He was a quiet man, but there was never a doubt in Janette's mind that her daddy loved her. Though he was stern and unyielding to any child who chose to disobey, he seldom raised his voice. He simply did not need to.

CHAPTER FIVE

Church

AMY TRIED HARD to get involved with the local church, but her only means of transportation was the team of horses. Since hitching them often seemed more trouble than it was worth, she frequently walked to church. And because the young children would not be able to keep pace on the two-mile walk each way, she sometimes went alone.

On one particular Sunday morning, when Janette was still small enough to be anxious about her mother leaving for even a short time, she became suspicious that something was in the wind. Amy had pinned her hat in place and pulled her fine black shawl over her best black dress, and it was evident she was going out.

Little Janette hung close to her throughout the preparations, but somehow Amy managed to sneak out the front door and start down the dusty country road. Finding herself outwitted, Janette ran howling after her mother.

The tired woman turned around and walked the short distance back to the yard, stooping to wipe the runny nose on her clean white hankie and muttering that since it was so hard to get to church she had a notion just to stay home. Though the small girl could not fully understand why, there was a momentary feeling of triumph. She was more important than "church"—whatever that was.

The feeling was short-lived. After seeing Janette settled back inside the house, Amy set off again, this time successfully.

The small Hoadley church had been started a few years before the Steeves family arrived in the area. Miss Pearl Reist, an "Approved Ministering Sister," was largely responsible for its beginning. The building, purchased in 1934, was a former pool hall and not much by today's standards, but able to supply a "meeting place" for the little community congregation.

The front of the building was used as the church, and the rear held a small parsonage. There was an outside entry porch at the back leading to a tiny kitchen and an equally small living room with a little bedroom off to the side. The church had wooden floors and was rather bare except for the small pulpit at the front, a pump organ to the side, and rows of roughly made wooden benches. There were no padded seats or shaped backs, just boards that quickly became uncomfortable.

By the time the Steeves moved into the area, Miss Reist had married a local farmer named Nels Lemont and had turned the pastoral duties over to Reverend Raymond Shantz and his wife, Esma.

To farm children in the midst of the Great Depression, they were people from another world. Dainty and petite, Mrs. Shantz was well groomed and soft-spoken. Reverend Shantz was always dressed in a suit and had a warm smile and courteous manner. They drove a team hitched to a buggy with big wheels and a cover to protect from the hot sun or falling rain. Janette had never seen anything so grand and was certain they were quite different from ordinary people. Soon, though, her awe turned to deep feelings of love and respect.

One day the Shantzes were invited to dinner. Being a preschooler at the time, Janette usually tried hard to mind her manners, but during the saying of grace she embarrassed herself by burping loudly enough to be heard by everyone at the table.

For a moment Janette wrestled with what would be proper to do. She had been taught not to speak during prayer—but she also knew she was to ask pardon if a burp should slip out. At last she said a quiet but audible, "Excuse me."

When the prayer ended, adults at the table exchanged glances and then gentle laughter rippled around the group. Janette was still uncertain if she had handled the situation correctly, but she was not scolded for it afterward.

Mrs. Shantz taught a Sunday school class for the younger children. It was held in the back quarters of the church where a small, backless bench had been placed. Since there were not many in the younger age group, this bench held everyone.

Amy's children attended regularly as they grew older, and though Fred preferred to stay at home, he saw to it that the youngsters arrived in church on the occasions when Amy was away.

Mrs. Lemont was also still busily engaged in the church. She led the adult Sunday school a good deal of the time, standing at the front and reading from the register in a clear voice, "Preschoolers present: five. Primary department present: six. Juniors present: eight. Adults present: fifteen. Teachers present: four." And though Janette waited from week to week for the "presents" to be revealed, she saw none. It took quite some time for her to conclude that it was all a hoax to keep people coming to Sunday school. Later she learned the truth: Mrs. Lemont was simply keeping a record of attendance.

Mrs. Lemont was a big woman, with a stern look for misbehaving children. She wore stylish hats and lovely dark dresses trimmed with bits of fancy lace at collar and cuffs. She often carried white lacy handkerchiefs tucked at her wrist, and though Janette admired her, she was a little frightened of her as well.

Since she was one of Amy's best friends, the family often saw her other than at church services, though the couple had no children to play with. Her husband, Nels, was an interesting character, having more stories to tell about his horses and dogs than anyone else Janette had seen. In fact, some of his stories sounded so farfetched it took a patient man to stand politely and listen to the tales.

Nels would often tell of the time that he harnessed another man's team and claimed that, since he was unfamiliar with their particular equipment, the horses had chosen the proper pieces from the selection of complicated harnesses. Nels said he held a piece up to them and that the horses would whinny and nod, or shake their heads and neigh. No one was certain whether or not to believe what he claimed so insistently, but what could they say? The horses truly had been wearing all the proper pieces.

Nels was quite outspoken about the quality of his animals. Whenever he passed the Steeves' house, dust flew from the dry roads and whirled around the lively hooves and fancy buggy wheels. Perhaps they were an excellent team, but most of the community believed he likely whipped up the horses just before passing a neighbor's farm.

CHAPTER SIX

Siblings

SINCE BROTHER JACK was four years older than Janette, she would play mostly with the younger Margie, who was a soft, plump, sparkling little girl. Whenever visitors would arrive at the house, Margie seemed to take the spotlight. She knew songs like "Jesus Loves Me" and "You Are My Sunshine," and her baby voice could carry a tune quite well. John Mann, a sturdy little Scotsman from Mann's store, enjoyed her especially, often singing songs back to her in his Scottish brogue.

Margie seemed to thrive on attention, whereas Janette was shy and withdrawn. But as a small child, Janette was most familiar with Margie's temper. Perhaps it was aided by the fact that, out of necessity, she had been allowed to have her way frequently during her bout with whooping cough. At any rate, Margie usually knew what she wanted, and she wasn't above using fingernails, teeth, or anything else it took to get her way. And she could squeal! Her loud, piercing cry would bring Amy, and then Janette would be scolded for making Margie cry.

Janette did not feel resentment toward Margie, since it seemed to her that this was just what babies did. And Margie's "stage" did not last for long. Before she was even off to school, Margie had changed into a gentle, compassionate, sweet-tempered little girl, and the maker of many friends.

Though the Steeves family was far from wealthy, it was accepted that a mother with a number of little ones would have a "girl" to help her. Ruth Chapman had come north with the family and stayed with them for a time, and Margie was Ruth's pet.

One day young Margie was standing on a chair beside the kitchen stove when Ruth walked by. Margie reached for her, lost her balance, and fell with one little hand on the hot surface of the stove, her other hand pressing her weight on top. There was a great deal of scampering and screaming, but the tiny hand was badly burned.

For several weeks the burn was dressed and cared for by the family. Two people would work on it at a time—one holding Margie and trying to distract her with some kind of goodie while the other carefully clipped away dead or damaged skin with a pair of tiny manicure scissors. Somehow she was spared infection but the scars remained, and though not at all her fault, they were an ugly reminder to Ruth of the terrible incident.

Margie was given a puppy one Christmas and he was named Pal. A mixed breed of mostly collie, he was a cute, fluffy little thing that grew to be quite smart, and even though he had been given to Margie, all of the children claimed him.

He joined Pooch, the family's older black-and-white mutt that was anything but a watchdog. Pooch typically ran and hid if things looked at all dangerous, being especially afraid of thunder and lightning. Janette could not fault him for that, though. She shared his feelings completely.

On the few occasions when Amy and Fred were away from home in the late evening, Pooch would sit and howl mournfully, sending shivers up Janette's spine as she slid farther down beneath the covers. To her young imagination it sounded like a death call and always made her worry that Pooch might know something she did not. She would lie silently, holding her breath until the familiar sound of her parents' return would reach her. Then, at last, she could drift off to sleep. Their howling prophet had been wrong again.

Pooch had one thing in his favor. He could pull a small sled—although not without a great deal of coaxing. In fact, the youngsters really worked much harder than the dog, since someone had to lead the way, calling and urging and pleading with the animal. But he did give some fair rides, pulling against the simple homemade harness.

Pooch lived to be quite old, and eventually the time came when it seemed wise to put him out of his misery. Fred preferred not to do the job himself, so he accepted the offer of help from one of the neighbors. Even though he was a bird dog by breed, Pooch was afraid of guns and the young man was forced to coax him away from the farm site. Fred had been very specific that the children be kept from learning of the incident. For all of the limitations of the silly old dog, the family had loved him.

In 1940, when Janette was five, Amy was expecting again. The children were allowed to place their hands on their mother's growing tummy and feel the baby kick. Amy told them that the baby was saying, "Let me out! Let me out!"

For this birth, Amy returned to the Champion area to stay with her mother, Grandma Violet Ruggles, and, in exchange, Grandma Kathryn Steeves came from Calgary to stay with Fred and his six offspring. She was a full-figured woman, well dressed, well mannered, and very dignified.

Grandma Steeves made no secret of the fact that Fred was a pretty special son in her thinking. While she was in his home, it was evident how much she loved him by the wonderful care she gave him and his family.

Kathryn had not lost her sense of propriety, however, and would tolerate no misbehavior. Although Fred did not use swear words and the children heard little of it from others, it was discovered that her penalty for what she called "bad words" was for the culprit to have his or her mouth washed out with soap.

After letting a word slip that she feared might fall into the "unsuitable" category, Janette stole quietly inside to get the soap and then hid at the end of the clothes cupboard, squeezing herself in the little space between the cupboard and the wall. Not realizing that it was unlikely Grandma heard of the incident at all, she scrubbed her mouth out with the ill-tasting foam, sure that if she did a proper job, it would be unnecessary for Grandma to do it.

After what seemed like many weeks, word came that the new baby was another sister, and when the day arrived for Amy's return, excitement filled the little home.

Janette was playing in the trees of a nearby pasture. When she heard Mommy was home with the new sister, she ran as fast as her short legs could take her, the younger Margie right behind.

After rushing to reach the family cluster, she was suddenly overcome by a sense of shyness. Mother had been gone for what seemed like such a long time and to see her with this new and strange baby felt awkward at first. When Janette finally brought herself to sneak a peek, she was surprised at how tiny the infant was.

Then it was announced that the whole family was invited to submit names for the newest member, and both Margie and Janette were asked for their choice, too.

It was easy for Janette to pick a name. A girl who went to their Sunday school class was Janette's ideal of all that a girl should be—she always wore nice dresses and had her hair neatly combed. Janette may have even envied her a bit if she had been old enough to know those kinds of feelings, but as it was, she just admired her. So little Janette picked "Joyce" as her choice for a name.

The choice was easy for Margie, too. She had not forgotten all the special attention she had received from the hired girl, so she chose "Ruth."

Each family member put a slip of paper into the container and two names were drawn out. The two youngest sisters were thrilled when they "won" and the new baby was named Joyce Ruth. Janette and Margie were sure that since they had chosen her name, she was even more "theirs."

Kathryn Steeves packed her bags and returned to Calgary shortly after Amy and baby Joyce were settled, and the children did not see her again. In the following year, 1941, word came that Grandma Kathryn was very sick. Fred and Amy left to visit her in a Calgary hospital. She soon died of cancer—the children's first introduction to the dreaded disease.

After the time spent with Grandma Steeves, Janette was better able to understand her own father. She had always been so proud of him. Even with clothes often dust-covered and smelling of sweat, the

JANETTE OKE: A HEART FOR THE PRAIRIE

hard-working farmer remained a gentleman. He knew how to doff his cap when meeting a lady on the street, and how to rise to his feet when a woman entered the room. He was the first to offer his seat if it were needed, or his condolences with sincere feeling. And he always acknowledged the presence of friend or stranger. Janette would never forget the pride she felt as she walked down the street holding his hand, watching him nod his head slightly, touch his cap, and say "How'do" to those who passed them.

Now she knew he was all those things because of her grandmother. Janette had a daddy to be proud of, and for that she would always be grateful to the older woman who, in a way, still seemed like a stranger in spite of kinship.

Kathryn's picture graced the living room wall during Janette's growing-up years and was still there to see whenever she returned home. She always looked at it with admiration. Grandma had been a special woman.

Four years later, Grandpa Robert Steeves also passed away.

Joyce was still very new when Janette came into the big farm kitchen from playing outdoors and found her mother bathing the baby at the kitchen table. She was small, chubby, soft—and stark naked—and Janette thought that she was quite the cutest little thing she had ever seen. The sight of the tiny arms and legs waving wildly made Janette giggle, until Amy's question caught her by surprise.

"Do you want to hold her?"

Janette was sent to stand by the opened oven door until all the chill had left her clothes and hands. Then the squirming baby was placed in her arms. She would never forget the wonderful sensation. Joyce was so little—so cute—and *hers.*

For the first few months it was the older sisters who got to spoil baby Joyce, and they took full advantage of it. As soon as she would begin to awaken from a nap, Betty, Jean, and June would race to reach her first. But the older she grew, the more the sisters were expected to share her.

Joyce turned into the family comic. Even as a little tot she was "full of ginger." She was tiny and wiry and always climbing and getting into trouble. From Mother's point of view, Amy felt it was a wonder that Joyce ever lived to grow up, but to Daddy, she was the household entertainer.

Sometimes Joyce's energy got her into trouble. Once she wrapped the roller towel around her neck and jumped off the kitchen chair where she had been standing. Another time she climbed out the upstairs window and onto the roof of the house. Then she proceeded to run down the sloped roof and jump off, yelling "Whee!" as she fell through the air. Her guardian angel must have been especially busy that day—she landed in a mud puddle instead of on the picket fence. Even so, the wind was knocked out of her.

Little Joyce certainly helped to keep things lively as she grew, putting on her own little shows and coaxing others to join her. Laughter was common in the home, and it seemed to ease tired shoulders and wipe away furrowed brows.

One of Janette's favorite pastimes was making play "farms" and "roads" in the hardened dirt near the back door. The path was so well worn that the grass for several feet around the area was completely gone. The chickens would scratch there, and the children used it for play.

All that Janette needed for her game was a few handfuls of her dad's nails from his shop, a hammer, and some string. Then she would begin pounding nails into the ground a few inches apart, trying to keep them in a nice even line. String was stretched and wrapped from nail to nail until it had formed fence lines. Whole farms with fields and pastures and farmyards would take shape. Then roads would be added, the whole structure sometimes becoming quite elaborate. Her immediate siblings sometimes joined her. The older ones in the family didn't seem to fuss about the construction sites as long as nails were pulled and returned and the hammer was put back in its proper place.

In the hours when she preferred solitude, Janette spent time walking the farm alone and making up songs or stories. She secretly longed for a doll carriage that would give her an excuse for the private walks, but there was none—not even a wagon to pull.

At times she sang some of her ditties to Margie while they were swinging together, but as hard as she tried she could never convince Margie that they were real songs. Margie would just dare Janette to sing the song again, and since it was never possible, Margie remained unimpressed.

At other times Janette spent quiet moments sitting with Betty, watching her work. Her oldest sister, who had then entered her teens, did some of the most beautiful and painstaking needlework. She often spent hours on a single piece. Janette considered Betty to be very grown-up, and the patience of her big sister amazed her.

Janette loved to crawl up beside Betty to watch—but she would also coax, "Let me pull the needle. Let me pull the needle."

Once the needle had been carefully placed where it should be, Betty would hold the cloth while Janette pulled the needle through the soft material, watching carefully as the tail of thread followed until the stitch was snugly in place. Then they would take another stitch together, and another. It was tedious for Betty, but she was patient and seemed to understand the thrill for her younger sister.

Betty also had a small treasure box of trinkets that she sometimes showed to Janette, who loved to finger the special things—item by item. Then they would carefully tuck them away until the next time.

Archie and Vi Ruggles, Janette's grandparents, did not visit often, but on those special occasions they always brought extra goodies with them and supper was sure to be a real treat. On one such visit, Janette was anxious to rush out with the others to meet their grandparents' car, but she had a rather noticeable problem—a big hole in her bloomers. Instead of joining the rest of the family, she hid in Fred and Amy's bedroom.

There was some laughter when it was discovered where she was, and then Grandpa Ruggles offered to fix her up. Cautiously she sent her bloomers out to him and then waited impatiently for them to be returned. Janette could hear a good deal of laughing while she waited, but she decided she must have a wonderful grandpa if he was willing to mend the bloomers of his granddaughter.

At last the garment was returned, and Janette could hardly wait to put them on and join the other family members. She reached eagerly for the bloomers and was about to maneuver her way back into them when she took a look at the mending job. What a disappointment!

Grandpa had mended the hole with paper, and even the small

child knew that would not work. The most difficult thing to understand, though, was the laughter. Janette knew it was coming at her expense, and her cheeks were hot with tears and embarrassment.

She sobbed and sobbed and refused to come out of the bedroom, crawling under the bed to hide from the laughter, feeling so ashamed. Grandpa Ruggles apologized, but ripples of laughter still escaped from some of the adults and it was difficult for the young child to forgive the act.

But Janette continued to love her Grandpa Ruggles regardless, and the two soon discovered a common interest. Grandpa was a writer. He wrote occasionally for a local paper, and he often wrote poetry. Janette was not very old when they began to exchange little bits of verse, and she still has one that he wrote to her.

> Way up north where the mosquitoes thrive
> Lives a little girl who is much alive.
> She is well covered with mosquito bites,
> Those little bugs that come out nights.
> This little girl I'll not forget
> For she is my sweet Janette.

At last the opportunity came to remodel some of the rooms in the house to better suit the needs of the family. Betty, though still a young teen, was the one who wielded the hammer. It seemed that the patience and thoroughness she exhibited while doing crafts carried over into a propensity for construction—an unusual trait for a teenage girl. She competently moved and rearranged walls, taking out one bedroom and dividing the extra space created between the kitchen and a remaining bedroom.

This room became the master bedroom, and after the walls were securely in place, the task of decorating it was undertaken. Wallpaper was selected, and the day for tackling the job arrived.

Janette stood against the kitchen wall, near enough to watch the proceedings and far enough not to be underfoot and sent away. The strange, gooey paste bubbled on the stove for quite some time and then was cooled. Soon the older siblings began to move in and out of the bedroom, measuring and cutting paper, then bringing it out to the kitchen table where they scooped up the paste in their hands and smeared it across the back of the paper. Then the whole mess had to be carefully maneuvered back into the bedroom.

It was all that Janette could do to keep from peeking into the room. Just as she would creep ever so quietly over to the door and catch a glimpse of the transformation taking place inside, someone would bump into her in the rush to retrieve whatever piece of equipment was needed. Several times she was chased away from the scene, but always she returned, fascinated by how new and different the room looked. When it was finally finished, dressed in color from the floor up and across the ceiling, it was obvious that those involved felt proud of what they had accomplished. Amy, Betty, Jean, and June stood back to admire the finished project. Janette could only stand and stare at the transformation.

CHAPTER SEVEN

School

IT SEEMED TO JANETTE that the time for her to begin school would never arrive. She had watched each fall as her older brother and sisters bundled into coats, collected lunch pails, and then hurried one another out the door in their rush to reach the schoolhouse before the dingling of the teacher's handbell.

At last came her turn to begin grade one, and she shyly but proudly entered the Harmonien school and a new era in her life. Little Margie was left to stand guard at the back door, waiting for them all to return home again.

The one-room country school was situated away from the passing road and reached by a winding lane that traveled over a small creek and up a rather steep little hill. In the springtime the creek often flooded the road, giving the pupils plenty of excuses for fun. Since the road could not then be traveled by foot, the ones who had not ridden a horse would be ferried across by those on horseback, going back and forth. This activity could be stretched out for quite a time, with lots of splashing and merriment.

In the winter every recess and noon hour was spent skimming down the school hill on sleds, skis, toboggans, or anything else that could be made to slide. Sometimes the games on the hill would get rather rough when the bigger kids took to playing their own form of cops and robbers. They would waylay a downward plunging sled, spinning it around and sending the occupant hurtling off into the snow.

Usually they were easier on the smaller children, but once Janette was hurt enough to cause tears to flow. It was her first year at school, and one of the "big" boys—perhaps in third or fourth grade—came to comfort her. He then offered to take her down on his sled in order to protect her—and instantly became her hero.

The road down the hill could be quite a rutted, muddy mess at the time of the spring thaw or if rains had been plentiful. The ruts would sometimes get so deep that the teams or cars coming up or going down would need to find an alternate route. There were few choices. It was too steep to go straight up and too narrow a track to swing very wide. The water washing down the hill often made deep furrows across the dirt road and the clay soil would turn to gumbo. If the road became too difficult to maneuver, only saddle horses and people on foot used the hill until things dried out again.

The Steeves children were largely unaffected by the road situation since they usually walked to school. The two and one-half miles in one direction could be fairly pleasant on a good day, but if it rained it was miserable. With no special rain gear they would arrive at school or return home soaked to the skin.

Since they were also without rubber boots, the worst muddy roads were conquered by simply slipping off their shoes and walking barefoot. Otherwise they did their best to clean their shoes in the damp grass and then let them dry by the kitchen stove before scraping them clean again.

In the winter the walk seemed longer. The frigid air bit against exposed skin on the face or where gartered stockings had slipped down to reveal bare legs. Colds and tonsillitis kept the children at home much of the time. The teacher spent a good portion of her busy day beside the old potbellied stove, drying out those who remained healthy enough to attend.

Janette was often the one left sick at home. Childhood illnesses seemed to catch her first, and she would pass them on to the other members of the family. During her early years she experienced whooping cough, mumps, measles, chicken pox, scarlet fever with an after-effect of inflammatory rheumatism, recurring bouts of tonsillitis, and many, many colds.

The report cards she brought home were filled with days marked "absent," sometimes absences outnumbering days present. But she did learn and was, in fact, the star of her grade. Of course it helped that her competition consisted of only one other boy. But the young teacher seemed to be quite proud of Janette's progress. In fact, in spite of missing so much, she finished grade one and took half of grade two her first year, then completed grade two and grade three in her second year.

Periodically, the school inspector would visit the school. When he came, he would stand at the back of the room, his tall, broad body encased in a dark suit, much more formal than the students were used to seeing. His head would be cocked slightly to one side, his hands clasped behind him, and his whole body teetering ever so slightly up on his toes, then down, up again, then down.

The inspector was neither harsh nor critical, but his presence was frightening just the same. His large frame and air of authority nearly made the children tremble; even the teacher seemed nervous whenever he showed up.

Thinking that Janette would be a fine example of her teaching ability, the young teacher asked her to stand and read aloud for the awesome man. Fear clouded Janette's thinking, and instead of "showing off" she stammered and stuttered through a miserable job of reading.

When his car was at last heard chugging away down the winding, rutted hill, everyone heaved a big sigh of relief—the teacher's sigh perhaps bigger than anyone's. Yet she could not refrain from speaking of her "disappointment" to her star pupil. Not only was Janette shamed by her embarrassing performance but also filled with remorse at letting her teacher down.

CHAPTER EIGHT

Farm Life

FRED WAS A BUSY man. He worked about the farm, usually with something in his hands, fixing harnesses, mending fences, cleaning grain, or sharpening tools. When he was doing field work, those same hands held a set of reins. For the first years on the Hoggarth place, the effects of the Depression were still being felt, and parts and gasoline to operate any farm machinery or vehicles could not be obtained. At this time, all the work was done with horses, several of them. And for the years that followed, Fred continued to utilize this source of "horse-power." Janette remembers each one as special in its own way.

Sam and Sandy were a gray team that Fred used for many years—Sandy had a few more "freckles" on his rump than Sam. Not fast, they usually traveled in low gear, but they were reliable and steady. Fred also used them in the bush for skidding out logs where there was little room for the antics of a skittish horse.

When the family was young and Amy needed to drive some-place—to church, the country store and post office, or a neighbor's house—it was Sam and Sandy that were usually harnessed to the rubber-tired wagon.

Even the children could harness the pair because they were so pa-tient with the fumbling of inexperienced hands. Since the horses were taller than the children were, it would take many stages of lifting, tug-ging, pulling, shifting, and practically climbing on their backs to get the harness over the top. Sam and Sandy stood quietly for as long as it took while the youngsters worked over them.

Although they could be ridden if needed, they were not considered riding horses. There were times, though, when they did act as taxi. After Janette had run down to the field to meet her daddy at the end of the day, he would sometimes boost her up to the back of one of the horses and let her ride home. It was a giddy feeling to be so high above the world and look down at the earth jerking along beneath her dangling feet. Her hands clenched the harness hames for all they were worth.

One day while logging, Sandy fell and tore his haunch on a tree stump. The theory was that while he rested, he fell asleep and went down. Horses rarely do such a thing but Sandy was getting rather old. After he recovered from the incident, he was watched more closely.

Sam was the unfortunate victim of a practical joke. Jack and Janette had decided to have some fun, each later blaming the other for coming up with the idea. But it was Janette who climbed into the manger while Jack covered her with a sprinkling of hay. Then Jack let the horses into the barn.

Of course, the first thing the horses always did was go directly to their stall and stick their noses into the manger to feed. Just as old Sam thrust his nose down for a mouthful, Janette jumped from the hay, flinging arms and yelling for all she was worth.

They had no idea that the poor old horse had so much life left in him. It was the fastest they had seen him move in years. Later, when bringing him back to his stall, Fred could not understand why his calm and steady old horse was resisting the rope and pulling backward, snorting and acting as if something were out to get him. Jack and Janette sent silent messages to each other, snickering behind their hands over their private joke.

Beauty was a pony for the little ones. Her shiny black coat was bumped against and tugged at by many a small child climbing what seemed to be a tremendous distance to the Shetland's back. There were many times when several children would pile on together, trying to fit as many bodies as possible from mane to tail before one began slipping and sliding over the other side, pulling the others along.

During the game, Beauty held perfectly still. Even when some of the braver children would crawl between her legs and under her belly or butt her stomach while pretending to be colts, she never moved.

Occasionally, however, when a child was riding her and wanted to be taken some direction the pony did not want to go, she would stubbornly turn toward home. There were times, with Janette tugging at her reins, when Beauty won this battle.

One of the games they devised to play with Beauty was delivering the mail. There was no rural mail delivery, and the children knew little about mail carriers, but they set about making their own postal system. Someone would ride Beauty under a tree and pick off several leaves. These would be sorted and delivered a few at a time to the other participants of the game who were posted at various stations around the farmyard. Each child was given a turn at being the carrier.

Jack, being the only boy among six growing sisters, led a different life on the farm than the others and had less time to enjoy the games. Though each of the children had responsibilities, he carried an extra heavy load, even learning at an early age to drive a five-horse team to help in the fields. Choring early each morning and late each night, there was not as much time for fun.

For a bit of income, Jack had been the school "fire maker" for a while. It meant that after his early morning chores were done, he would hurry the more than two miles, often running most of it, in order to start the fire in the big potbellied stove at school to take the chill off the room by the time the teacher and the rest of the pupils arrived.

This position also required that he haul enough wood to feed the stove for the day and then clean out the ashes as needed. It was a difficult task and the pay was only a few dollars each month. To supplement this, Jack also sold pelts. Rabbits could fetch a few cents; a good weasel, perhaps a dollar or two. He set his traps and snares close to the path to school and would stop to check them as he hurried past.

One slushy spring afternoon, when the ditches were full of snow and puddles, the children were on their way home from school. Acting on a strange impulse Janette impetuously yelled out, "There's a muskrat!"

She was surprised at the response by Jack. She knew he would be thinking of the fur and how much it would bring, but a muskrat was certainly uncommon in the area—though not preposterous.

Jack was immediately excited and started asking, "Where? Where?"

and Janette found herself lying, "There! There! Oh, it just went under that ice."

They chased the imaginary muskrat for about a quarter of a mile, all the way to the corner where the two roads crossed, and where Janette further said it went under the culvert. Jack posted Janette at one end and set himself on the other. When it was beginning to appear that they would stand their positions for the rest of the night, Janette decided it was time to confess that there had been no muskrat at all.

Jack failed to see the humor in the little incident. He scolded her thoroughly for lying, but she could not help chuckling now and then on the way home. On the occasions that Jack was later reminded of the little incident, it continued to bring mixed responses. Janette still laughed. Jack still growled.

There had been another brother, Kenneth, who would have been only two years younger than Jack. It had been especially difficult for Jack to accept the loss. He had been confused and hurt as a two-year-old when he lost his little brother, and for many years blamed the local minister, Reverend Dawson, who had come and taken the baby away from the farm home after Kenneth's passing. Then after waiting for two long years for another baby brother, he got Janette. But as they grew older they found that they could usually enjoy each other.

Some of the closeness was because Janette was the one who helped Jack with the farm duties. All the children had assigned chores, and Janette was responsible to fill pails of water from the deep, cold outside pump and carry enough wood to replenish the wood box in the entry.

There were no electric lights, and in the winter months it was nearly dark by the time they arrived home from school and still dark when they left in the morning. This meant that Jack needed someone to carry the lantern so he could see to work about the barn. Janette was the lantern-carrier.

It was usually a good arrangement, but on one night when the coyotes were howling nearby and Jack and Janette were away from the farmyard searching for cows near the haystack in an open field, Jack began to tell scary stories. By the time the cows had been spotted, Janette was in tears, certain she would be snatched up by long, yellow fangs and carried off into the forest to be eaten.

In spite of the pranks each pulled on the other, there were few actual fights between them, though occasionally miscommunication led to trouble. Once Jack was forking hay into the hayloft from a hayrack and his foot went through a hole in the floor of the rack, hurting his leg. He began to moan with pain.

Janette thought he was teasing. Since Jack rarely cried, it was easy to believe he was pulling another prank, so instead of helping him, she began to laugh. Janette's laughter only made him angry, as well as hurt, and he picked up a swatch of hay and slapped her across the face with it. Now it was her turn to feel pain—and she did cry. The quarrel was soon over, Jack out of his predicament, forgiveness granted, and the chores completed.

Butchering was another chore involved in farm life. Fred would not allow the younger children to watch the slaughtering of an animal, but they were needed to be a part of the action. They were assigned the task of runner, taking the parts of the animal in to Amy to care for after Fred had finished his part of the task.

The whole procedure was exciting. If it was a pig, there was scalding and scraping to be done. If it was a steer, skinning would follow. To the young child, it seemed so strange to gaze up at the creature suspended between earth and sky. The animal always seemed much, much bigger than it had when it walked the ground on all fours. But the butchering did not seem inhumane. It was a part of life. One did not kill for pleasure but for food for the family.

Fred hunted, as well, and during most winters wild game was a large part of the family diet. In fact, they ate far more wild meat than farm animals and, in the years when the family was accustomed to the distinct flavor, it tasted just fine.

The Steeves' house continued to be expanded and remodeled. What had been another first-floor bedroom was converted to a utility room, and kitchen cupboards were added in place of the lost pantry. Where there had at one time been three very small bedrooms on the main floor, there was now only one. This meant that the upstairs was to be shared by all seven children, with beds crowded into the space.

The kitchen gained space, which was important since it was the center of most of the activities in their home. Janette remembers it as the workroom. Meals were made, laundry done, baths taken. Almost everything happened in the kitchen.

The table was the place where the family ate, but it was required for much more. Babies were bathed there, then dried and dressed on warm towels spread beside the small basin. Canning was done while the table was covered with pans of vegetables or fruits in all stages of preparation and jars lined up to receive the produce. Letters were written, laundry folded, and quilts blocked. Homework was done, dresses laid out and cut, and meat prepared at butchering time. Chickens were dressed and fish cleaned. Crafts, either adult or children's, were assembled. Sunday school lessons were prepared, jigsaw puzzles were worked, and company was served. It was truly the heart of the bustling country home.

CHAPTER NINE

Occasions

EVEN AFTER THE Depression had ended and the long struggle to recover had begun, all the money that Fred could manage was tucked away in order to pay the farm taxes and make mortgage payments to Mr. Hoggarth. Because of the difficult times for farmers and townsfolk alike, Christmas celebrations could often be quite skimpy.

Amy and her brood worked carefully with what little materials they had, coupled with ample creativity, so that no one felt really deprived. And there were times when the results were exceptional.

When Janette and Margie were small, their older sisters planned a lovely dollhouse for them to share. Hours went into fashioning a little table and chairs, cupboards, and the little stove, painted to look just like Mom's big kitchen stove. Everything was made of wood and painted with trim, and the resulting furnished house delighted the two little girls. They played with it for hours at a time, and it became Janette's most cherished childhood toy.

There was usually a new dress at Christmastime, even if it was a made-over hand-me-down. One Christmas in particular stood out in the mind of Janette, who was growing quickly in spite of hard times. This Christmas dress was especially wonderful. As she slipped it on and looked at the reflection smiling back at her from the mirror, she felt lovely and special.

The dress was made in two pieces—a pleated plaid skirt buttoning onto a white blouse. When the time came for the community Christmas concert, she was pleased and proud to be so dressed up. Amy's face mirrored her children's pleasure in the gifts she worked so hard to produce.

It was an earlier Christmas that Amy herself held as most dear. On an especially cold, snowy day there was a jingling of harness, and a team and sleigh pulled into the yard. The farm dogs barked and then old Pooch hurried away to hide. The door was opened in anticipation of a caller, and the heavy fur coat of a bachelor neighbor filled the doorway. In his hands he carried a rather large box.

"For the kids," he said and placed it in Amy's arms. Words could not express the emotions of the young mother, and a special place for the dear old neighbor engraved itself upon her heart.

When the youngsters were allowed to open the gift, they discovered all sorts of goodies. Exclamations and laughter rang throughout the house. Janette was particularly delighted with the oranges the box produced. Oranges were a rare treat during that time.

On several occasions the Ruggles uncles came for a visit. They were still working at the Guess Ranch, living close to each other and somewhat communally. With them always came fun and laughter, the whole house seeming to rock with activity. It was wonderful for Amy to greet family, bringing their "goodie boxes" of special groceries too. She would laugh and tease, so thrilled to be with her brothers again.

The children were glad to see them, though the younger ones often hung back, not quite certain how to take the pranks of the teasing uncles. The favorite trick seemed to be to scare the wide-eyed youngsters. One would pull out a jackknife, sliding his finger along the sharp flashing blade. They were either going to "cut off ears" or "cut out goozlers," and though Janette was not quite certain where her "goozler" was, she wished to keep hers and was certain to keep at least an arm's distance away.

After giving the small ones a good scare, the uncles would pull out a sack of candy. Older children were more than happy to accept, knowing the uncles better than the younger ones, and at last even Janette was willing to forgive the earlier threats after her mouth was filled with jelly beans and her hands sticky with mints. Soon she was sitting easily on the uncle's knee, being assured that she would never be harmed and laughing along at the silliness.

Some visitors who pulled into the Steeves' yard were complete strangers. Often Indians would pass by the farm either singly or in groups, usually riding horseback or using teams and wagons. A few dogs ran with them, and many times at a stern command the animals would retreat and actually run under the wagon as it passed over the dusty road.

Sometimes the Indians stopped at the house for a drink of water or to sell their wares, which were usually smoked fish taken from some deep, cold Alberta lake. This was always a treat, with the children often being allowed to break off pieces and eat it like candy. Amy would later boil the remaining smoked fish and serve it with cream sauce. It was wonderful either way.

Though the Indians never gave Janette reason to fear them, she found her heart beating quickly whenever they arrived. Perhaps it was just that they were so different or that she could not put the wild stories of her older sister June out of her mind. June had quite an imagination and created bizarre tales of how Indians liked to "catch little white kids and hang their livers on the tallest branch of a tree."

Though Janette was aware of rumors related to Indian atrocities, it was well understood that there had been no real skirmishes between the Indians and the white people in Alberta except for one brief fling connected with the Riel Rebellion. The Royal Canadian Mounted Police had been created to forego problems and were very effective in doing so.

The quiet people who visited were always polite, and yet, her fear having no ability to reason, Janette shivered with fright whenever she saw them and secretly nursed some amount of awe as well.

One day when work was finished for the time being and Amy allowed herself to visit a neighbor for a cup of tea, the girls at home heard a knock at the door.

Margie opened it and was startled to find an Indian man. She may have shared Janette's fears of Indians or perhaps was simply too young to realize what she was doing, but the choice she made turned out to be a poor one.

The day was hot, and the man and his horse probably had traveled for quite some distance.

"Can I have some water?" he asked.

Margie nodded in the affirmative and told him "yes." Then she shut the door behind her. Apparently she expected him to get his own drink. The pump was in the pump house in the nearby yard.

When Amy arrived home a short time later, she was very upset. The Indian man had been quite offended at having the door closed on him and went farther down the road to the next place where Amy happened to be visiting. There he told of the treatment he had been given at the previous farm, and Amy knew that the previous farm had been hers. Amy made it clear to each of her children that nothing like this was ever to happen again, good intentions or not.

All neighborhood news traveled quickly, even without the modern-day convenience of the telephone. So even the children were aware when little bits of information reached their ears of a death in the community. One of the local men had been killed in a farm accident, and by the looks on faces it had been something terrible.

Then one day, the widow came with some neighbors to the Steeves' house and children were sent outside to play. When the company left and the little ones were free to go back inside the house, Amy was still wiping tears from her eyes.

This puzzled Janette. After all, the man was not "theirs," and she asked her mother about it and why she was crying.

"The Bible says that we are to rejoice with those who rejoice and weep with those who weep," Amy answered softly. The words sounded very strange and Janette's childish mind pondered them for some time, trying to sort out some kind of meaning. At last she felt she understood the lesson in compassion, because it was not just *taught* by her mother, but *lived.*

Janette also learned early the meaning of service to others. Neighbors often called upon Amy at the time of sickness to help nurse the ailing back to health. There were even times when she drove off to a home where she prepared a body for burial, trying also to bring comfort and help to the grieving.

While she was still small, Janette hated those interruptions into their family life, and she would stand at the window and cry as her mother left the home.

Later she realized how unselfishly her mother gave of herself to others. And because her mother gave freely, she also "gave" her girls. When others were in need of help for one situation or another, Amy was quick to offer the services of a daughter.

"She'd be glad to help you," Amy would say, and they did—starting quite early to lend a hand here and there.

Many of the daughters developed this spirit of generosity. Times were difficult and needs in the community around them were abundant. The Steeves did not have a great deal to offer, but what they could do to help they did willingly and generously.

Jean was one of the first of Amy's daughters to capture the zeal that her mother felt for her Christian faith. As a teenager, her ardent desire to serve the Lord made her hold tenaciously to her beliefs, even when faced with sisters who were more concerned about having a good time. Sometimes she would argue until tears came for some point she considered important.

When at last there came an opportunity, Amy announced to the family that she was going to be baptized. The service was planned on the banks of a small stream in a neighbor's pasture, and the district superintendent was to be present, assisting the local pastor. Jean quickly asked to be baptized as well.

The day arrived, and it was cool. Nevertheless, the crowd of people made their way across the field and clustered near the muddy bank. One after another, the baptisms were performed and the shivering participants, their faces glowing, waded back to shore into the arms of those who loved them.

Janette joined in as they sang "Shall We Gather at the River," her eyes wide with wonder. It was a strange ceremony, yet beautiful too. Perhaps someday she would be able to participate.

CHAPTER TEN

Summertime

EARLY IN THE SEASON, just after spring buds had opened and birds returned to the northern trees, the yearly pleading would begin.

"Can I take off my shoes?"

"Not yet."

"It's warm."

"Not warm enough. There's still frost in the ground."

"Well, it feels warm."

"You'll catch your death of cold."

"No, I won't."

"Not yet!"

When at last shoes were abandoned to their summer resting place and bare feet once again reveled in the cool dusty feeling of the hard-packed earth, freedom seemed to return.

It felt especially good to run through the grasses and down the paths after a summer rain shower. The cool mud oozed between toes and then dissolved in the "fairly clean" puddles where feet were rinsed before the children were allowed into the house for a proper washing.

After one delightful rainstorm that filled the slough to overflowing, Jack was feeling particularly boyish, bragging about how good his "brakes" were. He had soon talked Janette into watching the demonstration.

Jack took a good run toward the slough that had risen well past its usual watermark, making the grassy bank wet and slick. Just before he reached the water, he did as he had bragged and slammed on his "brakes."

Unfortunately, he had forgotten to take into account how slippery the wet grass would be and his "brakes" failed to work. Janette watched as his feet flew out from under him and he slid on his backside right into the small pond. The walk back to the house seemed so much farther to a boy dripping with pond water and followed by his laughing sister.

Except for Sundays and special outings, shoes were not worn by the Steeves children. It not only pleased the young ones; it made it easier on the family budget if shoes wore out less quickly and were able to last through a greater number of children before needing to be replaced.

Although Janette enjoyed casting aside her shoes as much as anyone else did, it was more uncomfortable for her in the end. Plagued with very dry skin and with the added drying of dust or mud, her heels cracked into miserable, deep sores.

After a day of playing outside, wash time followed. For Janette it turned into crying time each night. The water would make the cracked heels sting. Amy scrubbed as carefully as she could but still the screaming and crying could not be helped. When the feet were clean, the strong-smelling Watkins carbolic ointment was rubbed into the open sores and they were given a night of rest and healing. The next day would bring the same treatment and the process would begin again.

Another hazard of going barefooted was stubbed toes. Time and again someone would jam a toe into a stone and soon the nail was black and blue until it simply fell off. A new nail formed underneath, but there was always a chance that the sore toe would bump against something else before it had a chance to fully heal.

Though going barefoot made the soles of their feet calloused and tough, sharp objects did hurt and slivers could still be a problem. Sometimes on a quiet evening, the siblings would take turns picking one another's slivers. If the daily washing of feet had not been finished yet, a wet rag would be used to scrub little by little across the foot, slivers being removed as they were found. Many of the feet had already become calloused so they no longer hurt, but if the slivers could still be seen they were picked anyway.

It was rather like monkey grooming. Perhaps not very refined or genteel, but more than a little necessary—and even quite pleasant to have feet free from thorns again.

All too soon winter followed and shoes were taken from their storage places—along with heavy stockings, coats, mittens, and scarves. On arriving home after a day of play during the brisk winter, Janette saw the neighbor's car waiting in the drive. Inside the house she heard sounds of rushing around; then someone came out with a pale Amy and helped her into the seat of the car waiting for a trip to the hospital in the town of Rimbey. Later, words of hemorrhaging and miscarriage were overheard. Though Janette knew nothing of the meaning of the words, the worried tones of the hushed voices filled her with concern. She was afraid that her mother might not be coming home again. The following days passed slowly one by one.

Christmas Eve arrived without Mother, but the family tried to carry on the best they could, so the stockings were hung as usual. Janette received two small gifts; one was a little tool with pegs and a hole in the center. The idea was to weave yarn in and out, creating a long, round something. Though she was never quite sure what to do with the product of her work, it did help to fill many hours while her mother was away.

Later, when Amy returned, Janette overheard her mother say that one of the gifts Janette had received in her stocking was intended for Margie. The sisters had given Margie another present in its place, but the sense of having something that belonged to someone else was difficult to shake, even though Janette had had nothing to do with the mistake. The feeling of guilt kept her from enjoying the simple toy.

On Christmas Day, Betty and Jean took over dinner preparations. It seemed to take so very long for them to finish. While Janette tried to occupy her time elsewhere, the teens scurried around in the kitchen.

At last the turkey was removed from the oven. Betty and Jean were horrified to watch it fall to pieces as they tried to lift it from the pan. Tears followed for their failed efforts, but Janette knew nothing of the catastrophe. When at last she received the call to come and eat, she ate well, though she wondered why it had taken so much time to make beans for Christmas dinner. There were other foods served, but Janette had perceived only that Christmas without Mother was laboriously prepared baked beans.

During Amy's stay in the hospital, eight-year-old Janette took it upon herself to write a little poem.

> Away down in Rimbey way
> Each day I pray
> For my mother
> For she is my lover
> Each night I dream
> Of the lovely scene
> When she comes home
> Together we will roam
> Although she's far away
> If I pray
> She'll come back someday

Janette thought it was a crazy little poem, but when her mother returned, someone showed it to her. Janette had been too embarrassed to deliver it herself.

Over the next days, everyone who came to the house had to suffer through hearing that poem read. And though Janette was uncomfortable with sharing her work with so many people, it was the first time in her life that she realized something she had written could bring pleasure to someone else. And for a child, it was a "special" revelation.

CHAPTER ELEVEN

Games

ON WARM SUMMER evenings, Amy had difficulty getting her brood off to bed. The sun clung stubbornly in the northern sky until past ten o'clock, and in spite of the droves of mosquitoes, the children begged to be allowed to play outdoors "just a few more minutes."

They enjoyed the usual games like Tag, Kick the Can, or Hide-and-Seek, and sometimes they played Gray Wolf, which sent shivers up the spine of anyone young enough to still be easily frightened. Whenever Janette was allowed to choose, she selected Run Sheep Run.

Another sport they liked was baseball, and there were enough family members to have a good game. At times, even Fred, on his way to slop the pigs or separate the fresh milk, would stop long enough to take his turn at bat or coach someone on how to hold his hands for successful catching. Without mitts or gloves, it was difficult to convince young players to reach a bare hand out to a flying ball.

Some rules were adjusted to better serve the family game. For instance, any ball hit over the fence was "out." This kept those who could hit the ball hard from doing so and evened out the chances of younger ones getting on base.

When spring arrived, the schoolyard would become a playing field for every game imaginable. There were no age distinctions at the small school—it took every one of the children to make a decent game. Teams were chosen for softball, and the bigger kids took the hands of those needing help to swing the bat. If the pair actually managed to hit the ball they both would run, the older one practically dragging the youngster to first base.

If the game were to be Pump-Pump-Pull-Away, young arms were nearly pulled out of their sockets being towed to safety. And if the choice were Anti-I-Over, larger hands guided small ones as they struggled to catch the ball.

With so many children needed for each activity, there was no time for major discord in the schoolyard. On rare occasions there might be a disagreement of some sort, but to allow real spats would have spoiled the game for everyone.

However, there were times when Janette observed the cruelty possible in children. A group of young fellows attending a nearby school turned somewhat into a neighborhood "gang," and they chose Bobby, a handicapped boy who lived in the community, as their target. At community picnics or ball games the local bullies teased him unmercifully until he would lose his temper and chase them on his crutches. Although he hobbled after them as quickly as he could, they would soon be out of his reach and then he would lunge and hurl a crutch in their direction. Of course without his crutch he fell down, which made the boys howl with laughter. Janette was horror-stricken over the display of cruelty and wondered why someone didn't put a stop to it.

Bobby did have some good times. One thing he seemed to enjoy more than anything else was Beauty, and the chance to ride the little pony always made him grin with pleasure. Fred would help him up onto Beauty's back. Once on, Bobby's twisted legs made it difficult to straddle her well, but he clutched a clump of mane tightly in his hands as he set out for a ride.

Sometimes he did fall off, but Beauty was a small horse and the young boy was never hurt. Then he would coax to be boosted back up again, calling, "Mr. Steeves, Mr. Steeves. The old bronc rider isn't dead yet!" and his grin would spread from ear to ear. Beauty was good for Bobby, and somehow the small pony seemed to know it.

Other schoolmates occasionally came to play at the Steeves' farm. The closest neighbor lived about a mile away, so it was particularly exciting to share play time with children other than siblings.

Perry and Grace Rhine lived almost two miles away and had a family of eight whose ages roughly corresponded with the ages of the Steeves children, though the sexes did not. The oldest was Perry Jr., always referred to as Junior, then Dale, Fern, Faye, and Leonard, called

Sonny. After them were Lylas, Harvey, and Alta.

Over the years there developed a great deal of teasing over one Rhine-Steeves match-up or another. Betty was linked with Junior, perhaps with some justification. After all, he had once given Janette a dime to "get lost." And he did seem to hang around a good deal of the time.

Jean was teased about Dale. If there was any basis to this, it was hidden much better. Janette was teased about Sonny, and little Joyce, who was still very young, was tormented about Harvey.

Poor little Harvey. He had done absolutely nothing to deserve the teasing and laughter, but on more than one occasion little Joyce declared vehemently, "I love everybody in this world—'cept Harvey and Hitler and the Devil!"

The Rhines had a number of horses, and many adventures developed around them in one way or another. There were bucking horses and shying horses, running horses and horses who threw their riders.

One day Janette was finished playing at the Rhine farm and was ready to start home. Dale, a teenager, volunteered to give her a ride home on horseback. He caught the horse, pulled Janette up to her place behind him, then they started off.

There was one spot on the Rhine road crossed by a little creek bed. Whenever it was filled enough to be flowing, that part of the road could be under water, and after the worst rains it became a marshy bog. Only during dry weather could wagons pass that way at all. Even saddle horses hated the spot. Rows of loose logs had been laid across the swampy spot in corduroy fashion, but horses often balked and fussed, refusing to cross the makeshift bridge of uneven, shifting poles.

It was unclear just what spooked the horse on that particular day, but at just that muddy spot she suddenly plunged off the road, across the ditch, and deposited both of her riders on a rough pile of logs left there for future use in the crossing. She then lit out for home.

Dale, a big fifteen-year-old, bulging with farm-earned muscles, blazed with anger at the jittery horse. He took off after her, lifting lengths of logs from the ground and hurling them at the fleeing animal. None of his missiles connected, but throwing them seemed to release some of Dale's anger.

"C'mon," he called to Janette, and the two muddy riders trudged off after the animal.

It was not until they reached the Rhine barnyard that they caught the runaway and mounted again. Determination clenching his jaw,

Dale advised Janette to hang on by locking her small hands together around his waist.

This time they made it safely to the Steeves' farm. Janette, a little sore from the fall, thanked Dale and then watched as he swung the horse around, ready to firmly coach it across the mud again.

Fred occasionally made trips past the Rhine farm to pick up grain or some other necessity. One day he asked Janette and Margie if they would like to ride along and get off at Rhines' for a visit. He also suggested that they tie Beauty to the wagon so they could ride her home.

On arriving at the lane, Fred lifted them down, nodded his farewell, and set out again on his errand. With the little horse in tow, the girls walked down to the farmhouse but found no one home. Now having no reason to stay, they mounted the pony with the help of a wagon in the yard and started back toward home.

After traveling about halfway, a sudden storm struck. The thunder, lightning, hail, and freezing rain would have caused most ponies to bolt in fear, but not Beauty. She sauntered along, eating tufts of grass from beside the road, nibbling this and that, as though it were a lovely summer day and it had been a week since she had eaten anything. She seemed to be enjoying the freshness of the rain-washed grasses. Janette tried to hurry her up, but no matter how firmly she spoke or how much she dug in her heels and slapped the reins, Beauty paid no attention.

In the meantime, the girls were soaked to the skin with icy rainwater and pelted mercilessly with hailstones. At last they slid off. Janette and Margie had come to the conclusion that they needed help—desperately. So they did the only thing they knew to do.

Kneeling down in the middle of the muddy road, rain still beating on their heads and running over their faces, Janette held Beauty's reins in one hand and Margie's hand in the other and they prayed. This done, they started off again, now leading the stubborn pony in order to hurry her the best they could.

Amy, assuming that the girls were safe at the Rhines, had not been worrying. When Margie appeared at the door, dripping with rainwater and shivering with cold, Amy could hardly believe her eyes.

"Where's Janette?" she asked anxiously as she snatched a towel and wrapped Margie snugly in it. The answer to Margie seemed obvious. Janette had gone on to the barn to put Beauty away. They had been taught to always care for their horse after riding. Neither of the girls could quite understand why Amy seemed to be saying that Janette should have left Beauty standing in the yard and hurried into the house herself.

It was hours before either Janette or Margie could make her teeth stop chattering. Amy stripped them of their wet clothes, bundled them in something warm and dry, and put them in bed with hot water bottles under the covers.

Not until later did the remainder of the story come out. Amy looked surprised to hear of their spontaneous prayer meeting, but she was overheard sharing the story with guests, even relating the details to Rev. Hallman, the district superintendent, and his wife when they visited the Steeves' home.

Janette wondered why the kind gentleman seemed so impressed about two little girls kneeling down in the middle of a muddy road to pray for God's help. There simply had been no other place to kneel.

On rare and wonderful occasions there were trips south over the long, tiring miles to visit relatives still living on the prairie. Three homes clustered together at the Guess Ranch. Grandpa and Grandma Ruggles lived in a little house with a veranda lining the two sides. A "cook car" had been acquired some time before, and the kitchen on wheels had been "semi-attached" to the Ruggles' home. Here the women worked together to provide meals for all the families and any guests. Uncle Ross, Aunt Hazel, and family lived down the hill by the caragana hedge, and Uncle Wayne, Aunt Violet, and family lived in the small house to the south.

It was a wonderful place to visit. Cousins abounded, and those who did not live in the immediate vicinity were not too far away.

The favorite activity of the cousins was swinging on Grandpa's homemade porch swing. It was a wide affair with double-seats that faced one another and made complete with an attached floor between them. The whole swing was suspended from the veranda rafters. Hours were spent getting the swing, loaded with youngsters, to go as high as it could. The whole house must have rocked at times.

Fresh fruit was a real treat, especially juicy peaches. On one occasion it became known to the kids that Grandma Ruggles had some in her cellar. Whispered word came to Janette that there was to be a raid.

Three or four of the boy cousins had decided that a fresh peach would taste really good, and they asked her if she'd like to get in on the treat. After momentary debate with her conscience, she agreed.

Soon she had joined the boys in one of the granaries and smacked her lips as peach juice dripped off her chin. As usually happens to offenders, they were caught and ended up having to face the probing but gentle eyes of their grandmother, Vi.

"If you had asked me, I would have given you a peach," she said, the disappointment in her voice hurting much more deeply than a stern rebuke would have done.

Inwardly Janette wished to say, "But, Grandma—look at all the people. If you had tried to give everybody a peach, there wouldn't have been enough to go around. And you couldn't give them to just some of us."

But in her heart she had the feeling that her grandmother, generous and giving as she was, would have found some way. Janette determined never to hurt her again.

CHAPTER TWELVE

Antics

THE RHINES' FARM HAD a herd of sheep in one of its pastures. Among this herd was a ram that presented a constant threat to anyone trying to cross his domain. Dale, along with some of the older girls, developed a game of wits with the hot-tempered animal. They would draw his attention and then stand directly in front of a large tree. At the moment he put his head down and charged, they deftly stepped aside and the ram would crash against the tree. As he walked away, shaking his dizzy head at how such a small person could be so solidly built, the spectators would run off laughing.

Janette, afraid she might not move at the right time, never tried this bit of sport. And besides, though she did not voice her true feelings to the others, she felt just a little bit sorry for the cantankerous ram.

One day three of the girls decided to go for a horseback ride. They caught a couple of horses and set off through the pasture, Fern riding one and Janette and Faye sharing the other. They had often been warned not to ride among the rest of the horses, but in one of the impulsive moments of childhood, they paid little attention until they found their own horses out of control and running with the herd.

Then one of the horses began to buck. Faye and Janette clung desperately for several jumps, finally being thrown from the animal. As they scrambled up and dusted themselves off, the pair tried to shake the fright enough to chuckle at their mishap. Faye took a gulp of breath and reported that at one point, she put her hand down behind her to try to grab a handhold and found *mane*.

Then they did howl with laughter at the thought of Faye riding almost between the horse's ears and Janette bouncing along on its neck just behind her. Fortunately, they were not hurt badly.

Far more serious consequences could have resulted from another misguided idea. On a day when riding *behind* rather than *on* a horse sounded like a good idea, an old mare was harnessed to a stone boat. This piece of farm equipment looked much like a large wooden sled and was used to haul rocks out of the fields.

Once all the straps had been fastened into place, all the children piled onto the stone boat. They set out on an off-road, a single-vehicle rutted track. Grass and even small bushes grew on each side and spread down into an easy ditch for drainage.

The group had traveled only a short distance when they met one of the Rhines' uncles driving a team and wagon with a hayrack. No one was quite sure who was first to make the challenge for a race, but soon calls and dares were sounding from all sides and the offer for a race was accepted.

The load of children was rearranged, several of the smaller ones being sent up onto Uncle Jesse's hayrack. Then the horses were maneuvered into starting positions. Since there was room for only one vehicle on the road, the group on the stone boat took to the ditch. At the given signal they raced off.

The driver of the stone boat leaped into action, trying to steer clear of the biggest bushes and stones. Uncle Jesse's team had a definite advantage on the track, but the heavy wagon made a difficult load for racing.

Janette and the others on the stone boat were assigned the task of grabbing for handfuls of clod or anything else they could find to throw at their struggling horse. With no clear winner, Uncle Jesse had a good laugh—until he looked back down the road and realized what could have happened. He soberly concluded that had there been an accident, he would have found himself responsible for the results.

One summer, relatives visited the Yerricks, the owner-operator of the small Hoadley store. While they were in the area, the cousins often came to the Steeves' place to play summer evening games.

On one of those evenings while playing Hide-and-Seek around the barn, Janette jumped onto a board with some rusty old nails, and one

ANTICS

pierced her shoe. Instantly she began to scream at the top of her lungs, and soon got all the attention she felt the situation merited. Kids came running from every direction, each of them exclaiming over her plight. Even in her pain she was pleased at drawing so much sympathy from the Turple boys, the visitors from the city. One nail had barely grazed the outside of her shoe, but the other could be seen protruding through the top, having obviously passed through her foot first. It looked quite terrifying.

"We've got to take her to Mom," one of her sisters insisted and the others agreed. The children did not dare try to remove the nail from her foot, so they carried her to the house, the board still dangling. To Amy fell the task of removing the nails and calming the patient.

Amy spent much of the night soaking the foot, applying oatmeal poultices, and comforting a crying child. The poultices worked. For the next few days Amy wiped rust and pus from the hole in the small foot, but there was no serious infection. And since Vacation Bible School came soon after the incident, Janette attended that year hopping on one foot and minus one shoe, unable to wear the other until the swelling had gone down.

Somewhere and somehow, though money was still scarce, Dale Rhine got a truck. It was old and needed a great deal of work, but by then he had become quite a "tinkerer." It had taken a good deal of tinkering to get that old Ford to run. Though the truck was still not in top form, and in spite of the crush of small bodies loaded inside it and the noise of them all talking at once, Dale set out for a test drive with the lot of them.

There was room for a few to sit in the front, and as many as would fit loaded themselves into the small open back. The few brave ones who were left jumped on the running boards and grasped any appendage that could be used for a handhold. Then the ride began.

Dale was struggling to hear the engine, but the racket around him was making it very difficult. In order to lean a little closer, he opened his door and tipped his head out to listen intently while the truck chugged its way down the rutted, dusty road.

What he failed to remember was that little Harvey had been riding the running board on the driver's side, gripping the door by the open window. The door swung open for a few moments and finally swung back. When Dale looked up, there was Harvey, still holding on for all he was worth, his eyes big and his knuckles almost white. Dale grinned—and the motley crew continued down the road.

When fall came, leaves rustled with each step along familiar paths through the woods, and it was time for the assigned task of berry picking. Amy sent the Steeves children out to pick, but they were never quite the experts that the Rhine kids were. These eight children would haul in pail after pail of saskatoons, blueberries, and cranberries every year, and Mrs. Rhine would have rows and rows of two-quart jars canned each fall. Often, especially during the war years, there was no sugar, but the berries were canned regardless. Then if they did have sugar by the time they opened the jar, they would sprinkle a little over the top. Otherwise they let the berries "sweeten themselves."

Amy was concerned that the neighborhood children needed more Bible knowledge and began to send out invitations to a new Sunday school class, to be held at the Steeves' home.

She soon discovered that the Rhine children would not be allowed to attend on Sunday. Mrs. Rhine was Seventh Day Adventist in faith, and though she shared with Amy the desire to teach her children to honor God, her family felt that Saturday was the appropriate day of worship.

The Steeves children, being used to worshiping in different ways than the Rhine children, could not understand some of their "rules" but did not argue with them or try to dissuade them. So Amy switched the class to Saturday afternoon and everyone was satisfied.

Mrs. Rhine was determined to see that her children were raised properly and understood the importance of what she taught them. Janette remembers one occasion quite vividly. Some of the Rhine children had been playing in the Steeves' house, and late in the afternoon, the visitors headed out for their long walk home. The evening meal and activities were well underway for the Steeves children and darkness had already crowded against the windows when, suddenly, they were interrupted by a knock at the door.

It was Mrs. Rhine with Harvey in tow. After he had arrived home and had begun preparing for bed, she discovered some pennies in his pocket. With eyes lowered to the floor, Harvey shamefacedly admitted that he had taken them from the Steeves' home.

The woman was not willing to allow such an offense to remain until morning. So she boosted Harvey onto a horse and led him in the dark, over the rutted road and across the corduroy bog, through rows of tall pine and spruce without a light of any kind showing for miles, until she reached the Steeves' door.

Janette watched quietly as the mothers worked out the problem and then heard the click of the closing door.

"They could have waited until tomorrow. Why did they come so late at night?" she asked.

"Mrs. Rhine wanted to teach Harvey the importance of never taking anything that didn't belong to him," Amy explained, and on that night the lesson engraved itself on *two* young minds.

One day, the Steeves heard that Fern Rhine had had an accident. The teen had dismounted her saddle horse in order to lead him across the stretch of corduroy, and the horse had balked, then decided to clear the dreaded spot in a single leap. As he jumped, his hoof struck Fern on her knee.

The leg swelled and went from bad to worse. Fern spent several weeks in the small Rimbey hospital and was finally transferred to another with more extensive facilities.

While Fern was still away receiving medical treatment, the Rhines decided to have a farm sale and move from the area. There was much sadness at the thought of losing such good neighbors and friends. The community quickly decided the Rhines should be given a surprise farewell party.

On the appointed evening, neighbors began to arrive at the Rhine home, and since the family had had no chance to prepare for their surprise guests and the home had no electricity, Mrs. Rhine was soon bustling around the house, searching for working lamps to adequately light the rooms.

On passing from room to room, Mrs. Rhine noticed many of the neighbors whispering soberly among themselves and was worried that the unexpected guests might be annoyed about her poorly lit home.

She resolutely set out her remaining lamps and turned to greet one of the last guests to arrive. This neighbor, late to the would-be party and unaware that the Rhines had no knowledge of the actual reason for the hushed whispers, extended his condolences to his hostess.

There was a little scream, and Mrs. Rhine fainted and fell to the floor. It was not until then the neighbor discovered that she had not yet been told about Fern's death. The tragic news had come shortly before, and the neighbors had been trying to decide how the mother should be told, and by whom.

Janette was horrified. The dimly lit house, the whispers, then the final revelation and reaction of her neighbor woman all felt like some strange chilling story. She had not seen anyone faint before and feared that Mrs. Rhine might be dead. Janette's immense relief when Mrs. Rhine stirred again was quickly changed back to dread with the despairing mother's sobs that followed. Janette was shaken to the core. It would be such a terrible thing to lose a child, and Janette wondered how Mrs. Rhine would cope. That night the walk home through the darkness was filled with sorrow and a strange fear.

The neighboring Lindberg family was very special to the Steeves. They lived on a farm about a mile away—if one struck out through the trees on the Robakowskie quarter and pursued the cow paths as far as they could be taken in the right direction and then followed his nose. If one went by the road it was a bit farther—but likely faster.

The Lindbergs had three sons. Dennis, the eldest, was just a bit younger than Margie and was always a most amiable playmate for the Steeves youngsters. Gary was next and close to Joyce's age. Vern followed a few years later and was enough younger that Janette does not remember sharing a classroom with him.

Mrs. Lindberg was the local schoolteacher for some of Janette's grade school—and a good one she was, too. Mr. Lindberg was a hardworking and prosperous farmer until they sold the farm and moved to Rimbey. All three of their sons leaned toward the academic and did very well in school.

There were many family visits back and forth for dinners or evenings of games and fun. Children had sleepovers and shared special trips to town or treats of homemade ice cream. Janette still has a photo of the "mock" wedding that Mrs. Lindberg fussed over, just to give the kids something interesting to do. Margie was the bride, Dennis the groom, and the rest of the little party filled in as attendants.

CHAPTER THIRTEEN

Family

THE STEEVES FAMILY was growing up, and sibling relationships and rivalries had to change along with new independence and maturity. Betty, the eldest and the sister who had been the carpenter and craftsman, grew into a quiet, somewhat reserved young lady.

The second sister, Jean, was more outspoken, more impulsive, and it was often Jean with whom Janette would clash. Jean wished to take charge when Amy and Fred were away from home, and although it was obvious that *someone* needed to be in control, Jean's orders were often not well received.

Jack rebelled against her. Janette rebelled right along with him. At times the little house shook with the results of a directive that was not accepted with cooperation.

Though it did not happen often, on at least one occasion Jean decided that a spanking was in order. Jean was seven years her senior, but Janette was big enough—and ornery enough—to resist.

Through the tears that followed, Janette shouted, "I'm glad I'm not *your* kid!"

June had her own place in the family's heart. She was the "neat" one who enjoyed having nice things. Her clothing was always tidy and her hair just so. She was attractive, popular, pleasant, and talented—in fact, the kind of sister that one might envy and feel put down by. Janette adored her, and there were no fights between them. But then, June got along well with everyone.

June had an incredible imagination, and for many years she was the family storyteller. As children, she and Jack had invented their own pretending game where the "horse-steppers" took them to far-off places and let them experience exciting things.

As June grew older her imagination developed soap operas and other exciting tales. Often on the walk home from school she produced her own "programs" and aired them for her own pleasure. Janette always chafed against being required to walk ahead or behind. She would have loved to hear those "radio" presentations. June was the theme music, the announcer, and each player by turn, and the action could be dramatic indeed.

June was also musical. Though she did not have the luxury of music lessons, she did learn how to play the old pump organ that sat in the family living room. Hours were spent singing together, the younger Janette doing the melody and June providing the harmony.

Later, June was able to obtain her own accordion, and she quickly learned to play anything she heard. The family loved to listen to her Strauss waltzes and energetic polkas with the difficult fingering for her left hand.

Because Janette and Margie were so close in age, it was easy for jealousy to crop up. At times there was subtle maneuvering to lure a friend to one "side" or the other. Most often, however, the girls were able to share school chums evenly. It did not help that there were few girls their own ages. Janette's two closest friends were a few years older than she was, while Margie was blessed to have a schoolmate her own age. Often, though, the two found themselves enjoying each other's company in their play.

Milder winter days were spent outdoors. The little nearby hills were used for sledding or even trying out new Christmas skis. Sometimes a horse was used to tow a toboggan.

When the temperatures plummeted well below freezing, the slough behind the barn would be transformed into an outdoor skating rink. The Steeves had no booted skates, but the older kids enjoyed strapping the bob skates to the bottoms of their boots, and Fred would give the younger children a thrill by pulling them on a scoop shovel tied to a long rope. The sensation of speeding across the bumpy ice in long arcs was enough to lure them from the warmth of the house time and time again.

Days were short in the winter, leaving little time to work and play before evening darkness fell and the lamps were lit. One winter night there was a knock at the door and a neighbor stood there with a solemn expression on his face. Beauty had somehow gotten loose, and had been on the road. She was a dark horse on a dark farm road on a very dark night. A car had come over a steep hill, and she had been hit and thrown several feet.

Fred hurried to hook the team to the stone boat, sure that every bone in the small pony's body must be broken. To the family's surprise, she was alive but had to spend many days recuperating in her stall. Though Beauty never fully recovered, she was well enough so the family had their pony for some time to come.

During these dark winter evenings when the wind whistled past the windows, driving snow against the panes, the family gathered at the table under the light of an oil lamp to entertain one another.

Sometimes they copied funny paper characters. June was especially good at drawing all the pretty girls like Daisy Mae. In fact, it was often decided that her girls were even prettier than the professionally drawn ones. Jack was better at the Katzenjammer kids and Popeye.

At other times they tried their hands at limericks. They would each take turns reading their own aloud to see who could get the best laugh. Line upon line was written and crossed out, each child doing his or her best to create a punch line that would send the others into peels of laughter. Groans were all that some produced, others ripples of giggles, and still others loud hoots.

At last it was time for Janette to read hers. She began slowly, sneaking peeks over the top of her page to judge the reaction she was getting.

> A smart city slicker from York,
> When dining, didn't know beef from pork.
> "This is lamb," he did say,
> Then he heard the thing neigh.
> Surprised? Well, he swallowed his fork.

The laughter that followed was all the applause she needed, and the spotlight was passed to the next child.

In the glow of the lamplight that splashed against happy faces, more than limericks were being created. The shared moments around the little table brought family members, though very different in personalities, together and gave them a secure place in which to share thoughts and creative efforts.

Soon the first of the children to leave home would be gone from the circle. But long after they had all grown and moved far away, the special bond that was woven between them in those early years would draw them back again and again to the little farm where they learned how to give and receive love.

One Christmas occasion brought unusual visitors. Amy had heard of an Indian couple who was camped in the area on their way through from one reserve to another. A bad storm had come up, blowing a tree over their tent, and, though neither was injured, their tent had been damaged. So Amy sent Fred off with the sleigh to invite them to share the small house.

The couple came, bringing with them their guitars and their skills at entertaining. Janette was still apprehensive about Indians, but this time she found she couldn't resist her curiosity and stayed close by, though still in the background.

Mr. Northwest was great fun. He talked a lot and played and sang and did funny little tricks of whistling into his guitar, which made it seem that the sound came from the ceiling. The woman, whom each assumed to be his young wife, was very quiet and shy. She scarcely said a word. Later, the family learned that they were not married but running off together.

Before the few days together had ended, Janette had left behind her notions that Indians were ferocious. And soon after they had gone, taking along a puppy from the litter in the barn, they sent word back of their safe arrival at the new reservation.

Mr. Northwest expressed appreciation for the family's kindness and relayed to them what had happened in the latter half of their journey. A second storm had caught them while they were still walking along the highway, but a trucker had stopped. Since there was room for only one passenger, Mr. Northwest had sent the woman on ahead in the truck and had continued to walk. Eventually they had both arrived at the reserve.

Mr. Peter Waldin was a young professor at Mountain View Bible School located in the town of Didsbury. This English gentleman visited the Steeves' farm and informed Amy that a summer Bible camp for children was being started at Gull Lake and even offered to supply funds if any of the Steeves children were interested in attending. His only stipulation was that each child attending memorized a given list of Bible verses in order to earn their week's stay. It was decided that Janette, now ten, and Margie would take advantage of the generous offer, and they set about learning the required Scripture verses in preparation for their week at camp. The current Hoadley pastor, Rev. Dyck, and his wife offered to drive the two girls to camp, and they were very excited. This was their first time so far from home without a parent along.

It was a new experience to be sure. The log cabins with their built-in bunks were shared with a number of other girls their age, including one of their cousins, Eva Ruggles. Their cabin counselor was a young pastor's wife by the name of Joyce Taylor. She was very nice and helped to put the girls at ease in the new and strange surroundings.

Once they had settled in and had a look around, they could not help but notice a big, boisterous group of children from Didsbury, the Alberta center of the Missionary Church. Others hung back and let these town kids take center stage. This they did easily and seemed to enjoy the spotlight.

One lad in particular, running around the campgrounds in knee pants, caught Janette's eye. She was not at all used to seeing a ten-year-old boy dressed as he was: carefully pressed clothes, neatly groomed hair, and shoes that looked almost new. She watched as he raced by, swishing a branch and making loud, boisterous noises. Just behind him came his mother calling "Edward!" and trying to make him settle down.

It was at this camp that Janette took the first steps on her spiritual journey. The camp evangelist was Mrs. Beatrice Hedegaard, and Janette thought she was wonderful.

During the week's services, Janette sat stubbornly through a few invitations to come to the front and receive Christ as Savior. Her heart throbbing, her palms sweating, she knew she had sin in her life that needed to be forgiven. She ached to go forward with the other children.

But everyone thinks you're already a Christian, the deceiver whispered softly. *If you go forward they will think you have been living a lie all this time.*

Janette had thought she was a Christian. Now she knew that just believing the Bible stories—believing that God truly existed, believing that Jesus came to die for the sins of mankind—was not enough. What she needed was to accept that sacrifice for herself, to ask His forgiveness, and to turn her life over to Him.

The end of another service drew near. Again Janette's heart was pounding. The weight of unforgiven sin was heavy upon her small shoulders. Should she bring shame on the Lord—and on herself—by admitting she had been a hypocrite?

This time Mrs. Hedegaard did not ask seekers to come forward. Instead, she asked those who wished to have their sins forgiven, their lives given to Jesus, to simply raise their hands for prayer while the congregation waited with closed eyes. That meant no public exposure. Janette felt that this would not "shame" her God, and she slowly lifted her hand.

But in the next breath, Mrs. Hedegaard asked those who had raised their hands to step forward. There was no stopping now. With the first difficult step behind her, the lies of the accuser were shattered. The Lord would not be ashamed by her admission of need. It had been a lie—just one more lie that Satan had tried to use to hold her back. Quickly, she made her way to the altar and knelt to make her peace with God. Margie was right beside her.

After the two small girls had prayed their own prayer and been counseled by one of the workers, they joined hands and went looking for the evangelist.

"Our daddy doesn't know Jesus," they told her, tears running freely down their cheeks. "We need to pray for Daddy."

For Janette, two intense emotions had followed each other, the wonderful realization of forgiveness and freedom from guilt, and then the powerful concern for someone whom she loved dearly who was still "lost."

They returned home by train, anxious to tell their mother of their decision—but still burdened for their daddy. It would be many, many years before the fervent prayers for him would be answered.

CHAPTER FOURTEEN

Changes

BETTY, THE OLDEST, WAS the first to leave home. She was nudged into independence early because the family needed all the breadwinners possible. Though still in her teens, her wages were counted on to help out.

She took summer jobs keeping house and caring for children while their mothers worked outside the home. It was hard work for a young girl and meant a good deal of responsibility. But Betty was already familiar with caring for children and working hard.

One of her jobs was at the nearby town of Winfield. After being gone for a while, a short visit home became possible. And when she arrived, bringing gifts for the younger siblings, the family felt complete again.

All too soon it was time for Betty to return to her duties. But it turned out there was no one to take her back, and she was expected to be at work the next morning. In the end, she had to walk several miles along the railroad tracks, through heavy forest at night. When the dim lights of the farmhouse windows faded behind her, she was alone in the blackness.

Towering spruce crowded in closely to the thin ribbon of train track through an area where timber wolves, lynx, and cougars often had been sighted. Janette observed her mother's tenseness and knew that she was concerned about her oldest daughter. It was a puzzle to young Janette. Why did Betty have to go back—especially so late at night? And why did she have to walk in the dark? Surely she could have waited until there was a ride or at least until it was morning. But her anxious thoughts could not make the long miles any shorter for Betty, and her big sister did survive the rather frightening experience.

Betty was a good student, and after two years of working she returned to the local school. Since Harmonien only offered up to ninth grade, she then went to Rimbey for further education. Rimbey was not particularly far from home, and she found her stay fairly easy to endure because sister Jean went along and shared her accommodations.

One weekend, Janette and Margie were allowed to take the short train ride for a visit with their two older sisters in Rimbey. As they boarded in Hoadley, they were given their few cents of fare money with the explanation that the conductor would be around shortly to collect the coins.

The train lurched and then, slowly, the rhythmic chugging came faster and faster, and the girls watched familiar trees and landscape fall behind. Sitting firmly against the seat, Janette and Margie waited impatiently as the conductor made his way down the aisle, stopping to collect the fares from the few passengers who had boarded at the small whistle stop. He was a cheery man, and as he walked the shifting aisle he nodded his special hat this way and that. After a glance toward the girls he moved on, and Janette was left with her money getting warm and sticky in her clenched fist.

There was a stop at the town of Blufton where passengers and freight were exchanged. Then the chugging began again until the train drew up alongside the water tower and the boiler was refilled with a great deal of accompanying hissing steam. Again they were off. The next stop was Rimbey, and the man with the hat had not yet taken their money.

Janette was older, so the burden of responsibility rested heavily upon her. Visions of her and Margie spending the rest of their lives in jail flashed through her mind. Her eyes darted around the railcar in search of a way out of the awkward situation.

When the train pulled into Rimbey, they both looked at the money still resting in Janette's hand and then into the other's eyes. What should they do? Should they just stay on the train until the fare had been collected? Did they dare to get off?

At last Janette took the fateful plunge. Gathering up the few belongings, she took Margie's hand and they made a run for it. Glancing back, they were surprised to find no one in hot pursuit.

But immediately the pair had another problem. The directions they had been given did not seem to work out. Perhaps they had gotten off the train on the wrong side, but whatever the reason, they walked first in one direction and then back again.

A man with a team and wagon pulled up beside them and asked where they were heading. They told him the name of the man at whose farm Jean and Betty made their little home, and he invited them to climb aboard. Soon they arrived in the proper place and, grateful for the stranger's help, were much relieved to find their sisters waiting in the small building they rented together.

Later they learned that children were often allowed to travel the rails free. But the dreadful worry they had experienced was difficult to put behind nonetheless.

Because of illness, Jean found the schooling situation in Rimbey too difficult, so she soon dropped out and went to work. Even though she was so young, her paycheck helped to supply necessities for the family.

However, Betty, after her stay for schooling in Rimbey, went on to Prairie Bible Institute, which seemed very far from the family home. Then she went to work at the creamery in Bluffton.

It was there she met George Cox, and they were married on Christmas Eve, 1945, when she was nineteen. Then she and Jean both spent some time working in nearby Bluffton.

One day Betty and Jean called home with a sad story. The woman who ran the local hotel had been hospitalized, and there were seven children in the family, the oldest only eleven.

Janette did not overhear the conversation when the decision was made, but when the girls came home they brought three children with them—Ronny, Teddy, and Patsy, the baby. This had not been the first time that Amy took in children, for one reason or another.

Ronny and Teddy did not stay long as other arrangements were made for them, but Patsy did. The family watched her celebrate her first birthday, learn to walk, and begin to talk. She became a "little sister," and they all loved her dearly.

But the day inevitably came when things would change. It was both a good day and a bad day, for Patsy's mother finally was able to care for her little girl again, and yet it also meant that the Steeves family needed to give her up. And it was like losing a member of the family. Patsy did not even know her real mother, and cried as she was taken away, holding out her arms to Amy, calling, "Mama! Mama!"

It nearly broke Janette's heart. She retreated to the upstairs bedroom to cry, where a little sweater left behind just added to her grief. She wept for the little girl who had been like family and then had to be uprooted from their home.

They did not even dare visit Patsy until they were certain she had had time to adjust to her own home. At last the day was announced that they would call, and everyone went along for the visit.

Patsy may have adjusted, but she had not forgotten. Janette took her small hand and led her away to play together. Soon the little one's pleas brought tears to her eyes and pain to her heart when Patsy said clearly, "Bike, 'Nette. Home." She wanted Janette to take her home on the bike. So the Steeves decided it was best for Patsy—and for their own adjustment—if they did not visit again.

One of Jean's jobs took her to Red Deer where she lived and worked at the Provincial Training School. There she made acquaintance with several girls. One good friend, Bernice Budd, had come from Rimbey.

It was during the time that Jean spent in Red Deer that the wonderful news burst across the radio waves and into every newspaper: The war was finally over and the boys were coming home.

Families gathered at railroad stations across the country, anxiously searching the crowds for the first glimpse of their own returning soldiers. Arms stretched wide to receive them; men pounding their backs in strong hugs, and women weeping with joy against their soldiers' weary shoulders.

Among them was Orville, Bernice's older brother, who had been one of the first to enlist and had served overseas in Communications. Bernice took Jean home for a visit, and while she was there, Jean met Orville. There was immediate mutual interest. At least, that was how the family perceived it when Jean then brought Orville to meet her own family.

The warm smile and quick wit of Jean's dashing young man made him easy to like, and he quickly earned approval. The couple had met near the first of the year in 1946 and was married on June 23.

Even though these two older sisters had not been around much for a number of years, their weddings following each other in such quick succession meant they had homes of their own and would no longer be coming "home" as often. And when they did, they would not come alone.

Christmas, too, showed changes, and though there was often company, there came a year when the Steeves found themselves alone and their numbers diminishing. Perhaps Amy looked forward to a less eventful Christmas, though her love for company made that doubtful, but Janette felt it was a strange celebration with the house so quiet.

The saving events were the annual Christmas programs that could be counted on as part of the season year after year. The local church usually had a special program, and the schools always put on a pageant. There were recitations, small plays, songs, and skits. Everyone in the school was involved in the presentation, and if ever one was to have a new outfit of clothes, it would be for the school program. Janette often found herself reveling in the feel of a new dress that night.

During Janette's earlier school years, the family had traveled by team and sleigh to those events. Everyone in the area did. Fred would spread straw on the bottom of the sleigh, and Amy would load the blankets. Then the family bundled up and snuggled down on the straw.

As they rode, they sang songs and told stories and watched the dark skies for shooting stars or Northern Lights. And there were little spats about who had the most covers, who was taking the most room, or who was smothering someone else by crowding.

The trip to the program usually could be managed without too much ado, but the trip home was sometimes less than a scene from Currier and Ives. By the time the horses pulled in at the front gate, some kids would be crying from cold and exhaustion, and Amy would be vowing she would never again make the mistake of dragging all the offspring out into the December cold for the sake of a community concert. But she always did.

At the school there were pre-Christmas fundraisers, so each student would receive a small gift and all children attending would be given a bag of candy. To the accompaniment of much merrymaking and laughter, Santa was always there to distribute the goodies and tease blushing young girls by coaxing for a kiss on his whiskered cheek before he would hand over their booty.

The entertainment itself was unsophisticated but enjoyable.

Especially when little unplanned and unforeseen incidents spiced up the show a bit. Little occurrences such as someone stepping off the make-shift stage, or tripping over a cord, or catching a foot on the sheets that served as curtains would be remembered well after the choice of songs was forgotten.

All the children did their little parts, gave the bow or curtsy as they had been taught, and scurried off the stage, glad to have it over but pleased with themselves as well.

At one such program it was Janette's turn to recite "The Twins." Her teacher had been impressed with her performance during practice and could hardly wait for the recitation, expecting the crowd to enjoy it. Since the poem was written from a male perspective, Janette was dressed as a man and had practiced changing her voice in appropriate fashion. It would be fun to ham it up a little.

After the proper introduction fanfare, Janette began quoting the poem, which went well enough. Then to her horror, her mind went blank! She scrambled and floundered and the poor teacher coached, but the whole recitation became a miserable flop. Janette was only too glad to escape from the stage.

After the night's applause had faded and people were clustering to give their congratulations and comments of the evening, the teacher searched out Janette and asked what had happened. There was little she could answer. Stage fright? Nerves? The poem had simply left her—and it never returned in later years in its entirety, though she mentally groped for it and even refreshed her memory by reviewing it. It stubbornly refused to be relearned and only snatches of it ever come back to mind, just as it was on that awful night.

After the Christmas concert, lunch was served. All the mothers brought sandwiches or cake, and coffee was made in a big boiler on the potbellied school stove. The blaze heated not only the coffee but the entire room as well, especially when the small schoolhouse was packed tightly on concert night. Still, on such cold winter nights no one complained.

CHAPTER FIFTEEN

Striking Out Alone

SHORTLY AFTER THE marriage of Jean and Orville, eleven-year-old Janette was asked to move in with the newlyweds, as Jean found herself quite lonely and suffering from morning sickness. Janette attended seventh grade that year at Monte Vista, another small country school. From then on, she lived at home only on and off. For one reason or another, she found herself staying with someone in her extended family—often for reasons having to do with school. Because of this she missed much of young Joyce's growing-up years. It was also during this time that the last Steeves' daughter, Sharon, was added to the family. Since Betty, the first daughter, already had a small son, the baby girl was born an auntie.

Sharon arrived while Janette was still staying with Jean and Orville. The plump, dark-haired baby was a change from the previous Steeves children. The others had arrived with not much hair at all, whereas this new family member had lots of it. Then, a few days after Sharon arrived, Jean gave birth to her first baby, a boy. So Steve and Sharon grew up more like cousins than aunt and nephew.

After spending the following year with Jean and Orville, Janette was back in the Harmonien school, surrounded by past friends. It was wonderful to be home again.

One of these childhood friends who became special to her in this period of time was Helen Eliason. She was a few years older than

Janette and an only child. To a young girl in the middle of a pack of eight, Janette thought Helen had gotten all the breaks. At the same time, she realized that she would not have enjoyed being all alone in the family.

Helen's father had wanted a boy, and Helen seemed to share his feelings. She didn't care for skirts and hardly ever wore dresses. There had been one dress, a dainty yellow one with beautiful frills, row after row, but Helen wore the dress only for very special—and rare—occasions, and Janette felt her friend never fully appreciated how lovely it was. The rest of the time Helen wore pants. Once jeans came into fashion for farm kids, she rarely wore anything else.

Helen had a pony that she rode wherever she went, and it seemed she was on the road a great deal of the time, running errands for her mother and father and visiting friends.

Since she preferred working outside, Helen was not required to do many household chores. But that was no problem, for her mother managed just fine without her, keeping a spotlessly clean house and cooking the best of Scandinavian food.

Janette loved to visit the home, and it helped that Mrs. Eliason was openly fond of her. Every time she was invited for dinner, the kind woman cooked Janette's favorite dishes: Swedish meatballs and tiny potatoes steamed in their jackets, pastries and fat blueberries smothered in rich farm cream.

Mrs. Eliason was a plump, cheerful woman who told stories of her younger years with a flare that made them fascinating. She always wore a kerchief tied over her thin gray hair and a big bib apron, clean and crisp, pinned to the bodice of her housedress and neatly tied in the back. Janette loved her so dearly that later if there was one person from her youth to whom Janette would have loved to show her first published story, it was Mrs. Eliason.

Helen and Janette spent hour after hour "pretending" with their own versions of "cowboys and Indians"—they were "wild west nuts," drawing most of their knowledge of the subject from western comics. Helen had the advantage of more spending money than Janette and amassed comic books by the score, removing the colorful covers and mounting them in scrapbooks.

Helen was even allowed to go to western movies on occasion and retold the entire plot to Janette as soon as the two could get together again. Then they lived the characters. Helen was always Roy Rogers, and Janette was allowed to be Gene Autry or Dale Evans, according to

Helen's dictates. Janette always went along with whatever Helen said. After all, Helen was the authority. But the creative efforts were always enjoyable for Janette as their intricate plots unfolded.

Janette did manage to get a few of the comic books herself and, following Helen's lead, put the covers with the glorious pictures of smiling Roy and Dale into a scrapbook. Their big white hats and flashing outfits in blues, reds, or whites were bedecked with long fringes and sequins, and the girls often compared pictures and drooled over the finery.

Helen had elaborate plans of becoming a writer—of westerns, of course. Janette listened and smiled, never allowing herself to share her own private dreams of writing someday. At the time, the dream seemed far too remote and impossible.

But Helen was serious. She filled notebooks with her stories, with much encouragement from her parents.

Meanwhile, Janette contented herself with reading all the books she could get her hands on. Since the school had little in the way of a library, books were precious indeed. The students brought their own books from home, exchanging them with one another and faithfully returning them to the owners.

Westerns were popular, and when Janette borrowed a new one and brought it home, Fred and Amy would often manage to sneak enough time to read it too, before it was returned.

As much as Janette and Helen loved their make-believe world— the West—they did not realize at the time that the characters presented in the comics and books were phony—that the white-hatted, white-fringed, sequin- and satin-bedecked good guys fighting against grubby, cattle-stealing, black-hatted bad guys did not really exist. Neither in the Canadian West, nor in America either.

Janette loved her farm life. And one of the best parts of that life was the animals—especially the horses. Perhaps some would say that a farm wasn't very exciting—but country kids seem to generate their own excitement. And for Janette, it was enough to have family for games, cousins who visited, friends who dropped by on long summer evenings, and horses to ride whenever she pleased.

Of the horses kept at the Steeves farm, Trix was one of Janette's favorites, even though he could not entirely be trusted. He was black with white markings and had so much energy that he never walked, he always pranced. The family used Trix exclusively in harness for fieldwork, but there was a young neighbor man who had taken quite a fancy to him and wished to buy him for "showing off" on the road. When he came to the farm for a trial ride, it was the first that Janette had seen a rider on Trix. She expected the horse to buck—but instead he pranced around, throwing his head in an attempt to survey the rider and saddle, as if they were some strange new harness that had settled over him. His coat glistened in the summer sun as he side-stepped and danced on nimble feet. Convinced that Trix would make a good saddle horse, the young man made another offer—but Fred just shook his head. Trix was not for sale, and Janette was able to continue enjoying him herself.

The Steeves children were allowed to harness and drive Trix only after they had learned to handle horses well, but even then he sometimes got the best of them. They learned that if he was paired with a slower, steadier horse he could behave, but if he was teamed with the wrong mate, he did not need much of an excuse to run away.

One cold winter day, June and some of the others had taken the closed sleigh and set off into the crisp sunshine. Since the prickling cold air crept even under their blankets and through their clothing, some of the riders had pulled off their shoes to warm their feet by rubbing them. It was just then that Trix and his teammate, Nell, bolted. June lost control, the horses made a quick turn, and the sleigh lurched and spilled. The young people tumbled out into the snow with only their stockings to protect them from the icy drifts. Their shoes were still tucked inside the blankets of the sleigh as it was whisked along behind the runaway horses. In the end they bundled themselves as best they could and began the walk back home, arriving with feet bright red but thankfully with no permanent damage done.

Another of the horses that Janette and her siblings used often was Midnight, a half Shetland with a white star on his forehead. Used both to ride and in harness, Midnight was as smart as a whip, and ornery besides. He seemed particularly well suited for harness, though small, and could do his fair share of the work. If he were ridden, he was full of tricks, and often seemed to remember his riders much better than they knew their horse, reacting to each in a way that brought the most upset.

With Jean his trick was to rear up. He had done so once, and she had panicked, slipping his bridle and letting him go home on his own. Since it had worked then, he tried it again. From then on Jean rode Midnight only occasionally.

More often, Jack and Janette rode him to school, and there were a few occasions when they hit the ground rather unexpectedly. Once Janette even landed on her metal lunch kit. With the throb in her side, it was easy for Janette to harbor some ill feelings toward this horse.

On another school day, Janette was alone on Midnight. The snowplow had been through the area and had left a little pile of snow near a neighbor's gate. Midnight, who had been plugging right along up to that point, suddenly threw up his head and glared at the small heap of snow. He stopped, snorted, and refused to take one more step. Janette urged him, kicked him, and then slapped him with the reins, but he would take no more steps forward. Instead, he backed up step by step until he had retreated right into the ditch.

The farmhouse door opened, and a young neighbor fellow called out, "Do you need some help?"

At the sound of a voice Midnight's ears flicked forward. Then he looked directly at the neighbor, started forward, and walked right over the very pile of snow that he had been making such a fuss about. Janette, fully embarrassed, would have gladly sent him off to the meat packers on the spot had anyone offered.

There were other instances when Midnight showed a streak that was as stubborn as a mule. While Janette was riding him to Hoadley one day she met a cream truck coming toward her. A young man was driving, and Janette, a teenage girl, was tired of being placed in awkward positions by the stubborn horse. Again for some reason, Midnight stopped right in the middle of the road and stared at the truck, refusing to take one step out of its way.

Janette was mortified. The driver was forced to stop and wait, then to call and see if Janette needed any help with the horse. At last, Midnight decided that he'd had enough of the sport, and moved off to the side. Janette, a deep blush hot on her face, averted her eyes as the driver pulled past her and was finally on his way.

At the opposite extreme, Midnight also loved to run. If another horse were around he immediately assumed it was a race, though he was a notoriously poor sport. If he got ahead he would often cut in front of the other horse to slow him down. If he got behind he showed his displeasure by starting to buck. In fact, he had earned sufficient reputation locally that some of the neighborhood boys felt they might like to take on the challenge of riding him. Claude Estelle traveled a number of miles out of his way home from school one day just so he could try his horsemanship on Midnight. Shifting the saddle from his own horse onto Midnight's back, Jack and Janette were left to ride Claude's horse bareback. The skinny old nag had a sharp backbone and no plump padding to cushion the ride. They realized then that for as much as Midnight lacked in discipline, his rounded sides certainly beat Claude's horse for comfort.

Fred, too, would sometimes ride the little black horse. One winter day, some of the livestock had strayed and Fred needed to begin looking for them. Midnight was small and there were many drifts of snow across the roads, but Fred chose him and set off, though his legs hung low on either side, almost dragging on the crests of the drifted snow.

They had been out for quite a while and Fred began to feel sorry for the poor, tired little mount beneath him. He had been making it just as easy on the pony as he could, noticing that Midnight was trudging with his head low, his steps slow and laborious.

Suddenly, without warning, Midnight shied right out from under him, and Fred was astounded to find himself standing on his own two feet. So the once sympathetic rider decided that if Midnight still had enough life in him for such a bolt, the two could hurry just a bit faster on the way home.

During one summer's rush to bring in crops and hay, Janette was given the job of driving a team made up of Midnight and Trix, while Jack and Fred performed the more strenuous work on the stack. They were haying a field at a neighbor's farm where the train track ran right through the field. Since the Steeves lived some distance from the tracks, their horses were not at all accustomed to the sound of the train.

Janette was operating the rake, a rather dangerous implement if one happened to lose one's seating and take a tumble. Jack was up on the stack, and Fred was forking hay up to him. Just then along came the train with its clacking wheels and shrill whistle.

Trix and Midnight lurched, and Janette, who was just a young teen and not overly experienced, was sure she would be unable to restrain them. Instantly, her muscles tensed and she instinctively worked to hold in the horses. All action on the stack stopped as Fred and Jack both turned full attention to her plight, knowing they were too far away to be any assistance. As the clatter and racket continued, Trix and Midnight lurched and pranced, hooves dancing and ears twitching at the strange noise. Miraculously, Janette won the struggle and was soon able to settle them down. Later, Jack teased her about wanting to put on a show, but Janette was sure he'd been somewhat proud of her, even though he would probably not be willing to say so.

When haying time and the scurry of activity had passed, there was time for more leisurely pursuits, which sometimes led to pranks. One particular day, Jack and Janette wandered into the barnyard, looking around for some kind of mischief—something they could enjoy while still avoiding any serious trouble. Spying a long rope and the nearby horses, the plan began to form. Soon the rope was tied to the gatepost and then stretched inconspicuously along the ground across the gate's opening, the second end hidden behind the woodpile. Then, they were ready for the real fun!

Janette was to shoo the horses through the gate while Jack held the end of the rope. At first, she had little success, and the horses were driven vainly back and forth across the "spot." Then, finally, things worked out as planned.

Just as Trix ran across the rope, Jack gave a mighty heave and the rope snapped up, hitting Trix squarely on the under belly. His reaction was explosive. Hooves flashed and Trix bucked while Jack and Janette rolled with laughter. He had had no idea what had hit him, and all the effort was counted as well worth it—there was great satisfaction in turning tables on the ornery horse.

Soon another horse was added to the herd. It was not unusual to buy or to sell farm horses, and one day a neighbor arrived leading a bay behind his wagon. Fred had gone to a farm sale, and Jack and Janette were told, "Your dad bought him. He'll be home in a bit."

The man handed the lead rope to Jack and the two looked over the new horse, wondering what he would be like. Was he mean? Could he be trusted? And what was the strange lump on the side of his jaw?

Jack led the bay to the barn and fed him. He seemed gentle enough. Later, when he was turned out to pasture, the other horses began to pick on him. It made Janette worry that he might be hurt. They nipped and kicked and chased him around and around. Her anger rose as she watched, but finally the herd stopped their initiations and Dan, as the bay was dubbed, was accepted.

He was a good horse, gentle and trustworthy, both in harness and to ride. He quickly became Janette's choice whenever he was available. She even liked to pretend that Dan was her own, though of course he was not. He was a workhorse that belonged to the farm and family, but she loved him deeply anyway. And Dan repaid her devotion by doing everything he was asked to do—or at least he tried. Once Janette made him plunge into a pond of cold spring water and urged him to climb aboard floating ice blocks. The idea failed, but not from lack of effort on Dan's part. The ice kept chunking off just as he extended his hoof and thrust his weight onto it. But he kept right on trying valiantly until Janette gave up the attempt.

There were other farm horses too. An old white horse named Jack died one cold wintry day and gave the coyotes a feast down in the pasture. And there was King, a dark brown horse, and Old Bob, who fell down a shallow, deserted well. The group of men who gathered to try and save him had a terrible time fighting with him until they were finally able to hoist him up. Horses were only a part of farm life, but they were an important part. And for Janette and those who shared her equestrian pleasures, not only were they depended on for many of the farm tasks, they became dear friends as well.

Fred continued to receive offers to buy Trix. His answer continued to be "no," but as the years slipped by Trix grew old. The time finally came when Fred decided it was best to get rid of him. More cold winters would have been hard for the old horse, and Fred was far more practical than the children would have been. Had they kept the animal until he dropped of old age as some of the other horses had done, his carcass would have surely been pulled down to a distant field and left where the coyotes would have squabbled over its remains. There was nothing to be gained by allowing the old horse such an undignified end.

So Fred sold Trix to a man who made frequent horse-buying trips through the area. Janette stood behind the living room curtains, tears spilling down her cheeks as she watched the dealer cross the yard, Trix in tow. The dear, stubborn old horse was still prancing as he was led out to be loaded on the truck, unaware that he was taking his last trip. And Janette was certain she would miss him, despite all his senseless antics.

Midnight, too, was eventually sold, this time to distant neighbors. He was no longer a young horse, and Fred felt that the family needed the money more than they needed him. He had never been a really "good horse," but the Steeves children had all learned to love him anyway, so it was hard to let him go.

It was even more difficult when, a few days later, Midnight appeared back in the yard, a piece of rope dangling from his neck. Apparently he had not cared much for his new home and had decided that no mere rope would keep him from returning to where he belonged. The girls pampered and fed him, soothed him and petted him, and begged to be allowed to keep him. However, they were old enough to know better. For, of course, Fred notified the new owner and Midnight was taken away again.

The day of the school track meet was fast upon them, and joyous excitement buzzed throughout the school building. A classmate, Alice Hurteau, the youngest member of a French Canadian family in the community and another of Janette's school companions, was athletic and ready to challenge whomever contested her from the other schools. Janette shared her enthusiasm, though not quite all of her competitiveness.

On the morning of the appointed day, Janette rummaged through her clothing, trying to find a blouse that would suit the slacks she was wearing for the special event. There was none. It was her sister June who came to the rescue. From her closet of carefully maintained clothes, she produced a lovely white blouse. Janette could hardly believe that she would be able to wear the snowy-white garment and promised fervently that she would do her best to take good care of it.

All day long she was conscious of keeping the blouse from getting dirty, or spilled on, or smudged from track dirt. At the end of the day, she looked at the blouse in triumph, confident that it was no worse off for her use of it.

Some friends gave her a ride home from the track meet in their car, and as they bounced along over the rutted roads they talked about the day and relived its most exciting moments. Their small school could boast of capturing a good share of the day's ribbons.

The car pulled into the Steeves' yard and Janette stepped out, bursting with news to share with her older siblings and parents. Just as she leaned back toward the car for one last farewell, someone inside reached for the door and pulled it closed. The sound of tearing cloth ripped through the air. Somehow, the car handle had caught the front of the blouse, ripping where it pulled against the buttons. Janette felt heartsick. She had spent so much of the day concentrating on the blouse and now, just at the last moment of it being in her possession, was to go into the house with it torn. How could she ever face June?

She knew she should be scolded, but June said nothing. Later she carefully and skillfully mended the tear. There was no money for the luxury of a new blouse, and Janette was sure that each time June wore it, she was reminded again of her little sister's carelessness, but June never said one word about it.

Janette had a number of boy cousins around her own age and one girl cousin just a few months older than she. She loved being with Eva. During their early years before the move North, Eva's family lived nearby on the prairie and the two girls had seen each other often. Later Eva's prairie family also moved north, and the two families attended the same country school.

It was fun getting to know each other again, and they shared many good times. When sometime later the Burt Ruggles family moved several miles away to Ponoka, it was still close enough so that the families could spend time visiting in one another's home.

On one such occasion when Janette was in her early teens and visiting with Eva, they attended a special service in the Ponoka Baptist Church. It became one of the pinnacle events of her young life, for it was at that service, prompted by an invitation, that Janette dedicated her life to be used in any way God chose. Many years before at Bible camp, Janette had prayed for forgiveness of her sins; now she was stepping out further in her walk with the Lord. Now she was giving over all the big and little decisions that lay ahead of her. It was a significant experience for her, and she felt her dependence on God and her desire for His will grow.

Church attendance was still a regular part of the Steeves' life, and their church was currently being ministered to by the Lloyd Torgersons, who had recently taken up residence in the small church parsonage with their two young girls. While they were with the church, Mrs. Torgerson lost the baby that she had carried to full term, and the stillborn baby was prepared for burial by the pastor himself.

Reverend Torgerson was a handy carpenter, so he made a little wooden coffin and lined it with soft white material. He then lovingly and sorrowfully laid the baby into it himself, and arranged the small frame and tiny limbs to look comfortable and peaceful.

For some reason Janette found herself at the parsonage, and after Reverend Torgerson welcomed her into their home, he asked if she would like to see the baby. Chills ran up and down her spine at the thought of it but Janette agreed. The young girl had never before looked upon death, and struggled to force herself to gaze at the tiny infant lying among the soft white folds of the casket interior. The impression stamped itself on her mind, and though the experience was in no way pleasurable, it had not been terrifying either. Perhaps a merciful God was even then preparing her for later years, when she would look into the face of another infant so newly born and yet so still.

When the Torgersons left the area, Neil Neufeld, a young bachelor, came to the Hoadley pastorate. It seemed that Pastor Neufeld did not find himself well suited to single life and he left shortly, returning to Hoadley with his young bride, Gladys. They made a good team and the local people enjoyed them. Neil had a hearty laugh and shared some of the loves of fishing, hunting, and picnicking with Fred and the uncles. Even the church prayer meetings, held at various houses, became times of fun as well as fellowship.

As the school year approached when Janette was to begin grade nine, word came that the Harmonien school was not able to provide a teacher and that correspondence courses were to be offered instead. Fred and Amy decided that Janette and her younger sisters should attend the Hoadley school. Not long into the year, however, the Hoadley teacher decided that she could not manage the work of a ninth-grade student along with the younger students that she was responsible for. So Janette was asked to withdraw and reluctantly switched her enrollment back to the Harmonien school—which meant she would need to order the correspondence courses. Just before Christmas, they arrived.

Once the hustle of the season had passed and Janette had just settled herself to the hard work of catching up from a lost school semester, news came that Aunt Laurine was sick and needed help with her family. Instead of returning to her studies, Janette found herself packing her belongings and moving south to Champion. In the busy months that followed, all thoughts of schooling were left behind.

As the following school year began, Janette was still living with Aunt Laurine and her family. And so she was enrolled in the Champion school where many of her pleasant teenage years were spent. In Champion there were friends and cousins aplenty. And in addition to school, there were parties given for every reason imaginable—but mostly just for the fun of sharing time together, including a particularly interesting pajama party at Arden Gardiner's.

The girls were having a wonderful time with their own version of Spin the Bottle when a sudden banging on the windows sent them into panic. At first there was the fear of not knowing what the noises had been—an animal, a crazy man, or a monster. Then followed the realization. The boys had crashed the party. Shrieks of feigned alarm followed, and girls scurried around the room, attempting to hide but all the while wanting to see everything that was happening. It took quite some time for things to settle down again.

In turn, Aunt Laurine allowed Janette to be the hostess for a party of her own, and the fun began again. There was a holiday trailer parked at the back of the lot, and the girls were given permission to use it for their pajama party. They had already donned the appropriate attire and were beginning with the preparations for a feast that would be shared together. Among other things, the menu featured French fries.

Hot oil for frying had just been set to sizzling when suddenly the trailer tipped to one end. Pandemonium broke out. The hot oil slid across the small cupboard and off the edge directly toward Janette. Though she did her best to dodge, sizzling liquid splashed down one side of her pajamas and scalded against her leg. She shrieked in panic.

A rush of girls scrambled to help Janette shed her pajama bottoms while Dorothy Brett ran to the door and began to scream judgment upon the prankster who had tipped the trailer, certain that the culprit was again one of the boys. Oddly, her cries brought no response. There was simply no one outside. It wasn't until later that they discovered they themselves had caused the accident. The trailer tongue had been resting on a block of wood, but the rear of the trailer was not secured with blocks or any kind of support. It held the trailer until the girls gathered to one end while preparing the food. Then, as the weight shifted, so did the trailer.

Janette slept little that night. The dreadful oil burn stung, and it was several days before she could fully sit down. Fortunately, it healed without any complications, but she bore the dark burn scar on her hip for many years.

Another good reason for gathering a party was to go ice-skating. And one outing in particular, to which Janette knew she could not go, became one she would never forget. She was aware of the planned party, but also painfully aware that on the same night was scheduled a practice for the church Christmas program.

She gathered her schoolbooks at the end of the day and casually asked one of her classmates if he was planning to attend the skating party. Secretly, she thought this young man to be rather special. However, his answer caught Janette completely off guard.

"Will you go with me if I do?"

At the moment, Janette would have died to be able to say yes, but instead she blushed and stammered simply, "Oh, I didn't mean that."

Immediately a story relayed to her by her cousin Richard rushed into her mind. There had been another girl who had asked the same young man for a "date," and he had not responded favorably. Janette did not want him thinking of her in the same way. So she hastened on in some kind of explanation, not sure later just how she had voiced it.

In the end, Janette went to the church Christmas program rehearsal, and the boy to the skating party. However, the incident still bothered Janette.

During the annual school Christmas program not long afterward, two other boys took seats behind Janette and began a conversation obviously meant for her to hear. They were discussing how Janette's possible "date" had been turned down and its effect on the young fellow. Their taunts grew to be more than Janette could ignore which, of course, was exactly what the boys had intended. She spun around to inform them that she had not been able to go to the skating party because of church practice.

"Well, will you go with him if we arrange another skating party?" they asked.

Janette was surprised by the question. And even more by the fact that they had known anything about the original conversation. She was not in the habit of gushing to other girls about her dates or her wishes to date any of her schoolmates.

Even with the help of these would-be matchmakers, it turned out that the two never managed their skating date. They did, however, have a chance to go to the local Chinese restaurant where they sat and sipped sodas. And that was just as good.

Dates with others followed. Relationships developed, then faded. None were serious, but most were enjoyable—and at times even humorous.

The pinnacle of Janette's teen parties was one that Aunt Laurine threw for her on her sixteenth birthday. It was held in the church basement, and almost everyone they knew was invited. It was wonderful. Janette had never been the sole recipient of so much attention and so many gifts. Between the neat presents and the fantastic lunch, the party was a hit with everyone—and a very special and memorable event for Janette.

Church Youth

THE EVANGELICAL FREE CHURCH at Champion was the main source of activity for its youth. Sports games and parties were exchanged with the Vulcan Evangelical Church, and the two groups of young people became quite well acquainted. Many of these outings included Janette and her cousins.

Even though the group was relatively small, it was exciting and active. The young church pastor and his wife, together with Amy's brother Uncle Harry and his wife, Marion, who were at the time making preparation for the mission field, were able to create many innovative ways to draw in young people. In addition to the fellowship times, there were youth services at church, where the group was involved extensively in the service aided at times by the adults. At one such function the group presented an elaborate duplication of an entire radio production.

On another night they decided to host a Bible Knowledge Quiz. Two teams were formed and each given turns, member by member, to ask a Bible question of the other side. The only requirement was that each questioner knew the correct answer to his or her question.

When it was Uncle Bob's turn, he stood very seriously and asked of his opponent, a proper lady in the congregation, "Why did God bury Moses on the north side of the mountain?"

The woman was proud of her Bible knowledge and struggled for several moments, but finally had to admit that the question had stumped her. Her face fell and her brow furrowed. At last she murmured the difficult words, "I don't know."

It was then time for Uncle Bob to give the correct answer to his own question. Without a flicker of a smile he said, "Because he was dead." Gales of laughter followed as he sat down.

Aunt Marie was also a lot of fun. In fact, she was a great sport at many things. In spite of her having two little girls to care for, she entered in with the young people and could always be counted on to supply some of her good Scandinavian baking for lunch.

There were informal times in one home or another when the family had little sing-alongs, often accompanied by Uncle Dorn on the steel guitar, perhaps with Uncle Wayne strumming along. Janette especially loved such times.

And, of course, Sunday dinner was usually at Grandma Ruggles' house. Archie and Vi had moved from the Guess Ranch into town—to a most convenient location, right across the street from the small Evangelical Free Church where the family attended. After church one did not even have to move the parked cars—just walk across the road to Grandma's and gather round for one of her sumptuous meals.

It was a big family to cook for, but aunts helped by bringing dishes, and many hands shared in the work. Family spilled out onto the covered veranda and down onto the lawn on most such Sundays, but all were bountifully fed—except perhaps Grandma. She was so busy waiting on everyone that it was often questioned if she ever got a decent Sunday dinner.

For tenth grade, Janette returned home to Hoadley. She found that much had changed. Baby Sharon, now three, had become quite grown-up, and Joyce had already turned eleven—but was still as big a clown as ever. Margie was fourteen and fun to share secrets with, and June, then twenty-two, was planning a fall wedding to a young music professor whom she had met while attending Mountain View Bible College. Twenty-year-old Jack came and went from their home as work dictated.

There was a new pastor at the church, too, and Rev. Orland Boettger was a man with a vision. With a great deal of effort and dedication, he supervised the building of a new church, and it was Pastor Boettger himself who spent hours and hours in back-breaking toil getting the lumber to build it.

Some of the school year was lost when Janette began having recurrent bouts of tonsillitis, eventually resulting in time spent in the hospital. The offending tissue was removed and then began the wait for the medication to clear her system of infection. Finally, she found that she could swallow again—without pain.

During the summer of 1951, Janette was able to attend another camp meeting service. It was especially exciting for her because she could spend time with June and her fiancé, John Wilson. While sitting in an afternoon service with her sister, June called Janette's attention to one of John's young students, Edward Oke (an old-English spelling of "oak"), who was accompanying the hymns on the piano. Apparently John was a fine teacher, judging by this student's ability.

June's wedding was set for September 20, and Janette was to be a bridesmaid. In her mind, Janette could already picture June speaking her vows, her glowing face even more beautiful than usual. John was a fine young man, handsome and full of life and laughter, and Janette was pleased with June's choice.

The one outstanding disappointment about John was that he was an American, and his intention was to return to the United States after completing his time of teaching at Mountain View Bible College. This meant that sister June, soon-to-be Mrs. Wilson, would go with him, casting a shadow over the otherwise exciting plans for the wedding day. Trips to and from their new home, so far from Hoadley, Alberta, would be few, and June would be sorely missed.

Family relationships could not help but change even more rapidly now that more of the Steeves children were reaching adulthood. As August slipped away and September approached, the last few days of summer gave them a few more precious opportunities to spend together under one roof.

Once while Amy was away, and June was left in charge of "keeping house," Janette was assigned a task. The problem was not in her willingness to do the task, but in the manner in which it was to be done. June had given one set of instructions and Janette felt inclined to follow her own ideas.

The two, who had never been prone to argue, found themselves locked in disagreement, each girl holding to her own opinion. As soon as June left the kitchen, Janette proceeded with the job—just the way she felt it should be done.

When June returned rather unexpectedly, Janette felt hot embarrassment color her cheeks. She knew she should expect a reprimand; instead, June brushed the incident aside.

"Okay. Do it your way."

Janette grinned, then chuckled, and they both ended up having a little laugh. There was no friction—no argument. She was still peace-loving June.

On the day of the wedding, Janette had little time to worry about impending farewells. She was a sixteen-year-old bridesmaid, still very shy, and with a long line of well-wishers yet to face. The receiving line became a blur of faces. Some Janette recognized, many she didn't.

Then came Mr. and Mrs. Oke from Didsbury. The Okes had hired June to work for them in weekly housecleaning and had been very kind to her while she was attending college in Didsbury. Janette shook their hands warmly and then offered her hand to the teenage fellow who followed, their son, Edward, John's piano student. Janette smiled and turned to the next person in line.

For many nights after June's wedding, Janette cried herself to sleep. The house was so empty, so songless without June, and she could not picture what the days of the rest of her life would be like without her dear sister at home.

It was so typical of the way life seemed to go. With the wonder of growth and change, there was always some measure of sadness about what was left behind and lost. Many wonderful days were ahead, but letting go of the yesterdays seemed so difficult. Life had been some-what certain and predictable. Now June was gone, as were Betty and Jean. Who was to be next? And where would Janette find herself when it was her turn to leave the family nest for good? Janette prayed often for wisdom to face the uncertainties that were yet to come. And with those prayers she found a measure of peace.

That fall Janette attended school in the town of Rimbey, traveling the distance first by car along with two other students, and then catching a school bus farther along the way. It was a long ride every day, and the students began very early each school morning and didn't return home until after five in the evening.

The traveling soon proved to be too much for Janette, and around Christmastime she was sent back to Champion to live with Uncle Jack and Aunt Laurine, where she finished the school term. But it was difficult for Janette to leave home again. Even though the reasons were very good and she had a wonderful family to stay with, there were sure to be times when she longed to be home again. Janette hugged each sister in turn, then her mother, and then her daddy. And as the car she was riding in pulled out of the little farmyard, she did her best not to think about how much the familiar faces would be changed before she returned.

Despite the distance, Jack managed a visit sometimes and was a special person in Janette's life even while she lived away from home. And, as her only brother, he took upon himself the responsibility of teaching Janette to drive, which required some amount of fortitude on his part. There were many lessons, but none more eventful than the one involving a car filled with boy cousins, a curvy hill—and pedestrians.

Janette had been driving a short time and had begun to feel she was ready for anything. Cousins Richard and Tom, and perhaps another one or two, climbed into the backseat, and Jack let Janette slide in behind the wheel of his car, which had a standard shift.

Of course, the boys began at once to razz her, yelling in feigned terror, covering their faces and all sorts of other antics. Janette tried to ignore them. She was growing used to their teasing, but this was not the proper time as far as she was concerned. And suddenly, it became even more serious.

They reached the river valley. The winding ride down the slope to the bottom went well, but the drive back up the other side was different. Just as the steep road rounded a curve, a group of people walking along the roadside came into sight, and, as the road was narrow, panic filled Janette.

She needed to shift gears, but shifting, being still difficult even on easy roads, became impossible. The boys' teasing was no longer at all funny, nor was it even bearable. In a rare moment of uncontrollable emotion, Janette quit. Instead, she buried her face in her arms on the steering wheel and struggled just to keep herself from crying.

Jack took over. His foot jammed on the brake at the same time that his hand grabbed the steering wheel, and an accident was averted. Janette climbed out shakily, and willingly relinquished the wheel to her brother. Unfortunately, the cousins had only been given more fuel for teasing, and the near-catastrophe was brought to mind more often in the future than Janette would have liked.

For all their teasing, Janette enjoyed her boy cousins, and they were good friends, often taking Janette with them on their own activities. Together they went to country and western music concerts, small town rodeos, and Youth For Christ meetings. Some of the singing groups that toured with Youth For Christ were among their favorites, like the Forseth Trio from Peace River, and Janette found herself traveling from town to town with cousins in order to enjoy more of their concerts. The cousins were also country music fans, and she went along as they saw most of the stars of the day. If the desired show wasn't offered locally, Janette and her cousins traveled to Calgary or Lethbridge to hear them.

Even with the shared enjoyment, there were tradeoffs that Janette knew she must endure for their times spent together. Embarrassing moments of crazy actions and teasing—like pretending to be drunk in a Chinese cafe. Everyone in the area knew full well that the family were not drinkers, so no harm had been done, but Janette blushed with embarrassment.

She was also aware that the boys had come by their sense of humor honestly. Janette's uncles had been known to embarrass her completely in public, as well. They once placed an ugly rubber finger into a plate of restaurant food and then grinned while the distraught waitress tried to remain composed enough to resolve the problem.

When Janette was in her late teens, Uncle Jack had a hired man from Eastern Canada who could play almost any instrument, and Janette soon began blending her alto voice with his, as they sang almost every western hit of the day.

Vic, the young singer, thought they sounded especially good together, so he suggested that they cut a record, and at first it sounded like fun. But Janette got nervous and took the first opportunity to escape the scene by fleeing home to her folks in Hoadley.

A letter from Vic soon followed. He was sorry she had left and hoped that they could still cut the record, and in the meantime, he had already made arrangements for backup with a western group touring in the area. Janette shared the letter with June and was teased about it. Though June did seem serious when she urged Janette to go ahead and do it. It seemed like harmless fun but Janette still could not feel comfortable with the recording venture.

She knew she didn't want to be part of a failed album, but she was also increasingly certain that she didn't want success. Vic was a talented musician, and though she did not consider herself to be exceptionally gifted, she could harmonize well. So there was a chance—just a small chance—that the venture might succeed. She had watched the traveling western groups close enough to know that theirs was not a lifestyle she was interested in, and believed that it didn't fit with her Christian commitment.

Vic soon slipped away to play backup guitar for a group that sometimes appeared on local TV, and Janette finally lost track of him altogether. Apparently, the opportunity had passed, though she continued to enjoy singing country music.

Uncle Ralph and the cousins had another friend who was a steel guitarist. At that time, a steel guitarist was as close to a hero as Janette was willing to allow, and she could have swooned over the man—if she had been the type.

One evening he visited and, of course, hauled out his steel guitar. Janette was still shy but very much enthralled with the music. There were many requests for various songs as the night went on, but the cousins hooted when Janette asked, without much thought as to how it could be interpreted, "Do you know 'I'll Hold You in My Heart'?" The singer was familiar with the song and he played it—in spite of the howling of the male cousins and Janette's searing red face.

During the time when Janette lived with her Uncle Jack and Aunt Laurine and attended the Champion school, it was expected that she would come directly home each day to help with the housework. One night, she strayed.

It was the spring of the year and she was walking with a couple of her girlfriends when they noticed that the spring thaw had made a sizable pond in a low area of town down by the railroad tracks. They also noticed a small raft sitting along the edge.

With a little persuasion, Janette decided to give it a try. She managed to get herself onto the raft and out into the pond, but it turned out to be much more difficult to maneuver the thing back to the edge again. She was stranded, and the friends on the shore could offer her nothing in the way of assistance. After many moments of coaching and struggle, she finally managed to get herself back to shore where she knew she should have stayed in the first place. By then it was late and Janette was both anxious and wet.

Aunt Laurine had been fretting, not knowing what might have happened to Janette. Her niece didn't have a habit of fooling around after school. And they both were well aware of the week's wash water waiting to be emptied and the back porch needing to be scrubbed. By the time the tardy Janette had finished her chores, she was also late helping with supper. After that experience, she was careful not to dally on her way home.

Just before Christmas, Aunt Laurine sent Janette downtown to the ladies' wear store to pick out a new dress. There were few opportunities and little money for new dresses then, and the occasion was a special treat.

Janette found a beautiful green dress with a full skirt of shimmering material that changed colors with the light. It was lovely, and she couldn't believe it might actually be hers. She brought it home on approval and to her delight was given permission to keep it.

The first opportunity to wear the dress was to a school party. School parties usually involved dancing, which Janette did not participate in, but on this night the dance was to follow a fellowship time. With the convenient break in events Janette did go. She and her new dress made quite a hit.

As she sat with her friends early in the evening, a young fellow, rather red-faced, delivered a soft drink to her and grinned broadly. Later, more than one fellow asked to take her home and she shyly accepted one of the offers.

The night's success made her feel a little heady. No small wonder her girlfriends enjoyed an evening "out" when there was such nice attention to be had. She was amazed at what a pretty dress could do and grateful for Aunt Laurine's kindness in giving it to her.

Other outings followed, one after another. In an area known as Wolf Coulee, a birthday party was planned. The deep valley was filled with interesting rock formations, and the group of cousins and friends from church thought a birthday party held at the coulee would be very exciting and a chance to do some exploring.

They packed the lunch and birthday cake, then set out for a hike. The triumphant moment when the birthday cake was to be unveiled arrived, and Dorothy Brett reached for it ceremoniously. Everyone howled their protest as it was discovered that sometime during the trip out from town the birthday cake had been sat upon. They ate it anyway, laughing at their own folly.

Then came other trips into the foothills toward the west. Lunches were packed and various groups headed out for a day of exploring streams and trails. On one trip, they came across some backcountry cowboys who had just shot a bear. The animal was stretched up in a tree and looked rather large to the group of wide-eyed prairie kids. One of the fellows was boasting about how he had shot the bear while it was running.

"Where was he going?" one of the young people asked in wonder.

The storyteller's eyes grew large, and he answered dramatically, "Toward me!"

After leaving the cowboys to their bear, the group continued on their way, laughing about the storyteller and his scare. Janette laughed, too, adding her own quip about the man "Lee."

The hiker beside her stopped short. "How do you know his name?"

It was really quite simple, she explained. It was stamped on a little leather patch on his pants. Everyone laughed at Janette's introduction to brand name jeans.

After the school year ended, Janette spent the latter part of the summer helping a woman who was experiencing trouble with her pregnancy. It was harvest time, and as the woman had been sent to bed, she needed someone to do housework and cook for the crew of harvesters. The couple had no other children, so it was a lonely place to work and carried a lot of responsibility.

Before the housekeeping job had been completed, Janette heard of a job offer in the Bank of Commerce at Champion. She was interested in it immediately but also very uncertain. In the first place, she had not graduated from high school. She was only seventeen, but because of transfers back and forth between schools she had lost precious school days. She would need two more years of schooling to get her senior matric, equivalent to grade thirteen in some provinces or first-year college in some states. Accepting the bank job would mean she would likely never complete the courses. Secondly, harvest was not yet finished and the woman she was helping was still bedridden.

So Janette took the difficult question to her daddy for his opinion and was surprised at his answer. "Sis, you need to be the one to decide."

It was the first she had been left on her own for such a major decision, and it was a little frightening. Her father was "cutting the cord," turning her loose to make her own choices. Though it frightened her, it was also an honor. He trusted her. He had told her so in those few words. In the end she took the bank job, and Margie, still a very young girl for such a big task, filled in as housekeeper and cook for the harvesters.

CHAPTER SEVENTEEN

Working Girls

JANETTE SOON LEARNED to love her job as a bank clerk. She enjoyed working with numbers, and it was fun to have things "prove up" and know that there had been no mistakes. The work was done manually, except for one adding machine for month-end balancing. The big ledgers were all hand-posted. With all the work done by hand—or rather, by head—it was especially fulfilling to get a "sight balance." That meant that all the entries for the entire month and the month-end listing had been done perfectly. For Janette a sight balance only happened on one occasion, but when it did there was a small stir. It was an unusual occurrence for any of the employees. An error or two managed to sneak into one's figuring on most months. Janette was soon promoted to teller, and she enjoyed that position even more.

It was nice to be known in the small town as one of the "bank girls." Sometimes Janette would go with her co-workers for a soft drink if they were off work early, and it felt good to be independent and out with the older girls. While working at the Champion bank, Janette was joined by sixteen-year-old Margie, who found work at Allan's General Store for the summer and then attended Champion High School. The two sisters got together with a friend, Vivien Deal, who also worked at the bank, and rented a small three-room suite just two houses down the street from Grandpa and Grandma Ruggles.

Independence, though pleasant, also brought weighty responsibilities. And for Janette there was the added challenge of supervising and providing for her younger sister, so she appreciated the support from the family. Grandma Ruggles kept an eye out for them, and Grandpa Ruggles waited for their daily visit when they passed his house returning from work.

On one occasion after Janette had missed a couple days' visits, Grandpa growled in his somewhat gruff way, "Thought you had died." But now Janette knew him well enough to know that it was all a front. She gave Archie a big hug and said that she had just stopped in to see her "favorite boyfriend." He laughed, and they enjoyed their visit together.

The cousins still came around often. One of them had an extra reason for his visits now. Cousin Don was engaged to Janette's roommate, Vivien, but when he arrived he didn't stay for long. It was usually just to pick her up for a date. Richard, Tom, and Larry dropped by often—at times bringing Uncle Ralph with them as well.

Visits home to Hoadley were infrequent, but on the occasions when it was possible, Janette found her way back for a short stay. Just as she had expected, the family continued to grow up and change, especially "baby" Sharon, now five. Janette felt it was her duty during one of these visits to explain some of the facts of life to little Sharon.

She was such a cute young thing, and sharp as a tack, but she was growing up as almost an only child—being the last sibling of the group and seven years younger than the next in line. Not being raised in the middle of the "litter"—especially in Janette's way of thinking— Sharon was given little opportunity to discover the need to compromise. There were few family members with whom she must learn to share, especially since easy-going Joyce was a number of years older. The family doted on their youngest, so among other things, Janette spent time trying to explain the dangers and perils of being a person who was spoiled and selfish.

After returning to Champion, Janette wrote home and encouraged Sharon to remember "their little talk." Amy was curious about the note and asked the little girl what the talk had been about.

"She said when I grow up, if I'm spoiled, no one will want to marry me," came Sharon's answer. When Janette heard the response, she could only laugh at the young child's version of the chat. Of all of the things they had talked about, Sharon had chosen to remember only that one.

Janette worked for two years at the Champion bank before

deciding it was time to look for a Bible college. Both June and Jack had gone to Mountain View Bible College in Didsbury, Alberta, but Janette was not certain that God wanted her there. Uncle Harry and some of the cousins had gone to Prairie Bible Institute in Three Hills, where Betty had attended. Perhaps she should apply there.

For some time Janette wrestled with the decision. And in the end it came down to funds. True, she had been working for two years, but the bank salary had been only $100 per month, and she had been paying her own living expenses. So she knew that she would have to choose her school according to her finances. P.B.I. was unable to allow her to attend classes on credit, as Mountain View had offered. This weighed heavily in the decision.

Then Uncle Royal paid a visit to Champion. He and Aunt Bea had been working at a little mission in the Yukon Territory at the time, and it seemed to be a good chance to hear some wise counsel. He and Janette discussed her desire for Bible college training and the two schools in question. His final comment before he left was, "Janette, remember. It's not the school. It's you."

She knew he was right. God could work in her life only if she was open to Him. The school, no matter how good it was, could only bring about as much maturity and spiritual growth as she was open-hearted enough to allow.

In the end she sent applications to both institutions, thereby putting out her own "fleece" to the Lord. She had prayed and promised that whichever college she heard from first, she would take as the college to which God was leading her.

By a twist of circumstance, Janette did not receive the mail-stalled letter from Prairie Bible Institute when she should have, offering her a spot in the freshman class. Instead, she received the reply from Mountain View, which was dated and mailed shortly after. So she accepted the offer from Mountain View, delighted that not only would they accept her as a student, they were also offering several days of cleaning work that would be credited to her student account as payment. So Amy and Janette spent time working on her college wardrobe. Although it was simple and inexpensive, it looked very nice to the two ladies, and they were proud of what they had managed.

Summer came to an end and Janette headed for college, while Margie moved on to another job. More than once over the year, Margie helped out by sending a little needed money. Janette always felt grateful, for she knew the money came through some sacrifice on her sister's part.

Several days were spent cleaning in readiness for the fall classes to begin. When school started, first-year euphoria set in and it took months for the feeling to wear off. Janette felt so blessed to be at Bible College and to be sharing so many things with other young people. She was very thankful to have been accepted and responded to many opportunities to testify in the chapel services. Soon she learned that other students had come to expect her to be one of those who jumped up each time an invitation for testimonies was given. From then on, Janette checked herself, allowing the privilege of sharing only when something really "special" had happened in her life.

Among her many fine teachers was Professor Peter Waldin, the same gentleman who had offered her money for summer Bible camp when she had been a child of ten. Janette enjoyed his classes and also became a part of the dramas presented by his yearly speech class. She enjoyed the experience and the creativity of acting out the part of a biblical character. Janette's roles included Mary, the mother of Jesus, and the young girl, Rhoda. With skill, Mr. Waldin wrote the plays himself. Janette learned to love and appreciate him as a fine teacher and the true English gentleman he was.

Each of the students was assigned a job "detail" at college. Janette had learned about the necessity of work early in her life and did not mind the tasks, giving the work her best efforts. For that reason, she was often assigned to clean the front hall, the offices, and the chapel. The dean seemed to be impressed with her work, and although she appreciated the compliment of sorts, it did seem that she got more than her share of the bigger jobs.

Dish crew, table setting, and other such chores were more enjoyable because there were others with whom to share the work. Janette enjoyed these details and took the opportunity it gave her to get to know other students better. Some of the best times at college seemed to happen during "detail."

One day as Janette was cleaning the front hall, a fellow student came along and began to help her work. He had not been assigned the task, and Janette was a bit puzzled about his help.

She knew him slightly, their paths having crossed a few times over the years even before they were fellow students. Edward Oke was a junior and rather hard to miss on campus. The student body was small, and he was a visible and vocal part of it.

In the girls' dorm she had already heard some reports about Edward. One of the girls had been his "steady" during the previous year. The relationship had, for reasons that Janette did not know nor ask, been terminated. But the girl had declared quite frankly that she intended to "hate whomever he starts dating."

Now, Janette wondered why he chose to help with her assignment, knowing that he had chores of his own. They chatted and became better acquainted. One of his off-handed remarks amused her somewhat.

"The fellows in the dorm have been trying to guess your age. They have you all the way from nineteen to twenty-three."

She didn't know why there should be interest in her age, but she admitted rather shyly that she was nineteen. He seemed a bit smug about the information. She judged that he must have been the one guessing her at age nineteen and felt good about being right. She didn't know that he had decided that if she were as old as twenty-three he would be reluctant to ask her out. Edward was also nineteen.

CHAPTER EIGHTEEN

Edward

SPECIAL MEETINGS WERE held at the local church, and all the college students were expected to attend. Rev. Norman Oke, an evangelist from the United States and also an uncle of Edward's, was the speaker. Janette enjoyed his preaching thoroughly.

Edward approached Janette one day and asked if she would be interested in joining several young people who were going to his parents' home for a snack after the evening service. It sounded like fun and Janette agreed. The arrangements were made with the Dean of Women. It was not a date. Freshmen were not allowed to have dates (known as S.P.'s—Special Privileges) the first semester.

After the service the group of young people met at the door of the church for the short walk to the Oke residence. It didn't take long for Janette to discover that all the others attending the little gathering were known around campus as "couples." Only she and Edward were unmatched. Was this a *date*, after all? She had never consented, but the only thing she could think of to do was to fall into step beside him.

By the end of the first semester she and Edward were "going steady" even though they had never been allowed an official date. However, the school had many functions and parties where the fellows and girls were allowed to mix freely, though one-on-one pairing was discouraged. In fact, campus rules were so strict that students were not even allowed to converse with a boyfriend or a girlfriend except during certain specified times of the day. Among these precious moments were the few minutes before mealtime while waiting for the last bell to ring for dinner—perhaps the faculty realized what an excellent way this was to make sure everyone arrived in plenty of time for the meal.

Janette and Edward came from quite different backgrounds. She had been raised in a large farming family that had needed to make every dollar stretch until it threatened to snap. He was raised with only one sister, Alta Mae, in a town where his father was a very successful International Harvester dealer. This meant that Edward had grown up with new clothes, piano lessons, and leisure time enough to rise through the ranks of his Boy Scout troop. He was outgoing, self-confident, and intelligent, even valedictorian for his high-school graduating class.

Edward had enjoyed many privileges that Janette had not. In fact, they had dated just a short time when she became quite strongly convinced that their relationship was not very practical and would hold too many adjustments. After carefully going over her intentions in her own mind, Janette launched into a prepared speech one day, catching Edward a bit off guard.

"When two people start dating—either they break up or they don't. For us—it can only be the one, and I think we should break up now before we get too involved instead of waiting until later."

Edward, who listened with furrowed brow, seemed to misunderstand the intention of the entire speech and brushed it quickly aside with little comment. In later years he even managed to turn the episode around and teased her about being the one to force a proposal.

They did not break up. When dates were finally allowed they took as many of those Special Privileges as they were given, though this was only a couple each month and included almost any occasion where they might be seen together. Whether it was a school function, a walk together, a meal off campus grounds, or just a chance to watch TV at the Okes' house, each counted as an S.P. When the school term ended and they took summer employment, they kept in touch faithfully. Though they had not made their intentions public with an engagement ring, Edward had already asked Janette to marry him and she had agreed.

The following fall, Edward left Mountain View and enrolled at the University of British Columbia to study engineering. Janette returned to Mountain View for her second year. Edward was a fine student,

Edward and Janette Oke
(1986)

The Enchant Nine—Fred Steeves is standing second from the right. Jack Steeves (Janette's uncle) is seated on the far right.

Fred and Amy Steeves prior to marriage.

Hoadley house—Janette is standing on the left with Amy and the farm dog.

Steeves family: Back row—Fred, Jack, and Amy
Middle row—Betty, June, and Jean
Front row—Margie, Joyce, and Janette
(Sharon had not yet arrived.)

Shetland pony
Beauty. Janette is on
the far right.

Janette at sixteen. Jean and Orville bought her the dress.

Edward and Janette's engagement dinner.

Graduation from Mountain View Bible College.

Wedding day—May 13, 1957.

Bringing Terry home to the
Calgary (Montgomery)
parsonage.

Lorne and Lavon at the
Didsbury President's
home.

Lavon and Lorne admiring their
sister Laurel.

Four little Okes. Terry
tries to read a bedtime
story.

Janette leading the Didsbury Sunday School.
Edward is playing the piano.

Laurel after her cousin
Janice's haircut.

Lavon and Lorne with
puppy Curious.

Lavon and Lorne's high-school graduation in Didsbury.

Edward and Laurel during her senior year.

Terry's wedding

Laurel's wedding

Lorne and Deb's wedding

Amy and her family

Four generations—Amy Steeves, Janette, Terry, and baby Ashley.

Family reunion in August 1986. Left to right is Betty, Amy, Janette with grandson Nate, and Aunt Laurine.

Jessica Logan's dedication. Grandpa Edward does the honors.

Janette and granddaughter Katie.

Kristie Oke's dedication in Mishawaka, Indiana.

Grandpa Edward and Jackie.

Nate and the girls!

Grandma blows bubbles.

Janette with Ashley and Nate during their first Christmas.

All eight grandchildren!

Grandpa Edward and Alex.

The first Christmas in the Calgary house.

The Oke family

The Steeves sisters at retreat at the farmhouse.

*Four generations: Front row—Edward, Grandma Steeves, Marvin
Back row—Jessica, Laurel, Janette, Nate, Grandmother Oke*

Janette's Bethel College doctorate

Lavon and Monica's wedding

Remodeling the Steeves' farmhouse

Janette

Berwyn Machonachie and son Randy

getting top grades in most of his subjects. He also enjoyed the study courses and was quickly adjusting to life at the large university and the journey toward becoming a good engineer.

Janette returned to Bible College with wistful thoughts of her fiancé being so far away, but these days were short-lived. She soon found herself ill and miserable for a good share of the college year, even struggling to finish the first semester.

At Christmastime Edward was home and she received her engagement ring. Family and friends were not surprised at the news and were all quick to offer their congratulations. However, Janette's condition did not improve. Her local doctor advised her against returning to college, but after losing a few weeks of classes she traveled back to Didsbury and worked hard to try to catch up to the rest of her classmates. She was determined to force her aches and pains out of her mind. Her strong resolve to continue pushed her through the many difficult days ahead.

In addition to her physical difficulties, Janette had another problem. She told no one of this private dilemma, but inside she was wrestling with mixed convictions about marrying Edward. For some reason she was feeling strongly that she was to be a minister's wife. Yet whenever she prayed about her relationship with Edward, she never felt he was the wrong person for her. The paradox confused her. How could she be a minister's wife and marry Edward when he was to be an engineer?

But the God she trusted was not a God of confusion and soon worked out the solution. Edward took only one year of engineering and returned to Bible College. He had decided, without a word from Janette, that the world needed ministers more than it needed engineers, and he was prepared to give himself to serving the Lord in that way. Upon his return to Mountain View in the fall, they were fellow classmates in their senior years.

During this third year at Mountain View, Margie joined Janette. When the younger sister arrived in Didsbury along with the other freshmen, she may have appeared quiet and reserved, but she soon livened up the place as she was discovered to be the most fun-loving member in the dorm. Margie was constantly dressing up in crazy outfits, or decking herself out in some outrageous garb, and didn't seem to mind the many pictures to prove it.

Good health had returned to Janette after surgery, and a summer spent recuperating at home meant she was able to enjoy all aspects of college life—but, to her, the most important was the opportunity to grow spiritually. From classroom discussions and lesson assignments to walks uptown in the crisp winter air, from chapel hours to work detail, from Gospel Team to bedtime chats, from Days of Prayer to Special Privileges, from frustrations and concerns to shared laughter and school parties—her college life was full and precious. Each aspect of it helped her to learn and grow in her walk with her Lord and in her relationships with others.

Jack often passed through Didsbury on his way between home and the prairies. He was now working at jobs as they turned up, as well as helping Fred on the farm. It was good to have him stop by for a visit, and Janette always looked forward to seeing him.

There were many times when he asked candidly, "Do you need some money?"

What could she say? It seemed that she always did. So he would reach into his pocket and hand her a few bills. She loved him for his unselfishness, but she felt a little guilty as well. She knew he needed the money just as much as she did.

News came that Jack was to marry Ila Strand, and though Janette did not yet know her well, she was confident that Jack would choose wisely and was thrilled for him. Everyone was certain that Ila would be the perfect match for Jack, and the years have proved it to be true. She has been a warm, generous, and hospitable mate—and perfectly suited for Jack's ample sense of humor.

During this final year at Mountain View, Janette proudly wore Edward's engagement ring. She often found herself fingering the ring unconsciously, allowing excitement and anticipation to rise as plans began to take shape for their wedding and life together.

Then an unexpected event dampened some of her excitement. The students did their own laundry using a rather old-fashioned washer with a wringer. Because Margie had a problem at times with eczema on her hands, it was decided that she should keep her hands out of the hot, soapy water and that Janette, who didn't mind swishing around in the suds, would help out. But Janette didn't want her "new" ring exposed to the heat and soap. The solution was to pass Margie the ring and let her care for it while Janette finished the laundry.

On this particular day, Margie teasingly slipped the ring onto her own finger "just to see how it looked." Janette smiled. She didn't mind letting Margie tease her about the ring. What harm could it do? But when the job had been completed, Margie reached to give the ring back to Janette. For some strange reason it didn't slip easily from her finger. At first there was no concern—but as she tugged and fidgeted with the ring it seemed to grow tighter and tighter on her finger.

The sisters soaped the finger, then tried ice to reduce the swelling, but still the ring did not budge. The more they worked with the finger, the more tightly the ring entrenched itself.

At last they admitted the inevitable. The ring intended to stay right where it was. They decided to go find Edward. He appeared on one of the college sidewalks, and by the time they discovered him, both girls were in tears. What were they going to do?

Edward tried to hush their crying and allay their fears. "It's insured," he pointed out in typical male fashion. That was hardly the point! The ring that should be on Janette's finger was stubbornly staying on Margie's.

There seemed to be only one thing to do, and Edward took it upon himself. He helped Margie into his car and took her straight to the local jeweler. The ring was cut from her finger and sent away for repair.

The days spent without the familiar feel of the white gold finally passed, and the ring was returned to where it belonged. All through the years that Janette has worn it, it has very faintly borne the scar as a silent reminder.

Edward and Janette graduated together at the end of April in 1957. Edward left with the choir for a tour, and Janette went home to prepare for the wedding. They were to be married in the small Evangelical Free Church in Champion, which had been Janette's church while she lived with Aunt Laurine, and later during the months she worked at the bank.

CHAPTER NINETEEN

Married

MAY 13, 1957, DAWNED to find the Steeves' household already bustling with activity. All the aunts had pitched in to help decorate the church and provide the reception in the local community hall, and, thanks to her wonderful family, the "broke" college graduate was to have a lovely wedding with no indebtedness.

Margie, Joyce, and Edward's sister, Alta Mae, looked lovely entering the church in their tea-length dresses in shades of coral, teal, and gold. Little sister Sharon followed them down the aisle with exaggerated steps while Amy looked on with pride—pride mixed with wistful feelings as she brushed tears away and turned to see her daughter-bride enter the sanctuary.

Janette's eyes were almost shyly hidden behind her cousin Vivien's veil. The wedding dress that she borrowed from sister June fell in soft folds from her slim waist, and she was truly a beautiful bride.

Though her wedding garments were borrowed, the feelings were all her own. Tingles of excitement and nerves shot through her, the quiet sense of confidence in being certain she was in God's will, and the warm assurance of looking into Edward's eyes and hearing him sing words of love and commitment and then speak his vows.

All too soon it was over. Janette was Mrs. Edward Oke and was leaving behind the crowd of family that called and waved at their newest couple. The busy aunts, the teasing uncles, the fun-loving cousins, the dear sisters, and a rather quiet set of parents were soon lost from sight as the newlyweds sped away in their car.

The honeymoon was spent in the Canadian Rockies near Banff and Lake Louise. Since it was early May, the ice and snow were still clinging tenaciously to the mountainsides and lakes. Wild animals entertained the visitors and pestered the town residents, seeming to hate the thought of leaving winter's civilization and going back up the mountains to their wild habitat. It was a relaxing time, but the couple was anxious to get back and settled in their own little place.

The first home for Edward and Janette was an extremely small one-room efficiency apartment on the upper floor of Edward's grandmother's home. Grandma Nannie Greer offered them the use of the room, complete with a small cupboard, stove and sink, closet, fold-out couch for sleeping, a couple of chairs, and a little table. The bathroom was down the hall.

Edward and Janette lived there for only four months while they worked summer jobs, Edward at a dairy and Janette at the Calgary branch of the Canadian Imperial Bank of Commerce. During this time they did their best to save money to go to the United States where Edward planned to further his education for the ministry.

At the end of August, Edward and Janette packed for an impending trip to Bethel College in Mishawaka, Indiana. Edward would attend classes to get his B.A. and Janette would look for work as some means of support.

For some time Janette had been growing anxious. At last, just before the trip was to begin, Janette alerted Edward to her suspicions of a pregnancy. It had certainly not been a planned event, but the doctor agreed that Janette was correct in her conclusions—and was about six weeks along.

What was a happy expectation was also a major concern. Janette's income had been counted on in the plans for Edward's education, and a baby would complicate the situation greatly. Placing their worries into God's hands, the couple continued their preparations for the long drive to Indiana.

Edward and his father, Harold Oke, had fashioned a rough trailer for hauling their belongings. Many of their wedding gifts had to be tucked away into boxes, hauled down to Champion, and left behind in storage until the couple would return. They were grateful, too, that Dad Oke had also given them an old black Chevrolet in which they would make the eighteen-hundred-mile trip.

And they would have passengers. Fellow students from Mountain View, Cliff and Eleanor Quantz, were to travel with them. The Quantzes, also Bethel bound, added their things to the trailer until it could hold no more. The car itself was stacked with boxes, leaving little space to spare for the two young couples.

On a Tuesday morning the journey began after a disappointing late start. But eventually Champion fell behind and spirits lifted as the pavement began to race away beneath the tires. Edward was somewhat concerned about one particular tire on the trailer, which bulged awkwardly, but they were hopeful that it would hold up over the many miles ahead of them.

After two hours they reached the American border and were met by the stoic guard. Once it was discovered that the foursome was crossing the border for the purpose of an extended stay, they were "invited" inside. Janette fidgeted in her chair, grateful at least for the comfort of the sitting area. At last, an hour and a half later, they were again underway. All four of the young adults were waiting for their visas to be processed, and were allowed to enter the country with only "temporary status." This meant that if for any reason there were difficulties with the documentation, they could be called back to their port of entry and required to leave the country should the problem not be solved. It was a frightening thought.

A long and tiring day of driving followed, punctuated by difficulty with the trailer during the evening. After spending the night in a hotel, the foursome ate breakfast in a local diner. There they noticed that the waitresses were excited and distracted. A new singer by the name of Elvis Presley was to arrive that evening and pay a visit to the town fair for about an hour. There was no debate on the part of the travelers— not one of them had an inclination to stay. After all, this young new singer was no Roy Rogers.

All was going well as they again got underway—and then came the sickening sound of a dying motor. Edward glanced at the gas gauge and admitted sheepishly that they had run out of gas. So Janette and Eleanor waited in the car while their husbands hitched a ride to the nearest town. The humor in the situation took a little effort to find, but they managed to coax it along at last.

When the old Chevy began to act up later during the day, there was no energy left to laugh. Three more hours were lost because of car trouble and two more with the time changes. With two days of traveling behind them, Edward pulled into Fargo, North Dakota, late at night and they searched for another hotel. There had been plans to camp along the way and avoid the cost of a hotel stay, but the weather was cool and rainy so they opted for the comfort of warm beds.

Thursday morning dawned all too soon, and Edward took the car to a garage as soon as it opened. Shortly after two o'clock they were able to get underway and arrived in St. Paul, Minnesota, that evening.

The trip through the Twin Cities of Minneapolis and St. Paul was a difficult one. The road they selected from the map lay directly through the heart of each city, and it was difficult to follow in the dark. Tension mounted, and by the time they were emerging on the other side of the cities there was no chatter, only brooding silence.

Just as the car approached a long extension bridge straddling the Mississippi River, the sound of a bell cut the night air and a red light flashed beside them. Edward pulled to a stop, and the four watched in awe as a large portion of the bridge before them began to swing away.

Coming from the Alberta area, they had not seen a large draw-bridge. After recovering from the strange sensation of watching the road before them move away, they climbed from the crowded car and stood beside the rail.

There was lighting enough to see a large freighter creep through the opening, its wake barely noticeable, but the hum of the engine cut sharply through the still night air. Though it took more time from the traveling, the chance to stretch, to escape from the crowded car, and to have the distraction of viewing the interesting event seemed to take the edge off the previous difficulties and strained emotions, and each was glad for the relief.

With Friday's arrival, more reinforcements were needed for the trailer. Hopes for arriving in Indiana on that day were left behind when they heard the clank of metal on pavement and realized it was a support piece from their own vehicle. Edward walked back along the roadway and picked it up, then stopped at the next town to have it welded back on.

Slow driving followed, and they spent Friday night in a suburb of Chicago. All efforts had been expended not to drive into Chicago itself. They had been warned to avoid the difficult streets and traffic of the large city.

Morning began with anticipation of reaching Bethel before noon, but a flat tire soon frustrated this. Not completely unexpected, the tire that had bulged before leaving Champion had simply not lasted the entire trip, and a replacement was necessary. Janette and Eleanor searched for a shady place to wait while Edward and Cliff went about repairs. It was hot—terribly hot, and the day was heavy and muggy. The Canadian ladies were familiar with neither the heat nor the humidity. In the shade of a large tree, Janette sat at a picnic table writing a carefully penned letter home—trying not to let her disappointment show at how poorly the trip was progressing.

On Saturday, after five days on the road, the tired foursome arrived in Mishawaka, Indiana, and immediately headed to Bethel College. The long trip was over.

On arrival at the campus shortly after noon, though, they found empty parking lots and buildings. They discovered that the faculty had gone on retreat to Winona Lake and, further, that there were no waiting apartments for them as they had expected. Leaving the trailer on campus, they began the tedious job of searching for accommodations, armed only with the local newspaper and a map of the city.

Rent was the first consideration. Budgets were tight and accommodations would not be fancy. They were prepared to take whatever they could find. After viewing one apartment after another, they wandered into a building owned by a local dentist, where a two-room apartment was available. It was small, but as soon as Edward walked in he muttered, "Let's take it and be done with it."

The long day had dashed some expectations, and they were all willing to take whatever might be workable. When the owner discovered that both couples were looking for a place to live, he admitted to having a second apartment, and spirits began to brighten.

They were told that the second flat had been vacated quite recently when its tenants had been evicted. The apartment owner explained further that they had left quite a mess, but he would give them a break on rent if they would agree to clean it themselves.

They quickly decided to take both apartments and to figure out later which couple would be in each. As it turned out, the caretaker had already started to clean the second apartment, so it was not in terribly bad shape.

Relieved at finally finding some good news, Cliff and Eleanor took the second apartment for $55 a month, including utilities. Edward and Janette took the first apartment for $65, and the work of settling in began, each thankful for being able to live so close to friends.

CHAPTER TWENTY

Indiana

HOT WEATHER CONTINUED, and without even a fan, Janette found it difficult to relax in their small quarters. With Sunday upon them, she knew she could not begin the mountains of work before her, so she and Edward went for a walk in the park instead. That evening they attended the Gospel Center Missionary Church and began to make new acquaintances.

Some other friends from Canada had been recalled to their port of entry, and Janette feared they also would need to return. The car might not be able to carry them back over the winding miles, and there would be so many complications. Surely if God intended for them to be in Indiana, He would provide the means for them to stay there as well. She prayed continually about it.

In the first week at the new campus, a student get-acquainted party was to be held at Bethel. Edward and Janette had planned to attend with Cliff and Eleanor until Janette began having trouble with her pregnancy.

She longed for her own doctor who might be able to give her advice during such a worrisome time. Instead, Edward called a local doctor listed in the telephone directory and was told that Janette should remain on bed rest for some time. It was likely that the long trip, along with the stress and the strains of unpacking had triggered the problem.

Janette obeyed and went to bed. Eleanor, being a true friend, refused to go to the party and leave her alone. So the two stayed home while their husbands went to meet the students who would be classmates during the year.

Janette did lose the baby. In the strange apartment, miles from her mother, and with no doctor's care, she lay on the foldout bed and cried at the loss of the infant. Though he would have caused so much inconvenience at this time had he lived, she felt "mother love" for the little one she never had a chance to see or know.

The following morning she tried to put her grief behind her. God was God, and there was nothing to be gained in fighting His will. There was more work to be done in getting settled in their new home, and though she was still required to rest for the major part of the day, Janette busied herself with plans and accomplished what little she could.

Edward began school as well as work at a local church. Twenty hours of his time each week, not including Sunday, went into pastoral duties under the supervision of Rev. Gordon Bacon at Beulah Missionary Church in Elkhart. Edward was thrilled to find that his pay would be $40 per week, which he considered "just fantastic." His responsibilities would include the weekly bulletin, scheduled visitation, and some duties with the youth group.

Life had begun to settle into routine, both for Janette and for Edward. Gradually the apartment had been put into order and days became familiar. Then the dreaded notice came. Janette's visa did prove to be a problem. Edward immediately began calling the various offices to determine what would be necessary to get Janette's papers in order. Fortunately she would be able to get it straightened out in Windsor, Ontario, a relatively short distance away.

The thought of traveling so far alone worried Janette—especially to such a large city. Edward was deeply involved in his work and studies by this time and could not accompany her. So Janette was delighted when Eleanor agreed to go along. After a short stay, the women returned with papers in order and permission to work in the United States, so the job search could begin in earnest.

Eleanor found a job in a bank, and Janette applied for an opening in the same department. In the meantime she began to reap some of the benefits of being a pastor's wife. Mrs. Bacon shared some of their "gifts of love" with her, including eggs, beans, and tomatoes. It felt good to have this practical support.

The job at Eleanor's bank turned out to be suitable for Janette. She was glad to be working in the same department as her friend, and since the men needed the car for their trip to campus, the two walked to work together. Days fell into busy routine.

Janette worked in the accounts department, which included the daily and monthly balancing of accounts and ledgers. Her first problem was to balance the ledgers that had not been checked for several months. It was a tedious task to go back through pages of work to find hidden errors. She spent many nights of overtime poring over old checks and pages before she finally completed the job, but her boss seemed very pleased with her efforts. Over and over he commended her for her work.

Apart from work, there were college and church events to attend until there was hardly any time to relax. Edward was busy with classes, and Janette still cleaned, baked, and canned in addition to her job. The days were full.

Once fully settled, the couple had applied for a telephone and now waited somewhat impatiently for its installation. Edward and Janette were planning a Halloween "trick" on his parents: they would call collect, giving themselves a "treat" in the process. But October 31 came and went, and the promised telephone still had not been installed.

Edward and Cliff had still not received their working permits, and their temporary visas had expired. Because of the delay, the church was unable to pay Edward for his hours. It was difficult to wait when the money was needed so badly, but they continued to hope and pray. Finally all the "red tape" was behind them, the paper work in order, and Edward received his check. Now they were both free to work their way through Edward's education.

At last the new telephone arrived, and a call was placed to Edward's parents. It was wonderful to hear their voices, and Janette found herself trembling with excitement as she placed a call to her own home.

She listened intently as the operator rang through to Edmonton, then Camrose, then Ferrintosh, and finally the Steeves' number. A stranger answered, and because of the poor connection, he and Janette were not able to understand each other. After struggling for as long as she felt she could afford, Janette was forced to hang up, and the disappointment was hard to shake. Thoughts of trying the call again were quickly set aside. It was too awful to think about failing again after so much excitement and expense.

The new church was beginning to feel like home. More and more faces were becoming familiar and the church services were fully enjoyed. During the years since Janette's conversion there had never been an opportunity for her to be baptized. The churches where she attended had not had baptismals, and there were few streams that were convenient as an alternative.

At the time Janette had joined the church, she had promised the Lord she would be baptized at the first opportunity. So she was thrilled when she discovered that the Beulah church had a baptistery. After her arrival in Indiana, when the first candidates were to be baptized, she joined them. It was important to her to fulfill Christ's command to His followers to "repent and be baptized." She had repented and experienced an inner act of cleansing through the blood of Christ—now she was also baptized as an outward demonstration to others of her obedience and determination to follow her Lord.

At Thanksgiving time, the church threw a "pound shower" for their young intern and his wife. Janette was moved and thrilled with the many canned goods and variety of other food items. Though it seemed a bit ironic that she had to come to the United States to discover "Canadian bacon."

Then the Christmas season drew near, and Janette felt the familiar excitement mixed with loneliness for her family. Parcels were mailed and Christmas cards sent. Counting faraway family and friends and local church people, she sent over three hundred cards, an incredible amount of work for someone whose life already seemed too hectic.

Her employment at the bank continued to go well, and when the bank's manager came through to personally hand out the Christmas bonus checks, he shook her hand firmly and said, "I've heard about you." Janette tried to hide her surprise. She had not felt she was doing anything worthy of special notice, but the attention and praise were appreciated—almost as much as the bonus.

Christmas Day arrived, and Eleanor and Janette teamed up to prepare the shared meal. It was the first time away from the family Christmas dinner table, and Janette felt her throat tightening with loneliness.

It also felt odd not to have snow for Christmas. The winter in Indiana was unusually mild, and they did their best not to notice. The newly acquired used television set in the Quantzes' apartment helped to make the day pass, as well as a visit that evening with the Dycks, another young couple who had been classmates at Mountain View Bible College. But throughout the day thoughts of family members and the missed activity of home hung heavily in Janette's mind.

Shortly before the New Year, snow fell and beloved sister June and husband, John, came for a visit. With them they brought their two young daughters, Karen and Cheryl, who seemed to think that sleeping on the floor of the small apartment was a treat. Janette and Edward slept on the foldout couch in the Quantzes' apartment, leaving room for their guests in their own bed. It was such fun to visit with June and to enjoy her little family. The girls were so sweet with their long curls and pretty little dresses. Perhaps someday Janette would have girls of her own. It was a lovely thought, but for now her place was in the work force.

CHAPTER TWENTY-ONE

Elkhart

FIRST-SEMESTER GRADES came and Edward had done very well. Out of a possible three points, his grade point average was 2.8.

Graduation was to be held in June, and Edward's parents announced that they would make the trip to the United States in time to be present. This was wonderful news, and the young couple waited impatiently for the term to end. For the entire year, letters, newspapers, and gifts of money had been mailed from home, and Edward and Janette were so thankful to have support and love coming regularly. It helped to bring home a little closer during the times of loneliness.

After Edward graduated from Bethel College in the spring of 1958, a move to Elkhart was planned. Both his work as assistant pastor and his seminary courses at Goshen College in the fall would be outside the town of Mishawaka, so it seemed to make more sense to move to the nearby town. Janette resigned her bank job, and they found an apartment in the home of Dorothy Yoder, a widow who worked at their denomination's office.

Mrs. Yoder lived with her elderly mother and was a wonderful landlady. Edward and Janette stayed with her for two years. Church responsibilities, classes, and work left little time to socialize with the landladies, but they were much appreciated by the Okes.

Soon after leaving her previous bank job, Janette was shocked to learn from the newspaper that her boss had been charged with embez-zlement. He had devised a nice system of skimming off money from "dormant" savings accounts and depositing it into his own "very ac-tive" checking account.

On thinking back, she wondered if perhaps that had been why he was so pleased to see Janette's ledgers balance. The entire department had been close to being invaded by auditors just before Janette was hired, and his activity was sure to have been discovered. Janette's bal-ancing of the backdated accounts had temporarily removed the threat. But eventually, as in most cases, "his sins found him out."

Now it looked as if the tight job market in Elkhart would leave Janette unemployed. After much searching she took a job at Adams and Westlake, a manufacturing company. Typing seemed to be a pre-requisite for the position, but the interviewer was convinced that Ja-nette could handle the work, even if she herself had some doubts. She had very little typing experience, and it had been a while since she had used her meager skills. Immediately she dug out the typewriter in order to practice for her new job.

The starting pay was $50 per week, with a possible raise in three months. Janette was thrilled with the income; it was more than she had been paid at any of the banks where she had worked. And the woman who would be training her and helping her brush up on her typing skills was reputed to be very patient and kind. Edward joked that it was pretty nice to be paid $50 while someone taught her to type, and Janette supposed he was right.

Edward decided that it was time to trade in the old black car with its mechanical problems and found a 1955 Chevrolet Belle Air. It was a lovely soft blue-and-white two-tone, and they were proud to drive it. The new car meant car payments, so Janette's new job had come at a wonderful time. God had been faithful and timely once again.

The day after Janette began her job, the company hired a second girl whose experience in typing far exceeded Janette's. So she was moved from the steno pool to the mailroom. Though she was a little disappointed at not having a chance to improve her typing skills, she felt mostly relief. The bookkeeping department would have been even better in her way of thinking, but there had not been an opening.

The mail arrived by bag in the morning, and the mail clerk was responsible for sorting it and opening any letters not specified as "private." Then the mail was sorted by department and delivered, first to the executive offices and then to the various departments of the factory. It was quite a walk since the factory covered two full city blocks.

This task was repeated twice a day—to deliver what had come in and then pick up the outgoing mail, all of which needed to be stamped and weighed. For the most part, Janette liked the work, but with no air conditioning in the factory buildings, it did get hot and miserable in the summer.

Fall at Beulah Missionary Church found new responsibilities ahead for both Edward and Janette. He was put in charge of more services and other tasks while Reverend Bacon was away at various times, and Janette found herself in charge of the teenage Sunday school class— quite a shift from teaching first graders. She had been told that it would be an easy job but soon declared in a letter home, "I've been took!"

The youth program was in need of a great deal of organizing, and she didn't want to rush in to "fix things" too quickly. The patience and tact that was required for the task soon paid off, and she found herself enjoying the new relationships with the teens.

Fall turned to winter and a second Christmas arrived, bringing another welcome visit from Edward's family. Janette had spent time in thought trying to devise a way to squeeze her parents-in-law, as well as Edward's sister, her husband, and newborn son, into their small apartment. But an unexpected and much appreciated answer to prayer came from the president of the denomination. Reverend and Mrs. Geiger had heard of the situation and, because they were to be vacationing elsewhere, offered their home for the visiting family members over the holiday period.

Following Christmas together, they all traveled to Kansas City to attend the wedding of Edward's cousin. The Alberta relatives returned to Canada from there, and Edward and Janette left for Elkhart, stopping in Chicago to visit June and John on their way.

While they were still enjoying their time with June's family some shocking news reached them. One of the youths from Janette's Sunday school group, Judith Yoder, had been overcome with severe pain in her head on Friday and by late Saturday morning had passed away of an aneurysm.

The church was stunned. Judy had been a wonderfully sweet girl, capable and responsible. The whole church shared the difficult loss, but God also used it as a time of growing. Many of the church young people made new commitments to the Lord as a result of Judy's death.

In January of 1959, Janette made an appointment with her doctor. She had not been feeling well and was told that her hormones may have been causing the trouble. After tests, Edward and Janette were advised that she might experience some difficulty in getting pregnant again and that they should go ahead and try to start their family.

It was sobering to think that there might be trouble having children, and though they felt they were not quite ready to begin a family, they were anxious about not being able to have children at all. So they once again decided to trust God for their future—both for finances and for their hopes of having children.

In February, Janette received a phone call from a distraught church member. The woman had been trying to find a way to be relieved of her responsibilities for the nursery, and as a last attempt had called the young intern pastor's wife.

Janette agreed to take on the responsibility until someone else could be found, and then set about to find that "someone." The previous nursery worker who had also been unable to find a replacement had already alerted Reverend Bacon. Now Sunday mornings were spent entertaining toddlers during the church service, while Edward scurried about with one activity or another.

It wasn't long until Janette thought she might be pregnant, though it had not been verified. Anxiously they waited, hoping time would prove them correct. If they were, she had experienced no problem becoming pregnant as the doctor had forewarned.

One evening Janette arrived home from work and was preparing supper when a rather flushed and sheepish-looking Edward appeared with a package. When she opened it she discovered the softest, most beautiful pale-yellow baby gown and blanket. He had needed to do a good deal of searching before finding the little shop that he "just happened to be going by."

"The clerk asked me if it was for a girl or a boy," he laughed, "and I said, 'It's a boy.'"

"Great! A preacher lying," Janette accused him as they hugged and laughed. "We aren't even sure I'm pregnant yet."

"I am sure—and it *is* a boy," he insisted.

Later, Dr. Middleton confirmed their hopes, and they plunged into the excitement of the coming event. In March, Edward and

Janette sat down to begin a letter home. With pride he typed out:

> Janette and I are sitting here at our little desk in the corner (for Janette has changed the furniture again) and writing both of our folks. If you will recall some time ago, I wrote that the doctor . . . thought that Janette would have considerable trouble becoming pregnant. Well, I guess we just fooled the doctor. . . . She is now two months pregnant. Looks like you will be grand-parents a second time. It should be born sometime in October. . . . Already Janette is talking of buying wool for baby clothes. We already have a baby blanket and nightgown to match that I bought Janette to sort of give her a premature thrill. She was thrilled. We shall try to keep you informed of the details as they arrive.

The letter was signed, "Mom and Pop Oke, Jr."

CHAPTER TWENTY-TWO

Expectations

IN APRIL JANETTE PUT in her request to be moved from the mail delivery department at Adams and Westlake, and under the circumstances, her boss agreed. It was a difficult pregnancy, and signs seemed to show that a miscarriage was again a possibility. After having already lost one baby she was very concerned. Dr. Middleton, who was also a member of the church and a good friend, fought as best she could to keep the baby for them, and after many scares and a good deal of medication, things seemed to settle down.

Over the summer Edward continued his part-time position in the church as well as taking on additional janitorial duties, earning extra income to be saved for fall. When an opportunity to sell Watkins products came, he took that job too. The summer was long with Edward gone so much of the time and Janette's own body feeling so unfamiliar and awkward.

After working at the factory for about a year, Janette finally quit because of the impending birth. She turned down the offer of pregnancy leave because she did not intend to return to work after the baby arrived. Her fellow workers took her to lunch and presented her with a lovely gift. The soft, warm blanket was delightful to hold and fold, and then hold and fold again.

Janette spent a week with sister June in Chicago and returned with June's knitting machine, ready to prepare some things for the coming baby. She started a baby sweater, and quickly noticed that the whole process had captivated Edward's interest. Soon the "engineer" had taken over the task.

The next morning, Janette awoke to the sound of the clicking needles on the machine. There sat Edward, still in his pajamas, working away at a second baby sweater. In fact, he was nearly late for work that morning.

Other preparations were also underway. They had received Mrs. Yoder's permission to paint the little apartment, making it fresh and clean for the baby. Then they purchased a secondhand crib and dresser, stripping the old paint and applying a fresh white coat. Though crowded, the baby's corner of the bedroom was beginning to take shape.

August's hot days were particularly difficult this year for Janette. In mid-month, the church gave them a wonderful baby shower, well organized and extremely generous. They received a high chair, car bed, playpen, bathinette, bassinet, diaper hamper, plus many smaller items and lovely baby clothes. It was amazing to receive so many new things all at once, and Janette thanked God over and over for such wonderful people and their expressions of love.

Everything was ready for the arrival of their little one. Church girls were arguing over who would get the baby-sitting duties. Because of the expense, they had not had a trip back home. But the baby was due in October, and they were going to treat themselves by flying home for Christmas so they might present their new baby to the grandparents and other family members. Though Edward had declared it to be a boy, Dr. Middleton was now predicting a girl.

As was often the case, Janette expressed her deep feelings about the coming child in a little bit of verse. It began:

> A baby's coming to our house
> An answer of God to a prayer.
> And if it be a boy or girl
> We do not know—nor care.
> We only know that in His love
> He's chosen this way to say,
> "I trust you to lead heavenward
> My child day by day."

The verse continued:

> His days like all shall be numbered

And the day will come when I
Shall return him to you. "God grant it
That he shall be fit" is my cry.
May he live in a manner that when, Lord,
He answers your call, "Come home, son,"
He can stand in your presence undaunted,
Cleansed, through the death of your Son.

A short time before her due date, while Edward was at seminary and Janette was having her devotional time, she prayed again somewhat casually, reminding God that their child had already been given to Him. But that day she sensed the Lord speaking to her heart very clearly.

"Do you really mean that?" He prompted.

"Yes, God, I mean it."

"Really? You really mean it?"

Suddenly she knew that she had not—not really. But before she had finished her prayer time, she had given her coming child totally to the Lord. With tears, she worked her way through the struggle.

The due date came—and went. Janette visited her doctor and made an appointment to come again the following week. Janette prayed that she would not need the appointment, but she did. And then another still.

She heard the remark, "Are you still here?" more times than she could count, especially on Sundays when she again showed up at church. The two full weeks of being overdue felt like a hundred.

When Janette returned to the car after having kept the second overdue appointment and scheduled another for the following week, she was in tears. Edward was immediately concerned. Was something wrong?

How could she answer that? How could he possibly understand that everything was wrong even though nothing was? It was so very difficult to wait.

At least Janette could turn some of her thoughts homeward that week as sister Joyce's wedding date of October 22 approached. Joyce had moved to the Champion area and spent some time in the same bank where Janette had worked a few years before. Here she began dating Elmer Deal, a brother of Vivien who had been Janette and Margie's roommate and later married cousin Don. Elmer had been a friend of the family for quite some time and had visited the Hoadley home with the prairie cousins on several occasions. Kid sister Joyce had "grown up" since that time.

With Janette too far away and in no condition to even dream of attending the wedding, it helped to ease the longing to be with family when the next day she began to think that it might, at last, be time to call her doctor.

CHAPTER TWENTY-THREE

Brian

EDWARD WAS IN HIS FRIDAY seminary class. Janette was home alone. For a while she debated whether what she was feeling was really "it" or not. Should she call or wait? At last she placed the call and was told that she had best get a taxi and come to Dr. Middleton's office. From there she was taken with the office nurse, June Embrey, also a friend, the remaining distance to the hospital.

She was pleasantly surprised to find a friend from church already there and in labor. They had often joked about sharing a hospital room, but Janette was to have delivered a few weeks ahead of Shirley. Now Janette was late—and Shirley was blessed with being early—so they were sharing a labor room, after all.

As soon as Edward arrived home from class and found Janette's hastily scrawled note, he hurried to the hospital and the long wait began. Janette had been admitted around four in the afternoon, but according to medical staff, not much was happening.

Later that evening Dr. Middleton asked Edward if he would like to see X-rays of his child and he assured her he would. When he returned, Edward shared what Dr. Middleton had discussed with him. If things continued to move slowly and nothing had happened by six o'clock the next morning, she would perform a C-section. It was then about ten o'clock at night.

Shirley was taken to delivery first. Coincidentally, both ladies shared the same doctor and were also both going to be delivering breach babies. Janette did not give Shirley much time with Dr. Middleton before she needed the delivery room as well. The doctor and nurses had to quickly care for the newly arrived baby Jody and rush Shirley from the room so they might get it prepared and Janette into it. Her baby was well on the way.

There was the scurry of switching patients, and then the gas mask was clamped over Janette's mouth, to her great relief. The next thing she knew, she was a mother. Their son arrived at 11:19 P.M., weighing nine pounds and three ounces, and though she still felt somewhat heady because of the anesthesia, the first sight of her new baby filled her with wonder and joy.

Janette could not seem to look at him long enough. Quietly she studied the precious bundle that the nurse held out for her to see. He had only a little hair, but what he did have was quite dark. The feature that drew immediate attention was his broad little hands. They were shaped just like his daddy's—even the doctor remarked about them. He was named Brian Edward, the name they had chosen before his appearance.

All too soon her new infant was whisked away, and Janette was taken to recovery. Though tired from the long wait, Edward greeted her with high spirits. He strutted about the room until the doctor happened to look his way and realized that the father would soon be a patient, too, if she didn't act quickly. Then he was given a chair and asked to put his head between his legs until he recovered from his faintness.

"Daddy" seemed none the worse for wear, and when Dr. Middleton was sure he was going to be fine, she promised him that he could drop by in the morning to see Janette and the new baby, though visiting hours were not normally until afternoon.

Edward finally went home to bed—and to make some phone calls to relatives back home to let them know that he had a son.

Janette was wheeled away and arrived in her hospital room, to her delight finding Shirley already occupying the room. The ladies laughed at how much of the birth experience they had shared together and then settled down for some much-needed rest.

All too soon morning dawned, and Janette raised up in her bed and propped a pillow behind her. Nurse after nurse paraded into the small room, but she was waiting rather impatiently for only one—the one who would bring little Brian back to her.

When at last the nurse arrived, she appeared somewhat agitated. Instead of placing the little bundle in Janette's waiting arms, she merely held him out for his new mommy to see. Janette reached out and took the tiny hand of her son.

It felt strangely cold. Janette was about to comment but then decided against it. She was a very new mommy and knew nothing about newborns or hospital procedures. When baby Jody was brought in to be nursed, Janette wondered further. It was around ten o'clock when Edward arrived, accompanied by Dr. Middleton. Janette still suspected nothing until the doctor began to speak.

"Janette, we're having trouble with your baby," she said, and with those few words a surge of fear raced through Janette's whole being. A quick glance at Dr. Middleton's trembling lip alarmed her even more than the words. Doctors were trained to hide emotions well, and Janette knew that something was seriously wrong to affect her trusted doctor and friend in such a way.

"We've discovered a heart murmur," Dr. Middleton went on to explain.

Then all the medical information spilled out. Dr. Middleton had been called back to the hospital by the nursing staff who were concerned at Brian's color. A pediatrician had been called in and had begun working over their baby at about six o'clock that morning and was continuing to do so.

The doctor spoke of a heart murmur and of an enlarged liver due to stress, but the reason for their son's condition was still a mystery. They were anxiously looking for answers.

Brian's brief visit to Janette's bedside must have been made with extreme anxiety for the nurse who held him, hoping that the new mother would not ask questions or delay his return to the nursery.

Shocked, Janette did not cry—did not even speak. She closed her eyes and prayed, but unbelievably her prayer was, "It's okay, God. You can take him."

Why was she not fighting? She knew that it could only be that a few days earlier she had fought the situation through and had honestly been able to say, "Yes, God. He's yours. I really mean it."

Janette had hardly finished her personal "letting go" when a doctor she had not seen previously joined them in the room and, as gently as possible, informed them that their baby boy had died. Tears flowed then—but there was still no fighting against the shattering news.

Janette was moved to a private room. She and Shirley and their two newborns would not be sharing a room together, after all. Over and over her heart cried, "I didn't even get to hold him. I didn't even hold him!"

With all her being she wished she had insisted that the nurse allow her to snuggle her son, but now it was too late.

"I still want to hold him," she told Edward. He may have thought her to be a little hysterical, but he went to find the doctor anyway.

Soon a nurse arrived with the tiny body bundled only in a simple hospital blanket. Janette unfolded it and there he was: all ten fingers, all ten toes, a perfect little baby, chubby and well formed. She held his little hands, those replicas of his daddy's.

After a few minutes spent with Brian, Janette was ready to give him up. The nurse came back and took him away, and Janette mourned quietly the loss of her son.

Edward told her later that Brian had not been easy for him to look at, his little body already discolored. Janette had seen none of it. To her he was a perfect chubby, pink newborn. God must have blessed her with rose-colored glasses, and years later when she read the account given by Corrie ten Boom concerning her sister Betsy's death, she understood perfectly. Edward had the sorrowful task of making more phone calls—difficult calls only ten short hours after he had joyously dialed the same numbers.

Flowers began to arrive in her hospital room. Janette's reaction surprised even herself. She had always loved flowers, but now as the lovely bouquets appeared, she did not even want to look at them. The flowers could not bring her baby back, and each new delivery was another reminder of what she had just lost.

Her arms literally ached for the baby she did not have—so much so that she was tempted to go to Shirley's room and beg to hold little Jody, but she thought better of that. What if something happened to Jody? Then she would feel it was her fault.

At the same time she ached for a baby to hold, the tiny cries from the nursery aggravated her. She was not sure she would ever be able to look at another baby without bursting into tears.

And then she had a visitor. Elna, a kind lady from work, arrived at her door with a big smile and a gift for the baby.

"You haven't heard?" she finally managed in disbelief. Poor Elna. She was shocked and embarrassed. Janette could read her own pain reflected in the woman's eyes.

Elna insisted that she keep the gift—for the next baby—and

Janette did not argue with her. She tucked the pair of darling baby shoes aside and prayed that one day she would be able to use them.

Even though she wished to be alone with her grief, Janette was still a patient in recovery, and there was the usual stream of nurses in and out of her room. Most went about their duties quickly and hurried from the room, leaving only the silence punctuated with noises echoing in the hall. One young black nurse hurried through the usual ministrations, but as she was leaving the room, she turned and said with such feeling, "I am so sorry." And Janette knew that she was. She loved the woman for her kindness, and though she saw her only once, the sympathetic face has remained in her memory.

In the dark days that followed, while Janette lay in her hospital bed and Edward struggled alone with funeral arrangements, Janette felt the prayers of God's people as never before. She longed for family members and, as one always does in times of sorrow, seemed to need her mother in particular.

Yet, over and over, a song kept running through her mind, and she sang it mentally again and again. It brought comfort.

> God's way is the best way
> God's way is the right way
> I'll trust in Him always
> He knoweth the best.

She clung to the sentiments of the song.

As much as she ached for her baby and yet suffered with the cries from the nursery, she knew she had to face her emotions. When she was given permission to be up, she steeled her resolve and forced her feet to carry her to the nursery window where she could look at the other newborns. God was with her. And she felt love, not bitterness.

The longer she stood, the more she was able to enjoy the babies. This is where Edward found her, and she wished to share her triumph with him, raising her hand to point out a certain baby, sure that she had found little Jody among the infants. He brushed past her without a glance at the bassinets, his eyes tear-filled. Taking her arm, he led her back to the room. Edward had just come from the funeral home and had seen his infant son ready for burial.

"He's just beautiful," he wept.

Reverend Bacon was out of town holding evangelistic meetings, so a retired minister from the church, Rev. D. Paul Huffman, readily agreed to officiate at the service. They had opted for a private ceremony at the funeral home, and only a few close friends and sister June from Chicago were in attendance.

June had come almost immediately on receiving word, leaving behind her two young daughters. Karen, about six at the time, had sent a handmade card for her Aunt Janette with all the love and compassion that a child can pour into a little piece of paper.

Little Brian Edward Oke was buried in the lovely soft yellow gown, bundled in the snugly blanket his daddy had purchased before they were even sure he was on the way.

Janette was released from the hospital for the funeral service but not allowed to go to the cemetery. Only his daddy and Reverend Huffman went with the hearse.

Instead, Janette went home with Maynard and Ruth Yoder. The Yoders had become Edward and Janette's Indiana "mom and dad," and they lovingly took care of the grieving couple. After being released from the hospital, Janette spent the first few days with them while Edward was in class and then went home when Edward picked her up at day's end.

Dr. Middleton did everything she could think of to make the time easier for Edward and Janette. She insisted that she would accept nothing for her services and stopped by their home to be certain Janette was doing well. Being a parishioner and also a friend, the loss of Brian was difficult for her as well. Brian was the first baby she had lost since setting up her practice.

Duties at church were resumed. In fact, they increased. It seemed that well-meaning friends had decided what Janette needed was "busyness." They may have been right, but she was left emotionally drained.

Janette was given the assignment of children's Christmas program director. It was a big job and took a good deal of time in rehearsals. She had not yet looked for another job, so she had extra daytime hours at home.

In spite of the distractions, she continued to grieve silently. On some days while Edward was at class, she would go look at the empty little crib and the drawers full of tiny baby things and weep. She whispered silently to God on one such moment, "I know that I said that you could take him—but I didn't promise not to cry." The crying times seemed to be good therapy and were times of slow healing.

There were friends who felt that it would be good for Janette to have the care of a baby. She was often asked to sit with this one or care for that one. Though she appreciated their concern, it was not *a* baby she wanted—but *her* baby. She did baby-sit the ones who were brought to her and gave them loving care, but those times did not bring the comfort to her heart that her friends had hoped.

Edward and Janette still planned to go home for Christmas. She could hardly wait. Of course, it would not be the same, but at least it would be a chance to see their families and share their grief.

To those at home, their baby boy would not seem real, Janette reasoned. They had not seen him, not touched him, and not attended his funeral service. All he had been was a little unknown "someone." Janette longed to tell them all about him so they would feel they had known him, too.

But the time home was a disappointment to her. Because of the rush and bustle of Christmas activities, no one had the time to sit down and hear the few things she could tell about the baby boy she and Edward had seen and known so briefly. Perhaps she had brought unrealistic expectations. What was there to tell? Maybe there was no way for her to really unburden the thoughts and feelings in her heart.

Time slipped by, and, as difficult as the experience was, Edward and Janette began to see that it had been a growing time—both in their relationship with God and in their relationship with each other. They were reminded again and again that if they planned to serve in the ministry, in years ahead there would doubtlessly be many times when they would be called upon to share the grief of someone in their congregation. They could now truly understand the sorrow of loss.

And though the pain was sharp and real, Janette was thankful that a loving God had cushioned the blow as only He could. He had prepared her heart so that there was no bitterness, and He was with her daily, helping her with her sorrow and tears. Slowly, she even began to believe that there might be another child—someday.

CHAPTER TWENTY-FOUR

Returning Home

AFTER CHRISTMAS JANETTE began to search for another job. Since she was certain that her mailroom job at Adams and Westlake had long been filled, she did not want to apply there and have them feel they should find another spot for her out of pity.

Soon she was offered a well-paying position at Miles Laboratory. But it was night-shift work, and had she accepted it, she and Edward would scarcely have seen each other. At that time in their lives, they needed each other more than ever. So Janette turned that offer down.

Eventually she found a job at the *Elkhart Truth*, a local newspaper. She told them frankly that she was hoping she would not work for long as she planned to have another child, but they accepted her anyway. She hoped and prayed for another baby, and it was not long until she was pregnant.

This again was a difficult pregnancy. During the first months, the doctor had to fight to keep the little one. At one point, Janette was sure she had lost the baby, but she was grateful to discover she had been wrong, and at last the pregnancy settled down.

After some difficult months, the Okes decided they would return to Alberta in June. Edward applied for a ministry position in their home district, and they were assigned a church in Montgomery, a suburb of Calgary.

Janette quit her newspaper job. She had not quite come to enjoy her work, but it had filled the days and helped pay the bills. She had also been exposed to something new and gotten a small bit of experience in the field, although she felt she had not been there long enough to absorb much.

The ride back to Alberta, again pulling a trailer, was a long one. Janette was about five months pregnant, and they were concerned about the baby. The roads were rough, and the trailer seemed to exaggerate all the bumps, jerking against the car.

They reached the Canadian/American border at an awkward hour and found it closed to people crossing with all of their belongings. Rather than sit and wait until the next morning, they decided to keep on driving on the American side.

Across Minnesota and North Dakota they went. It was raining and the trailer was beginning to leak. Hour after hour went by and the couple was becoming more and more tired, but they could find nothing in overnight accommodations. At last they pulled into a small town and Edward asked about a hotel.

He was told that the town had two, but the stranger giving the directions was interrupted by another man saying, "You shouldn't send them there."

They did find a room for the night. It had no lock on the door, the light was turned off by a string from the bare hanging bulb, the window had no blind or curtain, and the sheets and pillowcases had definitely been used—but they took it and were thankful. They desperately needed sleep.

Edward and Janette arrived in Alberta to new responsibilities and a new home. The Montgomery parsonage was a nice little house of four rooms and a bath. Having managed to save $1,000 from their stay in the United States, they were soon shopping for furniture and found a store in Calgary with reasonable prices. Soon they had purchased a bedroom suite with mattress set, living room suite plus two occasional chairs, and kitchen table and chairs.

The salesman who helped them also knew of a used dining-room suite. A couple he knew was going through a divorce, and he was helping them sell their furniture. Janette supposed it was not proper for him to be selling used goods for friends on company time, but they were glad to get the furniture. It was a lovely set for the money asked—table, chairs, bureau, and hutch in great condition. They were very thankful that God had helped the money stretch so far, and they had stayed within their $1,000 budget.

Then housekeeping began. Edward was excited about his first church, though the attendance was a little lopsided. Most of the approximately one hundred who came were children. That meant the few adults of the congregation had to "put in overtime."

It was a big year for Edward and Janette. Their first home with their own furniture and the nice things from their wedding which could finally be brought out of storage. They had their first church and all the responsibilities that entailed, and each day that passed brought them closer to the expected arrival of their second baby.

Because of Janette's medical history, she had been advised to seek out a specialist upon returning to Calgary. A friend had given her the name of a city doctor, and she was pleased to discover Dr. Buchanan to be worthy of his recommendation. They appreciated his care.

When at last the day actually arrived, Janette entered the hospital at about six in the morning. It soon became evident that it would be a long delivery. Edward had almost lost faith that the baby would ever make an appearance and began to feel that Janette was doing something wrong. But they were both able to quickly forget the long, miserable day when their new son finally did arrive.

Terry Lawrence was born around four o'clock on November 19, 1960. The fall weather had been gorgeous up to that point but turned nasty later that same night. Janette was glad that the special event had already happened and that the storm hit after she and her baby were tucked safely in a warm hospital room. Terry weighed in at eight pounds six ounces, a little smaller than his brother Brian had been.

He looked hale and hearty and Janette was relieved, though she had forced herself not to worry about his arrival. If she had been a bit more aware, she might initially have been panic-stricken, for the staff had some trouble keeping Terry breathing at first. He had needed his little "breathing machine" started more than once. Almost calmly, Janette watched, sure that he was in good hands and was going to be just fine.

Dr. Middleton had sent all the records along with a personal note. In it, Janette later discovered, the Indiana doctor also informed the Calgary doctor that because of Janette's past experience, it would be very important for her to be able to hold her new baby as soon as possible. The request was honored, and little Terry was placed in her arms as soon as convenient after they stabilized his breathing.

Those first moments spent with Terry were wonderful, and even after Janette had been returned to her hospital room and settled for a good night's rest, she felt satisfied. Her baby was fine. She was a mother.

However, a terrible scare happened to her the next day. It began with a crying baby. Janette was sure it was the voice of her new son. She made her way down the hall toward the nursery and saw through the open door a hospital intern and a nurse working over a newborn, suctioning fluids from his throat.

Convinced it really was Terry and feeling scared and sick, Janette returned to her room. Just as she had closed the door softly behind her, the intercom paged two doctors almost simultaneously. They were her own obstetrician and her family doctor. This was enough to absolutely convince Janette that her baby was in trouble.

A nurse arrived to show Janette to the scheduled baby-bath demonstration, and she followed obediently, not knowing what else to do. The class had not met for long when a nurse poked her head in the door and asked for a Mrs. Cook. Silence followed as each of the ladies in housecoats and slippers looked at one another and the nurses swept their eyes across the room. There was no Mrs. Cook in the class.

The nurse left, still apparently concerned about finding "Mrs. Cook," and Janette's mind launched into wild thoughts. It would be terribly easy to confuse two names as similar as Mrs. Cook and Mrs. Oke. Maybe she *had* been the one the nurse wanted.

The tension was more than Janette could stand. She was *sure* something was wrong and was driven to do the only thing that came to mind. She needed a phone; she was going to call Edward. But a recorded message that the number had been disconnected seemed only to add further panic to her mixed-up thoughts. Her baby was in trouble, and she could not even reach her husband!

Her mind hummed and buzzed in frantic confusion. What could she do? How could she help? She could think of nothing, so she returned to her room and waited, terror-stricken.

At feeding time, a familiar nurse pushed open the door and placed Terry in her arms. He looked fine. Janette was so relieved she could have cried. She was still not completely convinced that it had not been Terry out in the nursery under the doctor's fervent care; but if it had been, God had protected her little son. When Edward arrived for visiting hours and Janette told him of her experience, he could not explain the phone message that she had heard. Both the parsonage phone and the phone at the church office were in perfect working order.

The morning finally arrived when Janette was scheduled to take her new son home, and her excitement almost caused her doctor to keep her another day. It may have been her temperature or her blood pressure, but he hesitated to let her go. At last he consented and said she was free to leave, and it was a good thing. She was certain that if she had been required to spend another night in the hospital, she would have exploded.

CHAPTER TWENTY-FIVE

Motherhood

JANETTE AND BABY TERRY had a perfect "honeymoon" together for about two weeks. Janette sat at the little kitchen table writing out thank-you notes, filled with the wonder of a brand-new life and having such a good child, while Terry slept peacefully in the small bassinet given by the friends at Beulah. No fussing. No problems. He simply ate and slept.

Then everything changed, and Janette suddenly found herself with a colicky baby. He began fussing routinely at about two in the afternoon and by four was crying loudly. She may have been able to deal with the baby had the situation not been further complicated by a group of Pioneer Girls who met at the small house each week at four o'clock.

Janette did not have a baby-sitter, and it became increasingly difficult to juggle a crying baby and run the program at the same time. As she ended each of these frustrating days, Janette felt drained and nearly sick.

Terry's fussing got worse and worse through the evening hours until both he and his mother were exhausted, usually somewhere around midnight. Many nights Janette slept with him on her stomach, the warmth of her body hopefully easing the pains in his little tummy.

Sunday school class was another problem. Again, Janette had Terry in tow. There simply were not enough adults to teach the classes and provide a sitter. Most Sundays she and her baby fared well, but if he decided to be fussy, they were both miserable.

Janette was trying hard to accomplish her household and church-related tasks, all the while endeavoring to soothe her baby's discomfort. Often she would just manage to get Terry to sleep when the phone would ring and he would awaken and cry again.

And though it was well intentioned, the "advice" she received left her confused and frustrated. The first phone call would say to switch the baby to formula. Then the next caller would state emphatically, "Whatever you do, don't put him on the bottle." Though not aware of it at the time, Janette—a new mother—was undoubtedly tense after having lost her first baby. So all the conflicting tips simply couldn't be shrugged off as they might have been during better times.

To make matters worse, she was on her own. Edward was extremely busy with church duties, and Janette was trying hard to fulfill her role as pastor's wife. The closeness they had shared after having lost their first baby was suddenly gone in the face of all of the responsibilities and duties.

With Janette's difficulties, and the pressures on Edward, they both were near exhaustion. Edward confessed to having even fallen asleep in his little church office. Janette had no such quiet place to hide.

─────

"Little sister" Margie had graduated from Bible College and gone to work. In due time she began to accept calls from a fellow student from Mountain View Bible College. Janette was totally in favor and had already decided that the young man, Wilfred Wiens, would make a great match for Margie. They set their wedding date for December 28, and the family enthusiastically joined in with the preparations.

Janette had volunteered to bake cookies and squares for the reception, but Terry refused to cooperate. Still crying from his tummy aches, he insisted on Mommy's attention while she tried to concentrate on rescuing cookies from the oven before they burned.

Gradually the cookie tins filled up, and the fussing baby was none the worse for his fretting. Janette's nerves were a little frayed—but that eventually righted itself as well. They joined the family for the winter wedding, and Terry was fairly comfortable during the special day.

In his sixth month, Terry became ill and lost a little weight, which was quite a switch for the rapidly growing boy. Finally he was switched to formula, and though there was no way to be sure if the formula had been part of the solution, from then on he began to get over the colic. It was a relief to get a proper night's sleep again.

As Terry left colic and illness behind, motherhood became the wonder of childish accomplishments that Janette had dreamed it would be. Terry was energetic and advanced in many ways. With pride Janette pulled out his baby book and recorded each new milestone: when he began to talk, to walk, and to interact with his world around him, like standing little animals on his high-chair tray, and stacking his building blocks. Following Ma-ma and Da-da, two of his first words were "tractor" and "flower." A rather unusual combination, but Grandpa Oke sold tractors and Mommy loved flowers.

One hot summer Sunday, Terry was sick. Janette knew he had a fever but she had no one to substitute as teacher for her class, so she was forced to attend church anyway. After Sunday school he seemed even worse, so she decided to take him home.

Too late she realized that Edward had the only car keys and the service was about to begin. Edward was already on the platform and there was no way to get his attention without disturbing the entire service. So there was nothing for her to do but to walk home, carrying her sick baby.

The long blocks stretched on and on as Janette juggled Terry first against one shoulder, then the other. The day was so hot, and Terry, who quickly fell asleep, was heavy. She was sure she would never make it home. Finally she arrived, arms aching, face flushed. Terry, with medication, soon got over his "bug," as babies so quickly do.

Baby Terry walked at eight months. Before he was two he recognized many songs and choruses, could name all the animals in his picture books, and could count to ten. Janette quietly glowed with pride. She thought he was pretty smart indeed.

Besides all the new tricks, he was a fun child, usually happy and outgoing. He was very active, and people used to laugh and say, "Aren't you glad he isn't twins?" But Janette would just smile sweetly.

Edward had more seminary work to finish, so in the spring of 1962, he left for Indiana to complete the work—alone. Janette stayed behind to pack up for the move. After being in Montgomery for two years, they had accepted a call to the Edmonton church, farther north but also closer to her home.

Janette's sister Jean stayed with them off and on at the time. She had recently had cancer surgery and was in Calgary taking treatments at the cancer clinic. Jean shared little about how sick she felt from the treatments, and it was only later that Janette learned how difficult it had been for her sister. Janette and Terry would drive Jean over to the clinic and sit in the car until she was finished. While they waited, Janette kept Terry entertained, and then they would all return to the parsonage.

When the time neared for Edward to return home, Janette was to drive to Indiana to spend some time with friends while Edward finished up his summer school; then they would return to Alberta together. This meant that all their household belongings had to be packed before she left so the moving truck could pick them up after she had gone. Together she and Jean finished the busy task.

When it was time for Janette to begin the long trip to Indiana, Jean was not quite finished with her treatments. So she and Orville stayed on in the parsonage, then finished packing the last of the dishes and furniture that they had needed for their stay and did the final cleaning of the home for its next occupant. The pastor's wife who followed said that she had never moved into such a thoroughly cleaned house, and Janette knew that Jean deserved much of the thanks.

Janette planned to pick up the last paycheck from the church, pay off the final utility bills, and use the remainder of the money for the trip to the U.S. It sounded like a good plan.

However, once the bills had been paid, Janette discovered that she had only about sixteen dollars left. Even in 1961 this was not much money, and she knew she could be in for trouble. They had a gas credit card, but that wouldn't pay for food and overnight lodging—and there was always a chance of unexpected expenses.

Janette was to spend one night with Edward's parents before leaving, and she knew that if she asked Dad Oke for money he would gladly help out. Both he and Mother Oke had been wonderfully generous and often helped them over the years while the young couple was getting established in the ministry. But Janette hated to ask.

She worried a bit, prayed even more, and then around four o'clock in the afternoon began the almost-two-thousand-mile drive with a gas credit card and sixteen dollars. Her friend Eleanor Quantz, who planned to spend some time visiting friends in Indiana, traveled with her and helped with the driving. Eleanor, too, had a little money—about thirty dollars.

Janette brought one of Jean's growing boys along to entertain

Terry, who was now eighteen months and very active. Terry and the young boy played in the back while Janette and Eleanor did the driving. Since there were no car seats for the baby, he was allowed to bounce quietly on the seat, or climb onto David's lap for a story, or press his nose against the window to watch the scenery.

They drove the loaded car straight through the first night, then continued on until late afternoon of the next day. When they stopped for an early night at a little motel, Terry sprinted from the car like a wild thing released from a cage, stretching his chubby little legs as he ran and ran on the soft green lawn.

The next day they arrived in Chicago at June and John's home, spending the night there. They were almost to Indiana and the sixteen dollars was stretching just fine. The shared motel room and light meals for David, Terry, and herself were all Janette had needed to pay for.

But when they were ready to leave Chicago, it was discovered that, through some confusion, the car keys had been locked in the trunk in a small suitcase. They had to call the city police for help. On arriving and surveying the situation, the officer finally decided to remove the backseat from the vehicle and crawl through in search of the case that held the keys. Embarrassed though she was, Janette was truly relieved to be on the road once again.

In Indiana they met Edward and stayed at the home of some friends. The Freeds were away at the time, and it was a relief to have a place where they could spread out and feel at home.

Again, confusion led to trouble, this time with more serious consequences. Janette had kept her small suitcase locked because it contained children's aspirin. Edward was not aware of this, and after taking something from the suitcase, he had left it open.

Terry found the suitcase—and the aspirin. He remembered the taste of the little "chewies" from times past and proceeded to help himself. When they discovered him and the bottle, they were aghast, not certain how many he had eaten.

They phoned Dr. Middleton, who told them, "You'd better get him to the hospital."

No longer being U.S. residents, they did not have insurance to cover their costs—and what was left of the sixteen dollars would not begin to cover a hospital bill. When they arrived with Terry at the emergency room, they discovered a friend from the Beulah Missionary Church was on duty.

He tried to get Terry to bring up the pills, but to no avail. His small body refused. After several attempts, they decided that stomach pumping was the only alternative.

"I think you need to take a walk," their friend, Virgil, warned. "Mothers shouldn't be here when we do this." And it was good advice. They could still hear their small son from across the hospital parking lot.

Even after the stomach pumping, Terry's blood showed a large amount of aspirin. The hospital did let his parents take him home, but when he awoke from his afternoon nap, his bed was drenched with perspiration. Otherwise, he seemed to suffer no further effects from the incident, and the generous friend who had given him the necessary care asked for no payment for his services.

As is often the case on vacations and family visits, Janette, who was so proud of Terry and anxious to show him off to her Indiana friends, found him uncooperative. Her normally good-tempered, friendly little son had turned into some kind of little monster. He would cry for food, but when Janette gave him some, he would chew it up and spit it out. Then he would begin crying for more. She felt embarrassed—and disappointed. Their friends were not seeing the real Terry.

While they were having dinner with the Middletons, Terry repeated the same scene, only this time a doctor was watching.

"I think that boy has a problem," Dr. Middleton said and told Janette to bring him to her office. Sure enough, he had a sore throat and ear infection. Medication quickly cleared it up, but by then it was time to head for home.

With Edward to help with driving, they drove straight through on the way home—Edward needed to be back in time for his ordination service. They made it, a little frayed around the edges but, nevertheless, they were there—and on time. Edward was ordained at a service of the annual camp meeting in Didsbury. They took up residence in the Edmonton parsonage, and Edward began his ministry.

Moving in with a nearly two-year-old was an all-consuming experience. Janette was happy to see that the new home had a nice board fence all around the backyard. With a sigh of relief she looked forward to not worrying so much about Terry playing outside. The victory was short-lived. He learned to scale that fence the first day.

After a few spankings for climbing over it, Terry gave up. Then he discovered that he could simply open the gate. His mother did her best to discourage him from that activity also.

It was a nice and well-maintained house. The congregation had almost finished giving it a thorough repainting indoors, leaving only the wall registers to be replaced. As they moved from room to room surveying their new home, Janette heard a little voice call from behind her, "Bye, Mommy." She turned to see Terry climbing, feet first, down a large, open air vent! She rushed toward him, half-expecting to see him drop out of sight before she could get there, but it turned out there was a bend in the duct-work and he was only able to disappear from the armpits down.

The Edmonton parsonage was a two-story house, which was wonderful, giving a family with a two-year-old plenty of room. Edward and Janette immediately plunged into the work of the church, taking upon themselves the many responsibilities of the ministry. Janette's duties included Sunday school superintendent, director of the children's church hour, which she taught alone to about thirty children, and two Pioneer Girls clubs each week over the winter season. She also worked in the nursery while the choir rehearsed before the evening service and then stayed on during the service.

When they left the church one year later, there were many adults in the congregation that Janette had still not met. She had rarely had an opportunity to attend the church services.

CHAPTER TWENTY-SIX

Additions

EDWARD AND JANETTE had hoped for a baby brother or sister for Terry, spaced a couple of years after his arrival, but it had not quite worked as planned. When, much to her excitement, Janette did become pregnant, she carried the baby for only about six weeks and then lost it.

At the hospital, for a surgical procedure after the miscarriage, Janette shed tears of disappointment at the loss of another baby. She read that some women have an easier time becoming pregnant after having this surgery so, rightly or wrongly, she decided to ignore the doctor's admonition that she guard against another pregnancy for at least three months.

Soon Janette decided that she was indeed pregnant again. She simply *felt* pregnant. But when she called her doctor, a specialist in Edmonton who had been her family doctor in Rimbey when she was a child, Dr. Bugis assured her that she could not be pregnant. He was certain that things had simply not "settled" since the D & C had been performed. Janette waited a few days and called him again.

"I'm sure you're not, Janette," he told her. "But come on in and we'll put your mind at ease."

When she did go in, he was astounded. Not only did he discover that she was pregnant, but that she was much farther along than she should be for the time period. He called in a second specialist for consultation, who confirmed it.

Edward and Janette were about to move again, this time to Didsbury, where his parents were living. Edward had been appointed by the denomination to act as president of Mountain View Bible College. His father, Harold Oke, had served as vice-president for a period of time a few years earlier.

Hearing that Edward and Janette were moving shortly, Dr. Joseph Bugis was uncertain as to what to do. "If you weren't going," he told her, "I'd put you in the hospital and find out what's going on. As soon as you move, get yourself a specialist."

Janette decided to go back to Dr. Buchanan in Calgary, even though it was a fifty-mile drive. After they had settled into the college-owned house in Didsbury, Janette made her appointment. It turned out that Dr. Bugis and Dr. Buchanan had been classmates in their training years for obstetrics. Dr. Buchanan laughed at the "joke on Joe." He was convinced that she had miscarried one baby and that a twin had miraculously survived the D & C. He set her due date accordingly for the first of October.

It was not a comfortable pregnancy. Janette grew quickly—too quickly. And she often found herself tired and worn out early in the day, though thankful for the life she held inside.

In an inspired moment, Janette sat alone and wrote out her thoughts in a poem. Her feelings about the miracle of parentage spilled across the page:

> The hand of God . . . reached down
> Into a mother's heart
> And there conceived a thing of beauty
> And of wondrous art.
> The little babe—so perfect, pure in every part—
> A gift of love
> From the hand of God.

Not long afterward, Janette offered the poem to June's husband, John, to see if he thought it worthy to be put to music. John added the melody to her words and "The Hand of God" became a song. It was later published.

As she approached the established due date, she lay down with Terry for a much needed afternoon nap. When he awoke he sat up, rubbed his sleepy eyes, then reached over and patted her rounded tummy.

"There's two babies in there," he stated simply.

"No," Janette spoke reassuringly. "Just one."

But he shook his head. "Two," he insisted. She let the matter drop.

The next day, with two months to go, Janette went to the hospital for an X-ray. When Dr. Buchanan saw her after the X-ray, he was grinning.

"It's twins!" he announced. Janette was thrilled. Terry had been right—though she was sure he had never heard of such a thing as twins.

Janette was not as thrilled, though, when her due date was pushed back to fit the first doctor's assessment. He had been right, after all. Janette had lost a baby, then immediately become pregnant again, but with twins. She was not due to deliver until early December.

And further, because Dr. Buchanan was afraid to have Janette fifty miles away, she was instructed to stay in Calgary for the duration of her pregnancy. Cliff and Eleanor Quantz were pastoring the Parkdale church and graciously offered her accommodation. It turned out to be a visit of six long weeks. She was grateful for Eleanor, who helped to make the days a bit cheerier and shorter with her sense of humor and good nature, and for her sister Jean, who kept three-year-old Terry for the entire time.

Over the years, as Janette has looked back with affection, remembering that this was not the only time that Jean cared for Janette's children, she's been reminded of her defiant words: "I'm glad I'm not *your* kid!" Jean, a dear sister, could not have given better care and more love to the little Okes.

Despite everyone who was doing her best to help, Janette was miserable. By now she was so big and cumbersome that she could hardly walk, sit, or even lie comfortably. At night she had to turn over in stages. She even outgrew her maternity clothes, so Eleanor made her a large, loose-fitting garment, like a Hawaiian muumuu.

A great deal of the burden and discomfort was because of the amount of amniotic fluid Janette was carrying, but of course there was also a lot of baby weight. She had to resort to medication to ease the pain from the pull on her muscles, though Janette still remained quite miserable even with the pills. Every day she hoped that labor would begin, even though her due date had been corrected and she still had some time to wait.

On a maternity visit, Dr. Buchanan told Janette pointedly that he was concerned about twin number two. This baby was much smaller than the first twin, and a second twin was a bit more at risk during the best of times. Besides that, he had not been satisfied with the fetal heartbeat.

Janette prayed for that little twin as she had never before prayed for anyone. And she did not reduce her diet as she should have. She reasoned that whatever she ate, the "little girl" Dr. Buchanan had predicted she carried would get at least a bit of it. The larger twin he had thought would be a boy.

On November 22, 1963, radio stations across the country were repeating over and over again the shocking and very sad news of the assassination of U. S. President John F. Kennedy. That night Janette was admitted to the hospital in labor. The doctor said that the emotional event triggered labor for quite a number of women, and that maternity wards all over the U.S. and Canada were filled.

It was the following morning before Janette was taken to the delivery room. A big healthy boy arrived first. He weighed seven pounds, three ounces. Janette was sure that she saw Dr. Buchanan's brow furrow at the unusual size of the first twin.

It was a strange sensation to deliver and then to have to begin the birth process all over again—but only a short time later another boy arrived, and to everyone's surprise, he weighed six pounds, nine ounces. Janette would not forget the big, pleased smile on the doctor's face. He strutted about the room, proclaiming the size of both boys.

"You'd think he'd done it all," a nurse commented dryly.

So Janette had not gotten her girl. For a brief moment she felt a pang of disappointment. She had been thinking of this second child as a daughter, had even been praying and speaking about the baby as a girl. But she was tremendously thankful for two big, healthy sons.

The twins went directly to the regular nursery where they were duly fussed over. The nursing staff there was not used to caring for twins. Multiple births were typically underweight and cared for in the preemie nursery. Janette was certain that hers got special attention, especially from one nurse in particular.

"You'd think she was their grandma," stated one of the other nurses one day, sounding a bit peeved at all the fussing.

Edward was thrilled with his new sons. When he came to call, he spent more time at the nursery window than visiting Janette, but she didn't really mind.

"One will be my pianist," he exclaimed, "and the other my hockey player!" That in itself proclaimed Edward's two greatest loves: music and sports.

They named son number one Lavon Craig and son number two Lorne Douglas. Janette quickly forgot her disappointment over not getting her girl. In fact, she soon decided that twin boys was really the only sensible way to go.

Janette had crocheted two little sweater sets. She had embroidered little flowers on the fronts of the sweaters—one in blue and the other in pink. Now, as she lay contentedly in the hospital bed, she carefully removed the pink flowers and replaced them with blue as well.

The babies progressed splendidly and were taken home at the usual time. On the day they left the hospital, Janette dressed them in their little garments, complete with the two little sweaters and caps, and then bundled them up in their new blankets.

Just as she left her room, she heard someone call, "Come see the Oke twins going home." The corridor filled with nursing staff. Even the floor supervisor came from her office. Later Janette wished she had taken a picture. Here were her babies, ready to go home, and their mother could not even get near them as the nurses oohed and aahed and bid the babies good-bye.

Janette could hardly wait for Terry to get a look at his two new brothers. Jean and Orville brought him home, a new rattle in each of his hands as gifts for the new babies. He was thrilled. Even though he had just celebrated his third birthday and had been the sole attraction in his home for all three of those years, he never did seem to resent the new babies. He claimed them immediately, occasionally trying to take over their care.

Even so, at times both Mommy and Daddy were occupied with a baby in each set of arms, and when visitors came there was always a fuss made over the new little pair. Terry never did take it out on the babies, but he did have his own way of stealing some of the spotlight.

One day, Uncle Jack and Aunt Laurine came to see the new arrivals. While they were there, Terry and Uncle Jack were having a visit together. Terry loved the farm, and Uncle Jack was a farmer.

"You like cows?" Terry asked during their little chat.

"Oh yes," said Uncle Jack. "I like cows."

"Then close your eyes," said Terry, who had already developed the habit of praying about everything.

At this time, Janette's Uncle Jack, who had been like another father to Janette, was not a professing Christian. Many years would pass before he did make this commitment.

Terry closed his eyes, folded his hands, and asked God to send Uncle Jack "lotsa black cows."

"Just a minute," Uncle Jack stopped him, "I have brown cows." The uncle prided himself in his registered Herefords.

"Oh," said Terry, without concern. "Then close yours eyes again." He corrected his prayer. But when Uncle Jack and Aunt Laurine arrived back home, they found one of the Hereford cows with a little black calf trailing along at her heels. It was dubbed "Terry's calf," and the joke in the family for many years was, if you were serious about wanting something, have Terry do the praying.

On another morning, when Janette was ironing and Terry seemed to be having a difficult time finding something to do with himself, he finally decided that what he needed was a playmate and that he would go to his friend Karen's house. So Janette stopped her work and bundled him up.

The morning was dark and cloudy, and though he really wanted to find the courage to leave the house, his first glance outside brought him back.

"Mommy, it might snow on me."

Janette put aside her iron and went to assure him that it was not going to snow, that it was just a cloudy day, and returned to her work.

Soon he was back. "Mommy, will you take me to Karen's house?"

"No, Mommy can't go," she answered. "I have to stay with the babies."

Janette watched him start toward the door again and then turn back. "Mommy, please, will you take me to Karen's house? And then you can run right back home again—fast—to the babies."

Again Janette set down the iron and walked to the small boy. Crouching down and drawing him close, she soothed, "Mommy can't come. But Jesus will go with you."

His face brightened at the thought that followed. "Mommy, you come with me and let Jesus take care of the babies."

She laughed, hugged him, and wondered how she could explain that he should trust God when it seemed to his little mind that she was not willing to do the same. How would he understand that Jesus had given her the responsibility to guard the twins in those early days, and also the difficult task of teaching the little boy to turn his trust from her to the infinite God he could not see?

"Honey," she asked, "would you like us to pray and ask Jesus to go with you?"

"Uh-huh," he murmured, still uncertain.

Together they prayed, and then Janette reached over and opened the door while the little boy walked slowly out into the cloudy day.

"Mommy will be at the window," she called to him, and the little boots tramped quickly down the street, stopping at the corner for a wave toward home.

In the weeks that followed, Janette often repeated the story of Terry's struggle and was finally prompted by June to write it down. She tucked the completed pages away, along with several other things that she had written and wondered if, perhaps, someday she would be glad she had kept them.

For the most part, raising the twins was easy. After having one colicky baby, two good ones were a snap. She alternated feedings: one on breast, the other on bottle—then the reverse. For the night feedings when one awoke, Edward or Janette woke the other as well. Edward gave the bottle while Janette breast-fed. Though they were both weary, the nighttime feedings became a time to catch up on the chatting they could not find time for during the day.

In the early months there was daily laundry, but for the first time in their married lives, Edward and Janette had an automatic washer and dryer. The grandparent Okes had just moved to a new house and had purchased a new set. Edward and Janette were bequeathed the old one and were so thankful for the two wonderful machines, just perfect for a family with twins. Even with the extra work, they would not have traded the boys for anything, and Edward was convinced that every family should have at least one set of twins.

Perhaps the most difficult trick was getting the twins ready for anything on time. Janette enjoyed dressing them alike, but as surely as they were about to walk out the door, one or the other would spit up or manage to mess his outfit. That meant changing them both and yet be on time. It was especially difficult on Sundays. But then, Sundays were one of the few times Janette and the boys did go out.

When the babies were close to three months, they both developed severe colds. Janette thought Lorne was the sicker of the two until she lay Lavon down and saw that he was beginning to turn blue. She continued holding him until Edward returned from work, then bundled him up and took him to the emergency room.

Lavon was admitted immediately with pneumonia. While there he was given medication after medication, but nothing seemed to have any effect. Edward had a responsibility to be at a college retreat out of town and Janette had intended to accompany him. But the family doctor frankly warned Janette not to leave town. He wanted to be sure she was close enough to call if things suddenly took a turn for the worse. Of course she canceled her plans and stayed nearby.

All they could do was to hope and pray. Yet Lavon didn't seem to respond. Days passed into weeks, but the medicine wasn't helping. Finally they called some friends who were in the ministry and made arrangements for them to visit the hospital room together to pray over their small son. Almost immediately he began to improve. God had again answered prayer, and soon they were able to take him home to a twin brother, who was very happy to see him; they had been apart for three long weeks.

Lorne was the impatient one—even as a newborn. When he wanted something, he wanted it right then. He would lie on his tummy, his head thrown back so he could peek over his bassinet, and scream at the top of his lungs for Mother.

Lavon was much more content to wait. So he usually was cared for after his brother. Janette would whisper to him, telling him what a good boy he was and how much she loved his patience. Of course, he was still much too young to understand her words, but she hoped he picked up her tone of voice.

Edward was often gone because of his role as college president, and consistently those occasions fell over Sunday. It was difficult for Janette to get three small boys to church alone. There didn't seem to be a good way to do it. Which twin did she carry in from the car first, and what did she do with him when she went back for the other? She certainly could not carry both of them in at once, plus their diaper bags.

Then there was the service. Church nurseries were not as popular in those days. There was a small room at the back of the sanctuary known as the "cry room," where a fussing baby could be taken, and this is where Janette usually spent her time. One or the other twin could be counted on to be too noisy for the service.

She sometimes wondered why she even bothered to go, and then reminded herself that, hopefully, they were developing in their little family a lifetime habit of church attendance, if nothing else.

It was fun to watch the twins grow. They were not identical—only confusingly look-alikes. On at least one occasion, when one of the toddlers had seen himself in the mirror he became excited at seeing what he thought was the other twin. At first his parents failed to realize what all his excitement was about until they heard him call the reflection by his brother's name.

Their roles together developed and changed over time. First, one would seem to take over leadership of the pair, and then they would switch. But always, they were very close. Lavon was able to keep a little ahead of Lorne in size, but even that was insignificant.

They were quite different in personality. Lavon made friends with people quickly, while Lorne was shy and reserved. Edward's father, Grandpa Oke, used to worry about it. He came to see the twins frequently, often on his lunch hour, for Grandmother was teaching school and he was alone at noon.

"Poor little Lornie," he said to Janette. "Lavon will always get the attention."

But his prediction was not fulfilled. Lorne had a quick wit and was soon using it, and after some time he gradually outgrew his shyness as well.

Grandpa Oke loved to watch the boys wrestle together. They were like two little bear cubs as they rolled around on the floor. If one should be accidentally bumped a little too hard, the game would stop while his brother hugged and consoled him. Then they would go back to their rolling again.

They did play well together. In fact, Janette was sure they could have lived in a world composed of only the two of them and been perfectly happy. But they enjoyed big brother Terry, too, and he got along well with both of them.

As often happens with twins, Lorne and Lavon developed their own system of communication long before they could communicate with the rest of the family. In their shared bedroom, one twin was in the crib and the other on the bed. There was also a tall chest of drawers in the room. Since neither could reach the top of the chest from the floor, it seemed to be a safe place for Janette to store any items she did not wish them to have. But the crib was on casters, and the boys soon discovered a way to get all the toys, tissues, and other goodies way up high out of reach.

When they awoke from their naps, they jabbered back and forth, and then the first twin from the bed pushed the crib over to the chest while twin number two stood in the crib corner ready to reach the treasures as soon as he was within striking distance. When he had possession of the things from the chest, he willingly shared. It took only a few such excursions before the casters were removed from the crib, and their scheme was thwarted.

Lavon still wheezed like an asthmatic sufferer from his earlier bout with pneumonia, especially when he cried. Because of this, Janette was told not to take him for his immunization shots until he was at least two, and that she should wait for Lorne's shots as well.

By the time the boys did go for their shots, they were old enough to converse, and by the second trip, they could remember what was going to happen.

"Who's first?" the nurse asked. Lavon was chosen, and he took the nurse's hand and followed her toward the door. Everyone in the waiting room chuckled when Lorne called after him, very seriously and emphatically, "Don't you cry."

The boys grew into busy toddlers and soon developed a terrible attraction to the telephone on the hall wall. Over and over Janette had reprimanded them about leaving it alone, but there was Lavon at it again. He had dragged a kitchen chair to the spot and was methodically dialing someone—likely in Siberia or Hong Kong. Janette scolded him again and took the phone away from him. Then she told him to put the chair back in the kitchen.

To her surprise he looked up and said, "No."

He had never directly defied before, nor had he shown a streak of stubbornness. On that day her patient, compliant son was like another child.

Janette insisted. Lavon refused. She threatened. He balked. She spanked. He defied. She spanked again. He remained stubborn. Then, in the middle of the confrontation, there was a knock at the kitchen door.

"You wait here," she told her errant son—and he did.

It was Grandpa Oke at the door. "Dad, I'm sorry but I have a battle going on here," she told him and briefly explained the situation.

He did not ask to come in, just turned and started to walk away. "Keep at it," he called back over his shoulder. "You've gotta win."

Janette knew that it was true, but how she hated it. She had to keep reminding herself that it was better for her little boy to have a sore bottom now than a ruined life later. She prayed and fought back the rising tears, but she spanked until Lavon gave in, pushed the chair into the kitchen where it belonged, and then threw himself into her arms for forgiveness and consolation while they cried together. He never openly defied her again.

CHAPTER TWENTY-SEVEN

Complete

THOUGH SHE LOVED HER boys dearly, Janette still wanted a girl. She had concluded that "if I'm staying home with three—it might as well be four." Then the process of ordering their little family would be complete.

When the twins were twenty months old and Terry was four, she got her wish. "It's a girl, Janette," came the announcement, and the nurse held up the newest addition for Janette to see. A little girl arrived in July of 1965, and was named Laurel Judith, after Judy Yoder, who died while Janette and Edward were at the Beulah Missionary Church. And she outdid all her brothers, weighing nine pounds and fourteen ounces.

Janette could hardly believe it. It was *really* a girl, and she didn't even remotely resemble the boys, especially not the twins. They had been long and rangy; this new baby was short and plump, with little arms ringed with baby fat. Janette had a hard time convincing herself that the new baby was really hers.

In her mind, she had envisioned a tiny infant. Since this was to be the last baby, she wanted to keep her little for as long as she possibly could—but she was not starting out even looking like a newborn, and from there Janette watched her grow quickly and steadily. The July birth date brought her home just in time for camp meeting, which was hosted at the Bible College. During her first week she was bundled up to be shown off and fussed over by many people who knew and loved her parents.

Reverend Geiger was the special speaker, and after one service, his wife slipped over to the house to take her turn holding the new arrival. In her hands she held a package, a gift for the new little daughter. While Mrs. Geiger snuggled the baby, Janette folded back the wrapping to reveal a delicate white dress set off by small blue butterflies all around the hem. She could just picture it. How fun to finally have a little girl to dress up!

Laurel was a good baby, and that was just as well. Janette was not sure how else she could have managed with two energetic twenty-month-olds, plus a going-on-five big brother. She had three in diapers for a period of time—enough to keep any mother busy, even with an automatic washer and dryer.

Now there were three little ones and a not-too-cooperative five-year-old to get ready for church on Sundays, so Janette made sure that everything was ready and laid out on Saturday night. Shoes had to be cleaned, clothes laid in proper order, and coats ready to go. There would be no time in the morning to look for missing items.

All the boys loved their new sister, who was usually happy to sit in a baby seat or lie on the floor and watch them play. Janette's days were full and busy, and all too soon the early stages of childhood slipped away, making room for growing up.

By the time Laurel was one and camp meeting rolled around again, Janette was ready to show her off properly. She had purchased a beautiful powder blue, multi-layered dress, complete with beadwork and matching crinoline. The pudgy baby in the fancy dress now needed only one thing—a hair bow.

Unfortunately, Laurel was still without the required hair. Undaunted, Janette gracefully taped the tiny ribbon to Laurel's fuzzy head and set out for camp meeting. Friends laughed—but Janette didn't mind at all.

Margie's husband, Wilf, was also working at the college with Edward. This meant their family lived close enough to stop in for coffee or for the children to play together. One thing Janette could always count on about Marge, no matter the hour, no matter what she was busy doing, a visitor was always welcomed as though she had been invited and Marge had been expecting her.

Marge and Wilf already had three children. Gary was born after Terry, Joanne was born before the twins, and Janice was just a few months older than Laurel. Eventually Greg would come along, bringing each family to a total of six. This made the cousins good friends and provided many times of laughter while Marge and Janette observed their children growing up side-by-side, and also some moments when the two mothers would wince.

On one of these occasions Laurel and Janice had come up with the wonderful idea of giving each other haircuts. Laurel cut first, taking a couple of snips, then passing the scissors to Janice. The older cousin did a much better job than Laurel, cutting her hair right down to the scalp in several places.

Janette had been pleased when Laurel's hair had finally grown to where it could be combed or curled as she had wished and she had begun to duly fuss over her daughter. But Janice had fixed that. Janette's heart sank as she surveyed the mess. Daddy just laughed and said it would grow.

But there had to be some attempt made to straighten out the choppy hairdo. Janette set her squirming daughter on a kitchen chair and went to work, trying to even out the patches. When later asked who had cut her hair, Laurel tipped her head and answered smugly, "Mommy did."

One day Janette and her little brood walked down to Aunt Marge's house for coffee. As they said their good-byes before walking home, Janette paused a few minutes, still chatting. She allowed Laurel, now past two, to run on ahead with the boys, and she reached the house shortly before Janette.

On arriving home, she couldn't believe the sight that met her. In those few short minutes Laurel was already "baking" two cakes, one chocolate and the other vanilla. She had the cake mixes in separate bowls and had added all sorts of good things from the cupboard—an entire bottle of vanilla, chicken soup, and anything else that she had found handy. The whole mess wasn't just in the bowls, either.

While wiping and washing and sweeping up, Janette shook her head in wonder. She had been so pleased to receive her wish for a baby girl. But the nice, neat beribboned little lady she had envisioned was not the little girl she had discovered in the kitchen; and as the years passed, the differences between fantasy and reality became more obvious.

Janette had more than one occasion to be embarrassed at Laurel's less-than-feminine ways. One day they paid a visit to the Preschool Health Clinic. Earlier Laurel had visited her daddy's college and played on the tractor there. Janette had not seen it happen, but the little girl had slipped, scraping her back against the metal housing. When the clinic doctor asked for the shirt to be removed, Janette found a mess of scabs and bruises. She wondered what the doctor would think—and he did make a comment, though not with any accusation.

As a youngster, Laurel often insisted that she was not a girl but a tomboy, as though that was a third sex, and Janette could not help but be disappointed. Hair bows chosen so carefully were hard to position on the struggling, complaining child's head. Once there, they were sure to fall into the playground dust, somewhere near the monkey bars, and be abandoned. Bumps and bruises were always showing on the sturdy little legs, peeking out from under smudged dresses.

Janette knew she had a choice before her. Either she could make them both miserable, insisting that Laurel fall in with her mommy ideals of what a little girl should be, or she could accept the child that God had given her. So she let Laurel be herself—and watched nervously as the ambitious, energetic, imaginative, rowdy little girl grew up.

Besides having the steady demands of motherhood, Janette spent much of her energy in keeping up with her home. Saturday mornings routinely were baking times. With the many visitors that Edward's position involved, Janette kept a stock of frozen pies, buns, and sweet rolls ready for the unexpected. Soon her children were anxious to be involved in the process, and what had been orderly and efficient became difficult and time-consuming. She partially solved the task of "too many cooks in the kitchen" by assigning turns. Each child, in turn, was given a Saturday to be "assistant"—except on donut-baking day; then they formed an assembly line—with each child given one small step in the procedure.

Though she took each opportunity to involve her children in her activities, Janette felt the pressure of being the college president's wife. She did her best to involve herself by making appearances as she was able. She also continued to keep her home in order, keeping up with four active, growing children. Many nights found her falling into bed exhausted when she had been chasing after her lively youngsters all day, then making sure her home was clean, and her husband's meals and clothing cared for. Sleep was a luxury.

CHAPTER TWENTY-EIGHT

That Dog

TERRY WANTED A DOG in the worst way, so the Okes got a little pup that he quickly named Rover. Only later did the family discover just how appropriate a name this was; the growing puppy hated to stay where he was supposed to be.

Edward and Terry built a little doghouse, and Terry was thrilled with his "many-breeds-but-a-lot-terrier" dog. Rover proved himself to be very good with the kids. He loved children. In fact, he hated to be away from them. For that reason, he was always finding some way to slip out of his collar and take off after Terry for the local school.

Janette would receive another call: "Your little dog is here again," and she would load up the younger children and go to retrieve him. She never could figure out how this ingenious dog got out of his collar or off his chain.

Then Rover developed another bad habit. Perhaps he was simply being the protector, but as soon as Terry was home from school, the puppy chased anything that came along—cars, trucks, or bicycles. Janette was afraid someone would swerve to miss the dog and hit one of the children running after him.

And then Rover went one step further—he started barking ferociously at people. Although he never bit anyone, he did cause a good deal of alarm one day when he went after a dear, elderly neighbor man, giving him quite a scare. For some time, Edward and Janette had talked about Rover's problems, and the last episode was enough to convince them. They could not have Rover running around frightening people or risk the chance that he would actually bite someone.

They talked to Terry about it. Of course, he was devastated. He tried desperately to come up with his own solutions. It was heartbreaking to hear this little boy fighting to save his little dog.

"I'll get a book on training dogs," he begged, "and I'll teach him not to do it."

They knew they had already given the little dog too many "chances." And if he were too aggressive, it would not solve the problem by simply giving him away. So an appointment with the vet was made.

Edward drove the beloved pet the ten miles to the veterinary office. Terry had asked to go along, and held his dog in his lap, loving him for one last time. When they arrived, he relinquished the leash to his dad.

"Bring me back his collar," he asked through tears.

Janette wasn't sure who grieved more—Terry or her. Watching her son's pain hurt deeply, and she herself had liked the little dog, so she felt rather like a murderer. Often she glanced out the window at the now-empty clothesline where he had been tied, and wept silent tears for her small son and his little dog. She prayed that Terry would quickly heal from his traumatic experience. She also hoped he would not get the erroneous idea that when things in the home became difficult, they were simply disposed of.

In due time, a new puppy was adopted. A funny, shaggy little poodle-terrier cross. Terry watched with delight as the new pup sniffed and searched in his new surroundings. Without a moment's hesitation, he was named Curious George Oke after the storybook monkey. Curious provided many years of fun—plus a few headaches, too—though fortunately not any as serious as his predecessor.

He was a sassy little dog, never growing much bigger than a small terrier but willing to take on anything, be it Great Dane, German shepherd, or alley cat. But he, too, was wonderful with kids. Edward and Janette were confident that their children could do anything with him and he would never become aggressive.

However, one of the favorite games that the Oke kids played with Curious was called "Mad Dog." They would be in the basement or in the backyard and someone would call, "Let's play Mad Dog," and Janette would know she was in for a lot of racket.

Each of the kids knew just what to do, and Curious seemed to be aware of his special role too. The children would run around, jumping on furniture or fences, whatever was near, and the furry little scrap would dart to and fro, nipping at their heels and barking furiously.

In a moment, the quiet, compliant dog turned into a beast, flying around and catching pant legs or shoes, whatever he could grab. He growled and chased, barked and nipped, and was dragged along the floor or ground, behind anyone not quick enough to escape his teeth. But he never hurt anyone, and they all loved the game—Curious included. Janette was perhaps the only one who was not completely enthusiastic. There was the dreadful noise—and the possibility of torn pant legs.

CHAPTER TWENTY-NINE

New Home

WITH SUMMER CAME hopes for building a new house. Grandpa Oke had provided the lot, next door to his own new home, and also the funds for the basic construction. Perhaps there were those who held their breath, wondering if the new house was a bit too close to parents, but Edward and Janette could not feel happier about a chance to own their first home.

Terry was then seven, the twins four, and Laurel three. Edward and Janette held to the theory that "strong fences make good neighbors," and accordingly planned to build one. They did not want trouble from little people leaving toys or ruining gardens in the yard of these important neighbors—their own grandparents.

Another faculty family would use the college-owned house. The plan was to have the new house ready to move into by the time the previous house was needed. The plan started well, but time worked against it. As often happens in construction schedules, it turned out that the other family wanted to move in long before the new house was ready for occupancy, and soon household goods were packed up and stored in Grandpa Oke's garage. For the summer months the family lived from suitcases, bouncing back and forth between grandparents, Oke and Steeves. It was a lot of traveling for Janette. She would just get situated at the Hoadley farmhouse, two hours away, with her own mom and dad when she would be needed back in Didsbury for some decisions regarding the new house.

It was even more difficult for the kids—Lorne and Lavon in particular. On one occasion Janette took them to Hoadley to leave them with Grandma and Grandpa Steeves. She thought they understood the plan, but it turned out she was wrong.

After putting them to bed and staying until they were sleeping, Janette drove the one-hundred-plus miles back to Didsbury. When the boys awoke the next morning, they were horrified to find Mommy gone. Huddled together on the couch, they refused to eat, refused to play, and even refused to rouse. Grandma Steeves could not coax them to do anything but cling to each other.

Finally she phoned Didsbury. She was concerned about the little fellows and felt that their mother should come and either take them back to Didsbury or else be with them in Hoadley. When someone answered the phone, Amy was told that Janette was not there but that they would give her a message.

Janette never received the message. By the time she did return to Hoadley, her boys had seemingly adjusted, but for several years they did not have the same excitement as before at the chance to go to Grandma Steeves' house. Janette felt sick about it. She had not realized how difficult it had been for them to be bounced back and forth and then left on their own.

A new house simply was not worth that kind of trauma and confusion. So it was decided that the family would move in long before the house was ready. It was just too important to be together. Janette had no kitchen cupboards, the floors were bare, the walls unpainted, and there were daily piles of sawdust, but at least they were all together. And for the children, the unfinished home was extra exciting. Only Janette struggled daily to pull together a home from the chaos.

Edward was preparing for another college term, so he had very little time to be involved in the house project. Janette stained and varnished the wood trim, attempted the painting chores, which she hated, and swept up the sawdust daily. Even blankets needed to be shaken and beds remade before children could be tucked in at night. It seemed like forever, but eventually they had a home to live in. By that time Janette was emotionally and physically exhausted, and she vehemently declared, "Never again!"

Once the essential work on the house was done and Janette had given herself time to forget the frustration of overseeing it and doing much of the work herself, she began the enjoyable task of decorating.

Room by room, over time, she worked with what resources she had and carefully created a tasteful, warm atmosphere for her family.

Christmas, 1968, was spent entertaining extended family in the new house. A long table was set up in the basement, and family members from the Steeves' side crowded together, not minding that the room was still unfinished.

After the hustle of the season had passed, Janette began to sell Artex, a popular method of decorating household linens, for a little extra income. The liquid embroidery paint was sold at in-home parties, where Janette would demonstrate the painting techniques and then make the tubes and iron-on patterns available to anyone interested.

Selling the product was not difficult. Here was a way to enjoy the attractiveness of needlework without the hours or skill necessary for such an undertaking. Parties were scheduled often during the few years Janette was involved in this business. But after a while scheduling often became inconvenient, so she decided to give the business up.

When spring arrived, Janette turned some of her efforts to the garden. Raspberry bushes were added, rhubarb planted, and flowers placed carefully to enhance Edward's landscaping.

The long days of summer passed, and Janette began the seasonal bustle to process the harvest. Along with the canned pears and peaches, jars of jams, jellies, and pickles filled the new pantry shelves. Then garden produce was ready to be frozen or stored. Long evenings spent over a dish shelling peas brought aching shoulders and a stiff back. Still, the burden of feeding the growing family was eased by her work.

Laurel soon caught up to her brothers in size, so by the time the twins started off to kindergarten, they looked like triplets. This sometimes bothered the boys—but it was all right with Laurel.

For many years now, Janette had been kept more than busy with her active family. One day at her kitchen sink washing dishes, she noticed a new neighbor lady pass by on the sidewalk.

"Oh, God," she silently mourned in a short prayer. "I haven't even had her over for coffee. It seems that the kids take all my time."

She was almost startled by the clear, immediate answer she heard inwardly. "They're supposed to," God whispered to her troubled heart. With the wonderful release from guilt, and a reaffirming of priorities, she was free to give her time and herself to the children in her home.

Now that three children were in school for at least part of the day, morning routines developed. For the family this meant breakfast, which was all too often porridge, followed by family devotions. This devotional time changed over the years but usually included Scripture reading, singing songs and choruses together, and memorizing Scripture verses. At times family members got to "perform" on one instrument or another. Sometimes they all played together. Then each had a turn praying as well, or expressing words of thankfulness for things God had done. And, even at this early age, the children learned that there was much to be thankful for.

For one thing, there was never a time when the children felt concern or doubt about their home being divided or that their parents would ever separate. True, they had their differences—but these were settled in private. In the children's presence, Edward and Janette presented a solid, united front—two different people with different characteristics and personalities but who loved and respected each other and the security needed for a solid home.

<hr>

There had already been several stages in Janette's role as a mother. First the struggle to begin the family with its great disappointments, followed by the blur of early days of diapers and bottles. Then came the years of watching over busy toddlers, until each of these had been left behind. The children who now occupied her home were changing. Each day seemed to bring more and more independence, and the familiar calls to "Mommy" became less frequent.

For Janette this meant that less of her time was spent actively "mothering," though she was certain that she gave no less of herself emotionally to the task. There continued the complexities of raising the family and praying fervently that she was doing so effectively and correctly. And she also prayed for the many times when she could not be near. At those moments anything could happen—and usually did.

The same winter that the twins started kindergarten, Grandmother Oke bought them fuzzy red parkas trimmed with white fur. The pair made quite a sight as they wandered down the street on their way to school, and there were many comments to and about them.

At a small cafe on Main Street, the owner and several of the regular patrons began to watch for them to appear. Aware of the unwanted attention as they passed the window, the boys finally resorted to dropping down and crawling past so no one would see them. This delighted their audience, who always managed to know they were there.

Two years later, just as Laurel was about to start kindergarten, Janette was approached by the local Royal Bank of Canada to see if she was interested in working. They had heard of her banking experience and needed someone who already knew the job. She and Edward talked about it, and Margie agreed to baby-sit after the half day of kindergarten; her own daughter, Janice, was in the same kindergarten class. So Janette decided to give it a try. Certainly the extra paycheck would be useful to help meet the family's needs.

Shortly after, a neighbor stopped Janette on the street and teased her about how "tough things must be" at home. This person joked about Janette even sending her children out to "look for work." Upon checking out his meaning, Janette discovered that Laurel had gone up and down the streets, knocking on doors and asking if there was any work for which she could be paid.

One dear neighbor told the little girl that she had just swept her kitchen floor, but if Laurel would come back the next day, she could do it for her. The little girl did and was paid a few coins and given a little trinket. All in all she considered herself quite successful in her new occupation and couldn't figure out why her parents discouraged her from "working outside the home" for a few years yet.

Janette was more than willing to let her daughter help out at home, though this didn't seem to be nearly as interesting. When one of the boys was sick and the family doctor phoned a prescription to the drugstore, Janette was not able to pick it up so she asked Laurel to run to the store for her. When she asked about how to pay for the item, Janette told her to ask the clerk to "charge" it. It was not unusual for local stores to carry an account for the town people whom they knew well. Laurel asked for an explanation and Janette's answer was rather vague. "It means we take it now and pay for it later."

Soon Laurel was back with the medicine and no more was said. But on the first day of grade one, she received a little list of needed school supplies. So Laurel decided on her own that she would immediately begin her shopping at the drugstore and "charge it."

Happily gathering all the items, and feeling quite independent and proud of herself, she was just about to leave the store when the pharmacist pulled her up short. He took the items and then, to her dismay and bewilderment, turned her over his knee and spanked her "for stealing." It was many years before Janette heard of the incident and felt terrible about the bad experience. But she couldn't help but laugh at her daughter's interpretation of "charging."

One day while playing alone in the back alley, Laurel had decided to use a glass jar to carry her growing rock collection. But she fell and the jar broke beneath her. Fortunately she cut only her finger on the broken glass. Edward held her hand under running water in the kitchen sink while blood streamed from it and Janette snatched up her purse and keys, loaded the child into the car, and drove off to the emergency room. The doctor sighed at the prospect of sewing up another screaming child, and Janette was asked to help hold her while he began the process.

To their amazement, Laurel didn't scream or cry. She simply sat on the stool and watched the procedure, her eyes wide as blood ran down the finger and the doctor drew his thread in and out of the cut. Instead, it was Janette who almost ended up on the floor during the ordeal.

The boys were no sissies either. They would often comment about some "hurt," and then not mention it again. Later, Janette would discover that it was something which really should have received attention. She expected more fuss over an injury. Street hockey, hunting gophers with bow and arrow, shooting pellet guns at one another, riding bikes over carefully constructed hazards, or setting up "track and field events" in the basement. The brothers seemed to have a wish to injure themselves in one way or another, and Janette was frequently unaware of their efforts. So she prayed even more fervently and tried to discourage any senseless activities as she became aware of them.

CHAPTER THIRTY

Holidays

ALTHOUGH JANETTE AND her family had now been settled in Didsbury for several years, there were frequent occasions for trips north to visit the farm where she had grown up. And just a few miles down the road from Fred and Amy's farm, Jack and Ila were busy working a farm of their own. This couple had also been blessed with children—four sons and one daughter—ranging in ages just a little older than Janette's four. When the Oke family car rolled into the Steeves' yard, each impatient traveler anticipated good times ahead.

For Janette and Edward there would be leisure chatter and games, familiar laughter around the kitchen table, and the hustle of meals prepared by many hands to feed many people. There was also the contentment of watching children scurry off to play in the barn, the yards, or the fields nearby, certain that the many cousins could be both playmates and baby-sitters—of sorts.

Visits to Hoadley included trips for the children to the barn to look for new kittens, riding horses, playing in the hay, helping with the chores, checking out new calves, and playing games in the fields late into the evening. Everyone loved the farm.

Holiday celebrations were often spent with Jack and Ila, partly because they had the biggest house and also because family was always welcome there. Janette and the aunts filled available beds with cousins and then allowed the rest to scatter across the floor in sleeping bags or blankets. It was fine for everyone concerned. "Uncle Jack's" farm was one of the few opportunities to stay up really late, and the children took advantage of it, not returning inside until parents themselves were tired or the mosquitoes had chased them in.

In the winter months there was time for skating, hockey games, toboggan rides, and snowball fights with many aunts and uncles joining right in. After the fun was over, everyone streamed into Ila's big country kitchen for hot chocolate, fresh-baked bread, and homemade jam. Coats were stacked many layers deep in the entry, and boots piled in such a heap that it was amazing to ever make a matched pair again.

For Janette's family, Christmas was not Christmas without cousins. And it was usually celebrated twice—first with the Oke side of the family in Didsbury, and then with the Steeves. They had waited for Christmas all year long—so it was wonderful to be able to have two celebrations in a row.

There were as many wonderful times to be had farther south in Champion where Joyce and Elmer were farming. Kids loved Uncle Elmer—at least, they usually did. There was one occasion when he slipped on a Halloween mask and poked his head around the door at the unsuspecting twins. He was completely unprepared for their reaction.

The two screamed and grabbed each other, taking a very long time to calm down again. Uncle Elmer felt bad when he realized how terrified they were. But despite his best apologies, Lorne and Lavon kept a careful eye on him for some time after.

Joyce and Elmer's farm provided cousins with plenty of space to play unhindered by adults insisting on quiet and decorum. But occasionally, this freedom had hazardous results. While Janette was busy indoors one day with the other adults, someone burst into the house shouting that Lorne had tumbled out of the second-floor hay-loft door and landed on the cement pad beneath.

In a moment, all the adults were crowded outside near the barn where Janette ministered to her winded son. Then the whole story poured out. A group of cousins had been building a fort of hay against the loft door, and when one too many bodies entered through one side, Lorne had been pushed out the other. Everyone shrieked and ran to him, but after recovering his wind, he seemed to be no worse for the fall.

This farm was also where Terry broke his wrist. Joyce's son Dwain had a small motor bike, and, of course, Terry felt it necessary to take his turn riding it. When the throttle stuck, the bike went out of control and Terry ended up in a heap, not bothering to mention the mishap until they were in the car on their way home. Then he confessed grudgingly, "My wrist still hurts." Janette took her reluctant son to the hospital in Didsbury for an X-ray, and, sure enough, there was a hairline fracture.

When summertime did not find the family at one farm or the other, they were often headed to James River Bible Camp. The Missionary Church's camp offered weeklong meetings each for boys, girls, families, and youth, so everyone was able to find at least one camp meeting to enjoy.

Janette served as a counselor at girls' camp on several occasions. This meant that for one week she became live-in mother for several young girls. There were late-night chats and pillow fights, along with practical jokes and quarrels in the cabin. But amidst the activity, Janette began special friendships, some which would last for years to come.

When fall arrived the family settled back into life at school and work. College students once more converged onto the nearby campus, and this usually brought one or two Steeves relatives to Didsbury. One year Janette's youngest sister, Sharon, was among them.

Sharon was the family "student." She had dived into books early on and had always brought home good grades, even though schooling still was not easy to obtain in the Hoadley area. Sharon, too, had needed to board away from home in order to complete grade twelve.

After her time at Mountain View, she planned to get her B.A. at Bethel College in Indiana. When she entered the school, she had only a few dollars in her pocket but a mountain of faith. God saw her through, and she completed the year with her bills miraculously covered—though her willingness to work her way through had certainly helped her situation. She was looking toward missions, with linguistics in mind. Sharon had an aptitude for math and languages, and seemed perfect for work in translation.

When Sharon returned to Didsbury to work at the Royal Bank, she lived with Janette's family for some time. The house was not large but enough beds were found. The boys and Laurel slept in the basement, while Sharon was given the second bedroom on the main floor.

Though it certainly had nothing to do with Janette's well-intentioned exhortation when Sharon was small, she had not grown up spoiled, and she did marry. While Sharon was in Didsbury, a young man seemed to take quite an interest in her—a fine fellow by the name of Richard Fehr.

Richard and Sharon, after spending time working and taking courses in both North Dakota and North Carolina, and then training at jungle camp in Mexico, left for Papua, New Guinea. By then they already had two children, Shawna and Eric. In fact, Ricky was just a few months old when Janette bid him and his family a tearful good-bye.

While the Fehrs were still in New Guinea, they sent news home that baby Amy had joined their family. Then Richard began having trouble with severe allergies, and because proper medical treatment was not available, they were soon home again. Now they continued their ministry in their local church, serving in a number of capacities.

Shortly after Sharon had moved out of their home, Janette had begun plans to redecorate the main floor bedroom for Laurel. First, she gave the room a fresh coat of apricot-colored paint, then hung sheers in a darker shade of peach. She even hung a pair of full-length sheers above the headboard of Laurel's white bed where they perfectly framed a set of four matching pictures. Dainty girls in dresses and parasols smiled out into the cheerful bedroom. It was charming, and Laurel loved it.

The boys had rooms in the basement where three bedrooms, a "rumpus room," a half bath, a large pantry/storage room, and a shop for Edward's woodworking had been finished over the years. Lorne and Lavon shared a room with a bunk bed, and Terry had a room of his own. The third bedroom had no window but was perfect for a small office for Edward. It became his quiet retreat for many years.

CHAPTER THIRTY-ONE

Parade of Life

AS HER KIDS GREW, Janette saw the family travel through the typical stages of pets, music lessons, and school functions. A trip to the mall resulted in a cluster of children entering the house with a small box holding two small gerbils. A rather reluctant parent carried the cage in. Fortunately this pair turned out to be especially mild-mannered and even allowed the children to hold and pet them.

Janette read the brochure about how they played games with their little ones, and finally concluded that gerbils might be interesting and educational. But when they later failed in parenting and turned on their own babies, even though they had been given more than the recommended living space, she soon lost her fascination with them. She could not understand how a mother could kill her own offspring. Through death by natural causes and accidental loss, the gerbils eventually were gone, and their cage set aside.

Terry began the tradition of piano lessons, plodding up and down scales and counting quarter notes while he tried to talk Janette into letting him off early for the day. A ball glove beckoned invitingly on the seat beside him. Lorne and Lavon did their practicing in much the same fashion.

In second grade, Laurel followed in their footsteps, trudging to her piano teacher's house on her way to school. The University of Toronto's Royal Conservatory of Music provided examinations given across Canada. Edward had passed his "grade eight" level in piano, and Laurel began working her way through each level, spending her allotted half hour each morning with the attempt to learn and memorize some simplified classical piece.

Occasionally Grandpa Oke would offer his encouragement for the struggling musicians, promising to give a quarter if a piece could be played for him "perfectly." There were always a few mistakes, but he was a pretty easy audience, and somehow managed to judge that the effort was worthy of the quarter anyway.

When Terry reached fifth grade, he left piano behind and took up the trumpet. Soon afterward, Lorne and Lavon switched to the saxophone and the clarinet, respectively. Mornings became filled with wild noises. The loud blasting sounds of wind instruments rose from the basement, and careless notes crashed into one another on the living room piano. Janette and Edward's love of music must have been sorely tested, but the occasional recitals and the proud moments made it all worthwhile.

For many years Janette had allowed herself to feel justifiable pride in Terry. Of course, she knew he was not angelic, but he had always been very responsible and truthful. Even in the area of discipline, he seemed to accept his punishments as deserved and appeared almost relieved when they were administered. Janette would have staked her honor on Terry's word alone—until the day in his early teens when she found evidence that he was deeply entrenched in a series of lies. With shocked and wounded heart she went before God, letting her emotions tumble out.

How could Terry have done this? He knew how important truth was to her. She could accept childish mistakes and forgive errors in judgment, but the lies had cut her deeply. How could she trust this son again? How could she help him see the enormity of what he had lost?

Once her thoughts and tears were spent, Janette waited—and in the quietness her answer came. "Satan has desired to sift you as wheat, but I have prayed for you." Christ's familiar words to Simon Peter echoed in her mind.

Of course, the tempter also desired her beloved eldest son. In her disappointment she must always understand that Terry had been trapped in his own humanity. The inclinations to evil passed along to him by his parents also made him vulnerable to the lies of the deceiver.

But what could she do? Suppose he continued to fail? Suppose any one of her children turned away from God? How could she pull them back again? Surely she would give anything to ensure their eternity with Christ.

Once again she recalled the verse: "But I have prayed for you." What wonderful assurance God gave to her, reminding her that He was even more concerned about the spiritual well-being of her son than she herself was. She could trust *Him*. It was not in Janette's power to protect her children from temptation. Once again the Lord was asking her to place them each back into His hands.

There could be no hesitation. Her own imperfect ways could not hope to accomplish what her loving Father was waiting to do. She had submitted her own life and then the life of baby Brian; now she would submit again the lives of the children she had been allowed to mother. Peace crept quietly into her heart, releasing her from the burden of worry and confusion. And also releasing Terry from her standard that he be perfect.

Periodically, notes would arrive home from school that the children were to be involved in a school production. Lorne and Lavon were part of the cast for the musical *H.M.S. Pinafore*. It was thrilling for them to participate, although some of the stories that drifted home sounded a great deal like the "fun" had more to do with pranks than with performance. But the night of the actual event proved that they had worked hard. Janette was proud to watch the twins and their classmates perform.

Another source of activity for the growing family was the church youth group but, at least in the small town of Didsbury where everything was within walking distance, Janette was not called upon to provide taxi service very often. And many of the other activities—children's program practices, Christian Service Brigade, Pioneer Girls, and school sports—required little parental involvement.

Janette's own church duties included teaching Sunday school and superintending departments. For some time she served as treasurer of the Women's Missionary Society and was always an active member. There were occasional denominational district committees. At times she wished she could have been more involved in the community happenings in Didsbury, but there were simply too many other priorities that she felt deserved her efforts first.

One day while Janette was at work and Terry was home on break from school, he decided to do something creative with his time off. Being in junior high, Terry was old enough to be left on his own, but even the most diligent parent has overlooked giving some particular piece of advice and then found out too late.

The younger siblings in elementary school had been coming home with wax projects. Apparently it appealed to Terry, for he decided to fill some hours making a wax figure. He found Janette's canning wax and put some in a pan to melt. While waiting he went down to the basement to watch TV.

It was Curious who insisted Terry get back upstairs and check on his project. When Terry finally responded to the dog's insistent barking and opened the door at the top of the stairs, he found the kitchen in flames.

Janette received his phone call at work. Terry carefully told her about the fire, assuring her that he had gotten it out on his own. "But the cupboards are a little scorched," he added.

What an understatement! Janette had churning, conflicting emotions as she surveyed her kitchen. There were places where the cupboards had been burned all the way through several layers of the plywood. Terry had tried so hard to clean up the mess that it almost made her cry. As she studied the damage and realized how close she had come to losing the house—and more importantly—her son, she uttered little breathless snatches of sincere, thankful prayers for the provision of guardian angels.

As it was, all Terry had suffered was a blistered finger where he had turned on the stove fan to clear out the smoke. If it had not been for Curious sensing the fire and making a fuss, he might have remained in the basement until it was too late.

Her other frightening realization was that Terry likely would have fought the fire alone, no matter how widespread it had become. Janette knew her son. He accepted responsibility for his own actions. He would have felt that the fire was "his fault" and so tried to handle it himself. She shuddered to think what could have happened, and thanked God with all her heart that they'd been spared the worst—even if He had used a little dog to help out.

Edward was pleased that each of his children had received early training in music, which had long been one of his own interests. He was also pleased to see their own interest in sports grow. All the Oke children thoroughly enjoyed participating in sports. Terry began by joining the local Tiny Mite hockey league. He had grown quickly, gaining almost all his height by the age of fourteen. Though his classmates passed him by later, he was one of the biggest boys in junior high. He was also a good player and really threw himself into his games, giving his best.

Lorne and Lavon also joined the local hockey teams, but Janette was not pleased with what she observed when she went to watch their practice. The coach didn't seem to have control, and all the boys, including her own, were complaining and fussing and telling the coach how things should be run. When she heard one of her own twins swear, she had reached the end of her patience. She went home feeling heartsick and poured out her feelings about the hockey team to Edward.

Having participated in the sport for many years, Edward loved the game and felt somewhat that she was being a bit unreasonable and panicky about things. But the discussion became irrelevant when that very night the town arena burned down. In the following years, those who really wanted to be involved with the hockey leagues could travel to neighboring towns to use other rinks at unearthly hours. Even Edward agreed that it was not that important for their young sons to be involved. So there was no hockey for the twins, who soon found other school sports and were quite content.

When the rink finally was rebuilt, Lavon decided he wanted to get back into hockey, only to find that things had not changed during his absence. He didn't stay with the team very long, though neither he nor the other boys gave up the sport entirely. Later when they attended college they happily plunged back into hockey and, as one of them put it, could not "imagine a winter without it."

Because Didsbury was small, those who were athletic and interested in sports could usually make the team. School sports started in the fall with cross-country, then volleyball, went on to basketball, to badminton, and continued into track season. Janette had always enjoyed sports, although she found it hard to keep up with four enthusiastic participants at one time. Having kids so fully involved certainly exposed their mother to a variety of games and training strategies. But through it all, she and Edward were generally proud of their accomplishments. When the twins were fortunate enough to play on a volleyball team that was ranked as number one in the Province, they could not have been more pleased.

During the summer, the boys played slow-pitch softball. Cool summer evenings were spent sitting in open stands with other parents, cheering and hooting for the team of their choice—which of course was the one with their offspring. The boys played well, and Janette found it thrilling to watch them, especially in a game that brought back so many happy memories of when her daddy had played.

When Lorne was in junior high school, he had the chance to go with relatives on their annual camping trip to the mountains. Uncle Jack's family of seven and their guests would transport their horses to a corral near Mountainaire Lodge. There the horses would be unloaded, all the gear placed on packhorses, and the adventure would begin. After a day's ride, the campsite was reached and tents pitched.

Lorne was hooked immediately, and the following summers found him regularly making the trek with Uncle Jack or the church Wilderness Camp, which offered the same camping experience. There are assorted stories of these camping trips, such as bears wandering through their site, being chased off by whomever was found to be the bravest.

Lavon chose to become more actively involved in the band, attending occasional band camps. Perhaps Edward's wish of one musician and one sports enthusiast would come true—though each boy had talent in both areas.

The Missionary Church in Didsbury encouraged participation in the services by the children and youth in much the same way that Janette's Champion church had when she was a youth. Singing, reciting Scripture, playing instruments, and taking part in programs or youth services were a part of growing up. The congregation prepared for a good chuckle whenever something special from the youth was announced, for it was almost without exception that something unexpected would occur. And it was often not so much *what* was said or done, but *how*.

Lavon was to give part of the devotional at a youth service. The theme was love, and he began like this, "One day Adam and Eve were walking in the Garden, and Eve looked shyly at Adam, batted her long eyelashes, and said, 'Adam, do you love me?' And Adam replied," Lavon continued with a careless shrug of boyish shoulders, " 'Who else?' "

There were strict rules at the Oke house about evening curfews—when darkness fell, all were to be home. It was sometimes difficult to comply, however, when teenage friends were still out running around the town streets. If there were a special event or reason to be out, such as a sports game or a church youth function, the rule was waived, but otherwise the kids were expected to be in.

One night a bunch of the twins' friends were planning some event, and the boys asked Edward for permission to join them. But he wasn't convinced that the plans sounded valid enough to allow the twins an exception. Janette was working in the kitchen when Lavon came tramping through, muttering under his breath.

"What's wrong?" she asked him.

"Oh, Dad!" he complained. Then he followed the comment with, "If Jesus comes back after midnight, I'll bet Dad won't even let us go!"

Janette's chuckle helped to ease the frown from his face, and he was able to grin at his own joke.

The entire family was involved with the college where Edward was president. The children had practically grown up on the college campus and knew the students for many years in a row. They felt as if the college campus, which was just past Grandmother's house and across the street, was as much their territory as their own backyard. From time to time Janette would teach a course on historical books or work in some way with the college girls.

Another fall arrived, and this time June's daughter Karen attended Mountain View and quickly found her way into her aunt's heart. Karen had matured into an absolutely beautiful, as well as talented and warmhearted, young woman. She married a fellow student, and together they prepared for a ministry in Northern Canada.

Later when the tragic news came of Karen's unexpected death, the family was stunned and gathered in Hoadley to comfort one another. Apparently, Karen had become ill on a car trip. It was during a stop along the roadside that the fumes already accumulating in the vehicle caused Karen to be asphyxiated.

June and John were heartbroken. The loss of their daughter was so hard to accept. Karen and her husband were so young and intent on beginning their missions work, and Karen was expecting their first child. It was all so difficult to believe. After the funeral and their return to Chicago, John wrote a song dedicated to his daughter. It said, "Oh, the love of Jesus, it won't stop," and proclaimed the ultimate words of comfort, "I have life forever . . . it won't stop." How treasured were the promises of God when life delivered its cruel blows.

Janette had worked at the Royal Bank for only a few years when she decided to take some time off and see how things *really* were at home. She needed to sense the "pulse" of the family firsthand, and was not sure if her working outside the home was a negative for her kids or not.

But she was relieved to find they were just fine. They didn't seem to have suffered from not having her there when they came home from school and were old enough now to take responsibilities and have a bit of independence. After a couple of years being at home, she went back to her work at the bank.

Then a businessman from church asked if she would accept a position in his office at the Reimer Concrete Company. Another lady at the bank agreed with Janette that it would be nice for both of them to work part time. So she and Barb worked out an arrangement with Mr. Reimer so they could alternate weeks at the new office job. Their position involved answering phones, dispatching the trucks, and keeping the books. The arrangement worked well and provided a nice variety.

In 1976, Grandpa Oke passed away unexpectedly. He had been having little spells that the doctors found difficult to diagnose. They seemed to be miniature strokes and would come and go, usually lasting for only minutes at a time. He had been on heart medication, but the family had no reason to think his condition was life-threatening. Then he was admitted to the local hospital to regulate his medication.

It was not the first time he had been hospitalized, but he disliked those little visits.

The day of his father's death, Edward was to preach at the Didsbury church during the Sunday morning service. After the service he was to pick Grandpa up from the hospital. But around nine o'clock, there was a call from the hospital saying Grandpa was gone. He had awakened early to visit the bathroom, then returned to his bed, and soon passed away in his sleep.

It was a terrible shock to the family. They had thought he would be coming home—but suddenly he was gone. Everyone missed him, and Janette cried many tears of loss. She was firmly convinced that never had a woman been blessed with a better father-in-law.

Grandpa Oke had been a very special person in Janette's life. With Edward busy at the college over lunch hours and Grandmother teaching, he would often pick her up from work at noon and take her out for lunch. Janette and her father-in-law would have just enough time to drive to a favorite restaurant in a nearby town, eat, and get back to work again.

They didn't always agree about things, but their discussions were always amiable. Janette felt free to express her opinions, knowing that he respected her right to give them and would accept, agree, or reject them without condemnation. They could debate a view in perfect harmony, and it was wonderful to be able to sort out and express her views openly, knowing she would not be misunderstood.

The kids loved Grandpa, too. He was the one who occasionally took them out for Sunday dinner, bought them their first bicycles, sent them to the local ice-cream stand with money, passed on his used cars to the family, and kept a close eye on their daily lives—especially when Edward and Janette weren't around to do it. He was loving and generous, and his death left a big hole in their lives.

Grandmother Oke was now alone, and Edward and his family were glad she was just next door.

CHAPTER THIRTY-TWO

Writing

EVEN AS A CHILD Janette had enjoyed putting words together, but she had always promised herself that she would not attempt to write for publication until she received special training. Occasionally she chaffed against her self-imposed restriction. She wanted to get to writing, but certainly the training had not happened, and it was beginning to look as though it never would. There had just never been the time or the money for it.

Janette had taken a couple of writer's aptitude tests, one for a secular writing course and the other for Christian Writer's Institute. Though they graded quite differently, her grade was almost identical on both tests, and she had been encouraged to try their courses. However, she had not been able to follow through on either one. The secular firm had sent a representative to see her. He had appeared at the Royal Bank one day while she was working. After interviewing her, his conclusion seemed to be that she did not read enough to be a writer. She had answered their questionnaire with, "I don't have nearly as much time for reading as I would like," and the man had taken that as an excuse. For her own interest's sake, Janette decided to track her reading for a number of years afterward. She found that she usually read more than one hundred books a year—but she easily wished it could have been three hundred.

While she was still working at Reimer Concrete, now full time, a comment from one of the men started her thinking. Not that she liked the statement—in fact, though she had heard it before, she still found herself frowning.

"You're free, white, and over twenty-one" was the phrase. What caught her attention was the "over twenty-one" part. She was getting quite a ways over twenty-one—at the time, she was fully twice twenty-one.

Janette began to think more and more about finally getting on with her dream. Her mind went to the short stories she had stuffed away here and there, and she considered gathering them up under the title "Twice Twenty-One" and sending them to a publisher. She felt that by the time a person had reached her age, she surely must have learned *something* about life.

But she knew she would need more material to go with what she had, so she started working on additional stories. Gradually ideas began to formulate, but the story that was taking shape in her mind was beginning to expand on its own. Soon she realized that it could not be contained in a short story, and she began to pray in earnest. She knew she would need a lot of help—and as always, she knew that God was the best one to turn to.

In the beginning, her idea was simply to provide a clean, entertaining piece of fiction to fill a void in the market. She loved to read fiction, but there was so little Christian fiction available, and what she found on the secular shelves was not what she wanted or enjoyed, particularly if she was looking for a short work that could be read in a few hours.

Sometimes she picked up romances because they were billed as "clean," but the newer books were beginning to get pretty tainted in her way of thinking. She could not conscientiously read them since she did not like the messages they sent out, yet she knew that countless girls and women were doing so. She thought the Christian community should at least provide an alternative. Then it would be the reader's choice as to whether they would accept them or not.

Janette also hoped that in writing fiction, she would be given the opportunity to share her faith. For that reason, she considered trying to connect with a secular publisher.

But all of that was in the future. First she had to *write* her book. She spent many nights lying in bed, working through the plot, living with the characters, thinking of the theme—and praying.

"God, I'm going to write this book," she informed the Lord at last. "And if it works, and if I discover that I have talent, I'll give it all to you."

It sounded so good at the time she said it, but God got her attention immediately. She knew He was not happy with her little arrangement, and she could sense Him speaking to her heart.

The message went something like this: "Just a minute. Haven't we got things a bit backward? I'm not interested in your book after you're *done* with it. I'm not even particularly interested in your talent. If you are really serious about writing as a ministry, then I want it all right now before you start."

At first Janette tried to argue. It was very important to her to see if she had talent. For some reason she felt that her true person was somehow interwoven with her desire to write. Though she had accepted the Lord as her Savior when she was ten, had dedicated her life completely to Him as a teen, had endeavored to walk with Him as an adult, and had thought she had committed every area of her life to Him, she found that she was still hanging on to what she dreamed would be a talent for writing.

She did some more praying, and when she finished she could honestly say, "Okay, God. We'll do it *Your* way. I will write to the best of my ability, seeking to bring glory to Your name, and whether something exciting happens—or absolutely nothing at all—that's entirely up to You."

She knew deep down within her heart that when one gives something, really gives it to the Lord, it's a "hands-off" commitment. It could not be a case of her saying, "I give it to You so You'll be free to bless it, Lord." No, it would require her to totally give it, leaving the results with God. It wasn't an easy thing to "let go," but afterward she was thankful so many times that God brought her to that all-important decision.

She was free. She was free to write without worrying about the outcome. She was free from the pressure of getting sales. She was free from the temptation of pride. She could admit that through the years Satan came along periodically and whispered in her ear, "You've done a pretty good job."

But she could quickly respond, "You know, and I know, that is not the truth. I've given myself, my imagination, and my stories to God. Get out of here, Tempter." When God gets the credit He deserves, it doesn't take very long for everything to fall into proper perspective again.

In the summer of 1977, as she sat at her dining room table trying to get down in long hand the first draft of her book, Janette knew nothing except that she wanted to get on paper the story that was on her heart. What was to happen after that was a total unknown to her. It was in God's hands.

She wrote in little snatches. The story had been in her mind and heart for a long time, leaving little work to do except to put it on the empty pages before her. So she wrote—before she left for work in the morning, a few minutes at noon, after the house grew quiet in the evenings. Whenever she could grab a few moments she wrote, filling up unused pages of old school scribblers.

At the time there were four teenagers in the house. It was much easier than having little tots who constantly needed her attention, and her four were old enough to think that it was "quite a kick" to see Mom doggedly writing a book at the humble kitchen table.

Then vacation days arrived. Though Janette felt it was the wrong time for her to go, she climbed in the car with the rest of the family and drove around Alberta, touring several places of interest. While they drove, she wrote with her pad on her knees. There in the front seat of the family car, with Edward at the wheel and sitting beside whoever was unfortunate enough to be stuck in the middle of the front seat for his turn, her book began to take shape.

Just short of three weeks later, Janette was amazed to find that she had finished her entire first draft in long hand. Even *she* was painfully aware, though, that it was far from ready for a publisher.

She went over it a few times, making no major changes but trying to polish it up a bit. She found that the most difficult part was keeping the unusual dialect of her characters consistent throughout the book.

The next step was to get the manuscript into typed form. Janette was a slow typist and it took her hours. On a few occasions one or another of the boys typed a few pages for her. Even Edward, an excellent typist, took a few turns.

At first she didn't share her plan with many people. She had talked to her mother about it. Amy herself had always had an interest in writing and passed along the news of the project to one of Janette's former teachers. Mrs. Lindberg kindly offered to go over the manuscript if Janette would send it to her. The offer was appreciated, and the seasoned teacher did catch some grammatical errors that Janette had missed.

Jean stopped in for a visit one day while Janette was working. She gave her sister the story to read and then sat across the dining room table, busy at the typewriter. Hoping she was being sly, Janette sneaked glances now and then, trying to catch Jean's reaction. To her delight, she could see definite emotional responses as her sister went through the story. She was *feeling* something. A little spark of hope was kindled for Janette. The story was "speaking."

When Jean finished, she stated simply, "That's my kind of book," but Janette was encouraged by her comment.

At last Janette had what she considered to be a manuscript. Now she had the awesome task of finding out what to do with it. The very first thing she did was a blunder. She bundled up the pages and sent them to Bantam Books, thinking it might be the type of story they would be interested in. She had read some of their published fictional works, and she did not see hers as being very different.

But the manuscript was returned quickly with a nice photocopied note: "We do not accept unsolicited manuscripts." She didn't suppose they would be soliciting hers, so she tucked it aside.

The manuscript lay on the shelf for about six months, not because she was discouraged, but because she was busy and not sure of the next step. Looking back on that time years later, she was convinced that those six months were the best thing that could have happened. When she went back to the manuscript, it was as a reader—not the writer—and it gave her a totally fresh view of the story.

Although there was little she did in the way of further changes, she could see it much more clearly for what it was. Then she did what she now knew she should have done in the first place. Research.

Edward found a few books in the college library about how to get a work published and brought them home to her. She discovered some interesting facts about finding a publisher. First of all, one not only had to get his or her work to the *right publisher*, but it had to be there at the *right time*. Publishers work with schedules, and the number of books they can handle in a year depends on the size of the publishing house. New manuscripts are slotted according to wants and needs. And, of course, much also depended on the editor.

Editors, too, have likes and biases, preferences and prejudices. One book said that whether an author's work was accepted or rejected could depend on what the editor had for lunch. After some years in the business, Janette has concluded that editors are far more professional than that. However, that comment did make a distinct impression on her.

Other books said that editors usually have two piles of manuscripts on their desks: one from known writers and the other from unknowns. Since the former stack was considered first, it would be lucky if they ever got to the second one.

Janette knew in which pile hers would be stacked. She was definitely an unknown. All she had ever written was the pile of little stories and verse still tucked in drawers and a few published pieces in the denominational publication.

The books did give her very good advice, though. "Never send out a cold manuscript; send a query letter." The query is a little "sales job" telling the publisher what has been written, why, and who might be interested in reading it. It should also give an outline of the plot and approximate word count.

Janette sent off about half a dozen queries and then sat back to wait for the predicted six to eight weeks for an answer. It was much longer.

Finally a letter arrived from Zondervan. They said they would like to see sample chapters, so Janette picked out three and sent them off, carefully including a self-addressed, stamped envelope. She did not want to be branded as an amateur before the editor had read even the cover letter.

After another long wait, the chapters were returned. Along with them came a short letter stating that her work did not fit the "present publishing schedule." She assumed this was a nice way of saying they were not interested.

The next reply came from Bethany Fellowship, Inc. Now, Janette had not previously heard of Bethany, but when she had been praying about what to do with the manuscript, she had drawn a verse from her promise box. The Scripture verse was familiar, and on the flip side was a four-line verse. In the middle of a line was the word "Fellowship." That was not a particularly strange word for a religious poem, but though it was in the middle of a line, it had been capitalized, and that had drawn her attention.

Strange, she thought, and began perusing the library shelves to see if she could find any publishing house by the name of Fellowship Press or some such thing. Bethany Fellowship, Inc., was as close as she had come, so that was the rather unusual reason she had included them in her little list of publishers to query.

The reply postcard simply stated that they were interested in seeing the manuscript, and it was signed by Carol Johnson, Editor. This made Janette's heart beat a little faster. She had written her story for girls and young women. So she felt that if there was anyone who would understand what she was trying to say, it would be another woman, and Mrs. Johnson had asked to see "the entire manuscript." Quickly, Janette bundled it up and sent it off.

The weeks slipped by. Every day she visited the post office. She couldn't keep herself from succumbing to that temptation! Day followed day—and no answer. Little did she know that Carol Johnson was fighting for her manuscript, urging other members of the editorial committee to "give it a chance."

One day when Janette went for the mail, there was an envelope with an unfamiliar return address: Bethany Fellowship, Inc., 6820 Auto Club Road, Minneapolis, Minnesota 55438. She turned it over, looked at it, pondered inwardly: "I wonder how *they* got my address," and tucked it back in with the mail.

Later she couldn't believe she had gone to the post office looking for that *very letter* for weeks on end and then not recognized it when it had finally arrived. It was not until she got home and looked through the mail again that she realized what she had in her hand. She tore the envelope open and read the short letter. It was to the point, declaring simply that they had decided to accept her book for publication.

Janette laid her head on her arm and cried. Up to that point, she had had no idea of the tension building within. She had written a book, had given it to the Lord, and had endeavored to follow His leading to find a publisher. Now He had honored her prayer. He was allowing her the opportunity of sharing her faith through the medium of Christian fiction.

When word quietly leaked out that Janette's manuscript had been accepted, the assistant pastor's wife called up some of Janette's closest friends and arranged a little luncheon at a local restaurant as a surprise celebration. What a wonderful encouragement it was to Janette to have those dear friends share her excitement.

Love Comes Softly came out in July of 1979. By December of the same year it appeared on Bethany's bestsellers list. Family and friends were thrilled for her and proud to tell about her success to anyone who would listen. It was strange, though, to have people consider her "famous." She was Janette, yet her new success as a novelist was exciting and just a little overwhelming for her family of growing teens.

She was already thinking of her next story. It was to be the tale of an orphan boy, Joshua Jones. But reader requests began to come in the form of letters, wanting to know "what happened next" to the Davis family. After talking with Bethany, it was decided that perhaps she should write a sequel to *Love Comes Softly*. Though she had not considered that when she wrote the first book, she began planning the sequel. The whole thing was most gratifying.

Then Janette realized that she was scared. She knew she had relied heavily on God's help for the first book. What now? Did she think she was able to write one on her own? Instinctively, she knew that if she even dared to try, she would likely have the world's worst flop on her hands. So Janette desperately went back to God. She was sure she needed Him even more for the second book than she had for the first.

There was also a time factor now. There was a publishing date looming on the horizon. She had not had that pressure before, and she was still a very busy wife and mother. This time it didn't seem to work to use the dining room table. She would not have the luxury of months of thinking and plotting. This time she needed quiet. She needed to be able to concentrate totally on the task at hand.

Jean and Orville had a house with a small basement suite. They were not at home at the time and had told Janette that she was free to use the suite if she wished. The house would be totally quiet, and the offer sounded too good to be true.

She gathered her scribblers and pencils, packed a suitcase, and set off for some serious work. Again she wrote longhand, starting in the morning and writing all day with hardly a break for a snack. By the end of the day her arm would ache all the way to the shoulder. On one particular day, she wrote eighty pages, filled from top to bottom with her small script. That alone was about a third of the book.

Since she had not planned to write a sequel, she was uncertain how to go about it. She didn't want a carbon copy of the book that had just been published, so she set about deliberately changing the tone. The chapters were shorter and the book covered a longer time period. She hoped her work wouldn't be positioned in a confining way.

Edward called with news that Amy had been taken to the hospital. Janette forced herself to finish one more half-day of writing before packing up and going to her mother. The book had to be done, and she knew she would not get back to complete it once she left the small apartment. She had finished the first draft of the manuscript in four and a half days.

This incredible pace was a little miracle. She doubted she would ever be able to repeat the performance and could not believe she had managed to do it that once. Her only answer was that God must have steadied her hand, given clear thoughts, and "pushed the pencil."

When she arrived in Rimbey, she was much relieved to find that Amy was improving. After a hospital stay she was able to return home.

Love's Enduring Promise was published in September of 1980. Then Janette wrote the story of Joshua Jones, which she had planned, and it was titled *Once Upon a Summer*.

Janette's original pace of one book per year soon doubled. Then she wrote a children's story about a puppy, intending to submit it to a writing contest. She ended up sending the manuscript to Bethel Publishing in Indiana after clearing it with Bethany House, the new name of Bethany Fellowship's publishing division. Bethel, the denominational publisher for the Missionary Church of which Janette was a member, was just venturing into publishing fiction. Previously they had been involved in preparing curriculum materials for the denomination's use. They had asked Janette if she had something they could handle. So *Spunky's Diary*, the first of her animal stories written for younger readers, was published by Bethel in 1982.

Now there was a second publisher who was interested in her writing books for them regularly. This meant three complete books each year, but it was enjoyable to change style and write the third manuscript from an animal's point-of-view.

Soon after Janette began writing, she was surprised to learn that because one's name appeared on the cover of a book, it was assumed that the author was also a speaker. But since speaking was another opportunity to share her faith, Janette felt she should take advantage of those invitations. Unfortunately, she soon discovered that she could not possibly say yes to all the offers. This would have required her to be on the road constantly, and didn't fit with her responsibility to family nor leave her the required time needed for writing.

But it wasn't easy to say no. Each request seemed to come with the subtle prompting, "Couldn't you just take *ours*?" She wished she could, but it wasn't possible.

One of the really gratifying results from her books was mail from readers. It was rewarding to hear how they had allowed God's Spirit to speak to their hearts as they read the stories about her fictional characters. Janette laughed and cried as she read some of the accounts shared with her.

The letters that brought her heart the most joy told of individuals many miles away, people to whom she knew she would likely never speak in this world, but who had opened their hearts to the Lord Jesus and asked Him into their life. In some way the books were able to help them discover this truth. How wonderful to be able to share a very *real God* through the use of fiction! Janette enjoyed each of the letters, although it was with great difficulty that she found time to answer them.

As her writing career blossomed, she tried to picture each one of her books as a little "paper missionary." It had the potential, through the Spirit's working, to reach a heart crying out for truth and answers somewhere, and she prayed often as she wrote that this would be so. Then, she prayed again after the books were completed, and she knew that the people at Bethany prayed along with her.

The prayers were what made it all an exciting adventure. Writing was not just a dream, nor was it a marketable commodity of words— it was a ministry for a world hungry for the knowledge of the God who loves them. Janette thanked Him that He had allowed her the privilege of being involved in "one more way" to share the Gospel.

Proverbs 3, verses 5 and 6, became increasing meaningful to Janette. Though she had memorized them as a small child, she felt she was just beginning to understand their deepest message and the wonderful truth: "Trust in the Lord with all thine heart; and lean not unto thine own understanding. In all thy ways acknowledge him, and he shall direct thy paths."

Such a simple directive, she thought. Yet we so often try to work things out in our own wisdom or strength. But God can do little for us—or with us—as long as we insist on doing it our own way. When we truly trust and acknowledge Him for who He is, then we can have that wonderful "direction" for our path—our life—that He has promised.

CHAPTER   THIRTY-THREE

Moving Again

FOR A NUMBER OF YEARS, Edward had dreamed of completing work on his Ph.D. He had been putting it on hold because of the needs of the rest of the family, but as the twins neared high school graduation, it seemed a good time to pursue his degree.

Edward and Janette's preparations included another dreaded trip to Immigration. At this time, border crossings were hard to come by as the economy in both the U.S. and Canada was suffering. Edward would need to work, and Uncle Sam did not want him to take a job from an American. When he made his initial trip to the Office of Immigration it looked as if there would be no chance at all.

Edward had the promise of a job at Bethel College, the liberal arts school he had previously attended in Mishawaka, Indiana. This time he'd been invited on as a faculty member. But there was still the matter of getting across the line.

The lady at the Office of Immigration gave him a form to complete, and one of the questions asked if the applicant had a right, through parentage, to American citizenship. Edward brought the question home to Janette. "The clerk says that because your mother was an American, you might have right to citizenship," he explained.

"That's ridiculous! Mom has been a Canadian since long before I was born," Janette answered.

"Well, this woman says we should look into it. It's the only way we'll ever be granted permission to enter."

After much red tape, they were both surprised to discover that Janette was eligible for American citizenship. They were required to obtain three documents proving her mother had been born in the United States and was, therefore, an American. Because Amy had never actively relinquished that right, the U.S. still claimed her. Canada operated under British law that allowed a woman to automatically take the citizenship of the man she married. Thus, to them, Amy was a Canadian.

As they worked through the papers, they discovered that Janette was the only one of her family of eight who was eligible for American citizenship. Because of the changing laws over the years, she had managed to just fit the specifications.

A big factor was their former residence in the U.S. from 1957 to 1960, and even their tiny infant son entered in. Brian had been born to them while in the United States, and he had never left the country. In a bizarre case of "legal logic," it had not seemed to matter that the infant had not even lived a full day. Who would have dreamed that little Brian would "open a door"?

Because Janette was eligible for American citizenship, she could apply to take her family members to the United States with her. Laurel was the only one of the kids still in school and had always wanted a chance to live elsewhere. The timing seemed perfect.

Lorne and Lavon would stay behind to attend Mountain View Bible College along with Terry. Grandmother Oke lived just across the street from the campus and would keep her eye on the boys.

But it was hard for Janette to leave them behind, especially the twins. They were only seventeen, so young for breaking the close family tie. Though Edward and Janette knew they would miss him, Terry had already been out of the nest for a few years.

Edward and Laurel left with the hired van packed tight with household belongings, while Janette stayed to drive the car accompanied by Jean and the twins who would make the trip and then return in time for school. Dear little Curious, now old and arthritic, had been given to friends from church who had a farm. The family knew he would be well taken care of and happy there, but it was still very difficult to walk away that last time.

The van crossed east to Manitoba and then started south to the border. Janette and her crew drove directly toward Montana and met with a discouraging and lengthy fuss at the port of entry. The Chevy they were driving was not approved by U.S. emission standards, but after wasted hours and a promise that the boys would agree to return with the vehicle, they were allowed to cross.

Edward and Janette met in Minneapolis, where Bethany Fellowship had invited the travelers to spend a night as guests. It was their first trip to the facility, and they were all impressed. Bethany was developed as a training institution for young people wanting to enter missions work. The idea of a profitable business to support the ministry had evolved later.

Now the publishing company worked to expand and develop the training programs and to support missionaries sent out to various fields. It was as if there was a double bonus. First the publication of the Christian books themselves was a ministry, and then the profits from the book sales helped to train and support workers for mission fields abroad. Janette was sure she could not have found a better publisher and thanked God again for His leading.

In Indiana, arrangements had been made for the purchase of a house across the street from Cliff and Eleanor Quantz, who had returned to Indiana some years earlier to pastor a church. It seemed almost providential how the paths of the two couples continued to intertwine over the years.

The house needed a great deal of work since it had been vacant for a few months. Even the swimming pool in the backyard that had once been emptied now oozed with muddy rainwater and harbored a number of frogs and innumerable crickets. There was plenty of work to be done.

Jean pitched right in as usual and the house was made "livable," though it was some time before all the desired changes were made. The bank from which the home had been purchased had completely repainted the interior of the house, but the carpets and drapes were in need of immediate attention. Not long after the moving process was complete, Janette began using her decorating skills to make the home her own.

In the meantime, Laurel began her junior year of high school in the United States, and the boys returned to Bible College in Didsbury. Janette looked forward intently to Christmastime when the boys would drive down, bringing Grandmother Oke to celebrate with them. Those family times together would be all the more cherished as her kids grew older and went their separate ways.

In the spring of 1982, Edward was asked to speak at the graduation ceremonies at Mountain View Bible College, which prompted another trip back to Canada for a visit. It was so good to see those left behind again.

That Sunday evening, Janette and Edward were invited to a friend's home. When they arrived they were very surprised to find the gathering was being held for their benefit. Although their anniversary was not until May, the local church people would not miss out on the opportunity to share the celebration of their twenty-fifth anniversary. It was a wonderful surprise, and when they returned home, Edward and Janette put the money they had been given toward a patio set for the back deck.

The spring of 1982 brought exciting changes for Laurel, and yet somewhat nerve-wracking moments for Janette and Edward. She had begun dating a young man named Marvin Logan. Janette chose to wait up on the evening of their first date and was ready for a mother-daughter chat, anxious for all the details of this new friend whom none of the family had met. The mother in her wanted to be sure that Laurel was safe at home, but they had long been sharing confidences about Laurel's teen years, and Janette wanted to hear all about the evening. The first words were, "Was I ever wrong about him! Marvin and I will never be anything but friends. He didn't even walk me to the door, just stood beside his car and waved as if he was afraid I would misunderstand his intentions."

But the relationship did develop. Edward and Janette were concerned because Marvin had not made a commitment to the Lord. And though they wanted to make him feel comfortable and accepted in their home, they were wary of the possibility of the relationship becoming "too serious."

After talking one evening with Roy Souza, a youth sponsor at church, Laurel decided on her own to have a chat with Marvin. Even though she enjoyed his company very much, it seemed important to let him know that they could never start a long-term relationship while he was not saved. Janette was relieved to hear that they had talked for some time about why Laurel was so determined that this was necessary—and that Marvin had accepted her terms for the relationship. And even more pleased to hear that he had requested that she get him a Bible.

Janette and Edward were even more grateful when Marvin made his own personal commitment to Christ shortly after graduation from high school, though there was not much time to spend with him immediately afterward.

Edward, Janette, and Laurel were planning a trip with Aunt Jean and Uncle Orville. In a two-week period, they drove through the American states until they reached the Atlantic Coast, seeing several of the historic sites along the way, and then proceeded north to the Canadian Maritime Provinces. For the first time, they were able to visit the area where the Steeves family had first settled in Canada.

During this trip, they also had a chance to visit the home that Janette's grandfather, Robert Steeves, had built for his wife, Kathryn. Though the house stood empty and well past its prime, it was thrilling to be able to walk through it, admiring the workmanship and reveling in the stories that they knew of its original occupants. There were also visits to local cemeteries, the museum home of William Henry Steeves, and an opportunity to visit with distant Steeves relatives.

Though Laurel shared the excitement of the trip with her parents, aunt, and uncle, she was also anxious to get home to Marvin. And once there, all were astonished at how quickly things had progressed during their brief absence. Marvin had met regularly with Roy, the youth sponsor who had advised Laurel to set limits on the relationship, and had devoted himself wholly to his newly established faith. By the time they returned from vacation, he was committed to being baptized before the summer's end and was actively growing in his personal walk of faith. Almost immediately, Laurel agreed to commit to the relationship. They had graduated in early June and were engaged by the twenty-sixth. Marvin had a private little chat with Edward and asked for his daughter's hand in marriage—but not until after he had already discussed the idea with Laurel.

During the same summer, Edward and Janette traveled back to Canada, to Winnipeg where his nephew Brent Hannah was going to be married. Grandmother Oke was also there, as were Terry and his new fiancée. This was the first time Edward and Janette had met Barbara Dieterman, and they were very pleased. Barbara was lovely, poised, and charming. Terry had made a good choice.

It was with mixed emotions that Janette joined Laurel in making wedding plans. They feared that she and Marvin were too young and that there would be many hard adjustments ahead. But the wedding date was set for spring of the following year and that gave everyone some time to adjust to the idea. In the fall, Marvin went off to Purdue University to study engineering, and Laurel enrolled at Bethel College, even signing up for and thoroughly enjoying a course taught by Edward.

Lorne and Lavon moved to Indiana the same year, after completing two years at Mountain View, and began attending Bethel. Except for Terry, the family was together again, and when Christmas arrived and Terry came for a visit with his bride-to-be, the family was complete. The house seemed much more lively and full with the "extras" around that year.

After Christmas, it was time to dive into wedding plans. The problem was that whenever she had free time, Laurel preferred to drive to Purdue to visit with Marvin. Janette was frustrated to realize how much there was to do and to have the date creeping closer and closer. In the end, she decided to cut some time out of the planning by hiring a woman to do the decorating.

In May of 1984, Marvin and Laurel were married at St. Mark Missionary Church in Mishawaka, Indiana. They had four attendants each, and Laurel chose Janette to be her special "matron-of-honor." When first asked, Janette was reluctant.

"People don't do that," she said. But Laurel insisted.

"I'm supposed to pick my best friend," she maintained. "You are my best friend."

So Janette conceded, though she still worried about walking the aisle with the young girls. They eventually worked it out that Janette would be ushered in as the mother-of-the-bride and seated at the front. After the wedding party entered, she would slip quietly up and take her place beside Laurel. Then Edward, together with Rev. Cliff Quantz, was to perform the ceremony, and all three brothers were all involved as well. It would be quite a family affair.

Many relatives and friends were coming from Canada for the occasion, and Janette had been busy arranging for places for them to stay during the few days they would be visiting. Aunts and cousins had volunteered to help in whatever way they could and the decorations began. For each table, June had made centerpieces out of hurricane lamps and silk flowers; streamers, mints and nuts completed the table decor. June had also created a beautiful centerpiece for the head table, bearing the shades of blue they were using in the wedding.

The decorator was responsible for setting up the head table. The poor woman was devastated to find that the tables provided were smaller than planned for. She had already measured and cut the table covering before the mistake was discovered. She paced and worried, upset that she could not offer her usual perfect job.

It no doubt added to her distress that the bride seemed unconcerned and the mother-of-the-bride was clearly too busy and determined not to be upset by minor details to fret with her. Janette calmly suggested that the underlying blue be slightly overlapped to cover the table, then covered with lace, flowers, and ribbons. And no one even noticed.

At age eighteen Laurel and Marvin packed their few belongings and were ready to start for Purdue and their new life together. Edward's voice broke as he prayed that they would be blessed in their marriage and in the coming years. It wasn't easy to see the youngest of their family, and the first to be married, really leave home.

Just two months later, Terry and Barb were married in Calgary. This time it was Barbara and Mrs. Dieterman who had the last-minute bustle. Janette was able to relax and enjoy the wedding.

Barbara and her mother had done a wonderful job of planning, but Terry had the last word this time. When he led his bride from the front of the church after the ceremony, he did it in a style all his own. From what seemed to be thin air he produced white gloves, cane, and top hat—completely surprising Barb.

After a short visit home to Hoadley, Edward and Janette returned with Lorne and Lavon to Indiana where the boys continued their studies at Bethel College. Terry remained in Alberta, beginning work at the *Edmonton Journal* in their advertising department and displaying an aptitude for both graphics and public relations. This came as no surprise to his family. As a youth he had enjoyed making intricate designs of cars and other graphics.

Throughout these years, Edward was teaching full time at Bethel College and attending classes at Andrews University toward his Ph.D. Janette was increasingly involved with writing and speaking engagements. The book schedule kept her busy, and letters poured in that required answering. But the work continued to be rewarding.

CHAPTER THIRTY-FOUR

Daddy

"JANETTE, IT'S DADDY." Sharon was fighting to keep her voice under control. "He was taken to the hospital with serious heart problems. The doctors can't seem to do much for him. You probably should come home."

The remainder of the long-distance conversation with her sister was a blur for Janette. When the telephone handset finally dropped back into its cradle, she could not even begin to sort through her churning thoughts. The day's list of things to be accomplished lay unheeded on her desk and her cup of coffee had cooled before she finally stirred herself into action. Necessary telephone calls needed to be placed if she were going to travel the nearly two thousand miles from Indiana back to Alberta.

First she talked to Edward. Was there something she needed? She couldn't think of anything—but she was having such a difficult time making her mind work.

Next came the telephone calls to rearrange her other obligations so she would be free to catch the next available flight home. Everyone was accommodating, hoping that her father's condition would improve quickly—hoping that her trip would go smoothly.

Early in the morning, clutching the suitcase that had been packed in haste and with no idea how long her stay might be, she entered the crowded airport. Outwardly she could perform the necessary activities, say the proper things, and, hopefully, was not conspicuous in her heavy thoughts, but once the wheels of the airplane left the ground, time seemed suspended. Now the feelings that had been so guarded pushed their way back into her mind.

What was it that Sharon had said? That Daddy's aneurysm was actually larger than the heart itself? How long had he known? And why hadn't she been told sooner?

Long before the plane touched down onto its final stretch of asphalt, Janette's yearning thoughts had preceded her to the farm. She could picture him there—standing just inside the door, waiting to welcome her, his blue eyes sparkling, as if to make up for the few words he would say. But she knew. She had always known how deeply she was loved and how tender the heart was in the aged and weathered body.

His heart. Daddy had had a pacemaker for years. Now with nothing left medically for the doctors to do, he had been sent home again. Janette decided that might be good. Daddy would not be comfortable in the hospital—and yet it sounded so devoid of hope.

"Oh, God," she cried softly. "How could I ever stand to lose Daddy? But I trust You. And I want Your will," she whispered. "Please bring about Your will for my daddy."

God's will. What was God's will for Daddy? She was sure of only one part of it. *Oh, Father,* her mind agonized, *please make him ready. I'm not even sure if he's ready for—for eternity.*

Again her thoughts carried her back, this time through many years. The little gray house that would always be home appeared, followed by a parade of memories. There was Daddy, tall and strong—and covered in afternoon sweat. The tired horses trudged back with their heads down, wanting only a cool stall, chop to eat, and plenty of water.

But Daddy still had the strength for a smile. Even with the many chores that lay ahead that day, he had listened to her chatter and offered his affections with a gentle touch of her shoulder or a quick rumpling through her hair. He was such a wonderful father, and she looked up to him in so many ways.

Why, then, had he always struggled against the idea of God and salvation—he, who seemed to be such a good man at heart? What made faith such a difficult step for him?

Janette knew that life had dealt him some difficult blows. There was the struggle to maintain the family during the years of the Depression, but even as a child, she had never felt that any of the truly good things of life had been denied them. There may have been a lack of material possessions in their home, but they were happy together. And even though they had seen their share of sicknesses and deaths, she had been raised to view them as a natural, though difficult, part of life.

Later, Janette had become aware of much pain in her father's own family, but God had not been an outsider even in that home. Though, perhaps, He had not been quite as welcome as in the home in which she herself had grown up. Janette's mother had been totally committed to serving her Lord and to raising her eight children to do the same.

Daddy, though, had not participated in the family's faith. He had never stood in their way, and had even seemed to support their beliefs through the years, but something seemed to be holding him back from making this faith personal.

Whatever it was that kept her father from allowing God to become real to him, it was locked away inside the quiet man. She could only pray for him that in these days of poor health and imposed rest, he would be able to deal with his own heart and with God, who longed to be his strength.

Terry met her at the Edmonton Airport. From there they drove to the farm where Fred was resting after his hospital stay. With nothing for the doctors to offer as treatment, he had been advised to go home and take things easy, not to exert himself in any way.

When Janette met him, his blue eyes were shiny, and his hug just as warm. Then the good news was shared. Her daddy, for whom they had prayed for years and years, had made his peace with God while alone in the hospital room. Jean and her daughter Gloria had found a chance to talk with him.

"We wish we could make the decision for you," they had wept. "But you know you must do it yourself." Fred had only nodded weakly, but upon their return his eyes were aglow. He had made the decision for himself. He had accepted the gift of salvation, the gift of eternal life. The family had prayed faithfully, and now they were certain. God had given those extended days for Fred to find his way home.

Following the strict orders that he should not climb the stairs to his bedroom, a bed was prepared for him in the living room. There was no door to the entrance of this room, so the next day some of his daughters, Janette among them, went to town to purchase a curtain.

While they stopped in the local coffee shop, some of the other family members came to find them.

"Dad's gone," Orville told them softly. They couldn't believe it. They had left him only a short while before, and he had looked fine. It had happened just as the doctor had said it would. One moment he had been having tea with family and visiting friends, then he leaned forward with a pained expression. Sharon had quickly crossed to find out what was wrong.

"I'll be fine in a minute," he had answered, and he was. In the next moment he was with God. The verse on Janette's daily prayer calendar for October 4, 1984, said, "Ye shall not see me henceforth, till ye shall say, Blessed is he that cometh in the name of the Lord" (Matthew 23:39).

The family mourned and rejoiced all at the same time. They had lost much. The tender daddy of their childhood, the welcoming embrace whenever they visited home, and the gentleman who had given so much of himself so that they could become who they were.

Yet they could not help but rejoice that they would see him again when they also reached heaven. This wonderful, upright, moral example whom they had called "Daddy" had now been washed clean by the blood of Jesus and welcomed into the heavenly kingdom. Had his death come just days sooner as it perhaps should have medically—they shuddered at the thought, knowing the Bible is clear that it is not enough to be good or moral. Only accepting the redemption of Christ on his behalf could make Fred a citizen of heaven.

Fred had always been a nature lover—and now the land that he enjoyed was dressed in fall colors. The family chose not to order floral arrangements but to use things from his own garden blended with cut flowers to make their own personal pieces. June skillfully prepared the arrangements. The coffin was covered with a lovely spray in browns and golds. Because of his love for baseball, Amy arranged for one of the ribbons to say: "Safe At Home."

The funeral service was one of grieving, of rejoicing, and of sharing the Christian faith and Fred's recent conversion with the community. The congregation was admonished not to leave their decision until so late in life.

Janette wrote a tribute on behalf of his children, and Edward read it at the service. It expressed the family's feeling for the gentle man who had been their daddy, and their pride in carrying his name. The "love letter" ended with the words:

We'll miss you, Dad.
We're glad you're waiting there
In your corner chair in Heaven.
When we arrive
We know you'll meet us at the door
And we will feel your arms again
That warm, strong hug
That we have missed.
You won't say much
But the sparkle in your eyes
Will say to us,
"I'm glad you're home."

Janette knew she would miss her father, but she had no idea of just how much of a sense of loss there would be. She felt emotionally numb for weeks, perhaps even months, dangling somewhere between reality and nowhere. If it had not been for the love and presence of her heavenly Father, she may have despaired. With time she began to connect again with the present world. She still missed him, for he had been the biggest human influence in her life as a child and she had loved him dearly. But life had to go on.

CHAPTER THIRTY-FIVE

Going On

THE FOLLOWING YEAR was the busiest Janette had yet seen with speaking engagements, all crowded into a heavy writing schedule and homemaking responsibilities, each requiring time to prepare as well as the travel involved. By the time she returned home she was often exhausted.

During the summer, she and Edward were able to take a cruise of the Caribbean. They relaxed on ship, dined at tables filled with an abundance of food, and shopped in the interesting ports. They were glad to leave responsibilities behind for a while.

When they returned, they began the process of moving Amy from the family farm in Hoadley into Rimbey. Her children were worried about her being alone on the farm and away from help if it were ever needed, so they encouraged her to take a house in town.

Janette spent some time with a realtor in Rimbey, looking at available houses for sale. When they discovered one that could be made to accommodate Amy's wheelchair and realized that it was across the street from Amy's good friends the Lindbergs, Janette was excited to take the news to Amy.

With friends nearby and a home that would meet her needs, Amy agreed with surprisingly little hesitation. Then the work of packing and moving began.

Christmas that year came with not one but two grandchildren on the way. Terry and Barbara were expecting in February, and Laurel and Marvin were due in April. It was exciting for Janette and Edward to have the prospect of their own grandchildren.

Ashley Caroline was born on February 21. Janette, anticipating the birth, had booked tickets to fly back to Alberta to visit with Terry and Barb in March, but when word came that Ashley had been born, it was hard for her to wait for her scheduled flight date.

There were other considerations as well. Marvin and Laurel were now living in North Carolina, and though her due date was April 15, almost two months after Barbara's, Janette was busy juggling her calendar.

She felt sure that she could work in visits to both new grandchildren with no problem. She and Edward had even planned a short trip to Holland over the college spring break with friends from the St. Mark Missionary Church. They had never been overseas and looked forward to the weeklong trip abroad. Janette planned to be back in plenty of time to catch her booked flight to Alberta to get to know her new granddaughter. Then in a few weeks she would make the trip to North Carolina.

Lorne and Lavon stayed behind to care for things at the house. The plans had been laid out so carefully, but upon their return home from the trip to Holland, Janette and Edward were welcomed with astounding news. Not only did they have already have a granddaughter, they also had a grandson. Nathanael Edward Logan had arrived six weeks early but was doing fine.

Now the new grandma had a dilemma. She had already booked a flight to Alberta and would keep it as planned. Could she also squeeze in a trip to North Carolina before she was scheduled to leave for Canada? No, she finally admitted that was not possible. But the six-week-old Nate had not aged terribly by the time Grandma arrived, bringing grandmotherly boastings—and pictures—of his new little cousin Ashley.

Edward had completed his doctorate work the previous summer, so it had been decided that the home in Indiana would soon be sold and a move back to Didsbury was planned. Edward had been offered the presidency at Mountain View Bible College for the third time, much to the delight of his mother, who was still living in Didsbury.

This time, they left three of their four children in the United States, along with their first grandson. It was not an easy move to make, but they did have the excitement of Terry, Barbara, and little Ashley waiting at the other end of the line.

Edward and Janette purchased a home in Didsbury and settled in. They had not expected to face adjustments. So much was the same, and yet they soon discovered that much had also changed. Janette felt she didn't fit back in the familiar roles of the past, and for a while it was a very difficult move for her. Eventually, she began to find herself busy again with writing, college, and church, and gradually a comfortable routine fell into place.

Further complicating Janette's ability to reestablish herself, she couldn't ignore the fact that she was feeling increasingly poorly. It wasn't exactly sickness, though periods of illness—colds, flu, and such—seemed to come all too frequently. There was more to it. Something intangible. Her muscles ached almost constantly, and her head throbbed far too often. Sleep had become elusive, and Janette had also become aware that her mind seemed to have slowed a little. She mentally groped a little harder to come up with names, numbers, and facts—even words, sometimes. And she often found herself out of breath after short periods of activity—like climbing stairs.

Her best description seemed to be that her blood might not be circulating properly. That somehow it wasn't reaching her aching shoulders and head, and not delivering oxygen quite quickly enough to her lungs and brain. But none of the few doctors she had seen would give serious consideration to her own analysis.

Instead, she was given several medications to try, in a chemical attempt to alleviate her problems, but she was plagued with dreadfully negative reactions to the medications. It seemed easier just to tolerate the original complaints. Then she began to explore natural food supplements and various vitamins, and doggedly exercised in an attempt to get that blood flowing well. Still, there seemed to be few real answers. Janette could think of nothing to do but continue to push herself through her busy days.

Then exciting news came from the publishers that her book sales had reached the three million mark. She had determined to withhold more of her time for writing; so with the move, Janette had set her own cut-off point on speaking engagements, taking only those she felt compelled to meet after they had settled in Didsbury.

On one occasion, after she had boarded a train late at night to travel to where she would speak, she allowed her tired body to collapse against the seat beneath her and reached a hand up to rub at her weary shoulder. Leaning back against the seat, Janette turned her head to gaze out the window. Instead, her eyes fell upon the reflection of a slumped woman with a weary face and she shuddered.

"Oh, if only they could see me now! Could it really be *this* haggard woman that these ladies want to hear from?" And then, suddenly it was amusing, and she found she could chuckle softly at herself.

Edward began the awesome task of working on a merger of Mountain View Bible College with another Christian college of about the same size. The plan was to sell the two separate campuses, one in Didsbury and the other in Medicine Hat, and combine the two into one school in Calgary. This would take years of careful and tedious planning, and Edward, along with others, was very involved in the undertaking.

In the fall of 1986, Laurel and baby Nate were able to come home to Didsbury for a visit. It was so much fun to have Ashley and Nate, the little cousins of half a year, together. They seemed to know they belonged to each other and—even though they were too young to converse—did enjoy playing and tumbling around and over each other. Their doting grandmother took lots of pictures, enjoying each minute with her grandchildren.

In May of 1987, Janette was invited to give the graduation address at Bethel College in Mishawaka, Indiana. At that time she was also granted the honorary Doctor of Humanities for her work in literature as a member of the Missionary Church denomination. It was strangely humbling to be honored in such a fashion.

Lorne and Lavon were both graduating from Bethel College at about the same time—and each was entering teaching. Lorne would be coaching volleyball and teaching math, and Lavon would be teaching music. Edward's ideals of so many years ago seemed to have worked themselves out. Eventually, Lavon chose to further his education and completed a master's degree at Indiana University in Bloomington.

Meanwhile, Lorne had met a girl by the name of Deborah Sousley, and they were planning a June wedding. The family would fly from Alberta to Indiana to join them, but there was a complication. Barbara was expecting their second child—and Terry was to be in the wedding party. According to Barbara's doctor, the baby would arrive before the flight date, and they would be able to head for Indiana as a family of four.

Apparently the baby had not been told of the plan. The days passed one by one, and still no cooperation. It was finally decided that Janette and Edward would leave, taking one-year-old Ashley with them. Then, hopefully, Barbara, Terry, and the new arrival would follow, just in time for the wedding. But still nothing happened.

A few hours before they were to leave, Barbara was taken to the hospital. The doctor declared this to be a false alarm and predicted that nothing would happen for some time yet. At the very last minute, Barbara sent Terry to catch the plane—alone.

That was precisely when little Amanda Janette decided to make her appearance. Barbara's mother was with her in the delivery room as her "coach" and the "welcoming committee" for the new baby. It was a difficult time for Terry to be gone and, of course, for Barb as well.

Amanda was born on the twenty-fifth of June; Lorne and Deb were married on the twenty-seventh. Edward and Janette stayed for an additional week, so they could attend the wedding of their nephew, then went back to Alberta to get acquainted with little Amanda.

Ashley was thrilled with her baby sister. Only sixteen months old herself, little more than a baby, she was a very mature little girl for her age and did everything early, including talking. She called her sister "Manny" and loved her dearly. Whenever Ashley awoke from her nap or came in from an outing, she would head for her little sister. The family all shared her joy at the new blessing.

CHAPTER THIRTY-SIX

Farm

ONE DAY A REALTOR friend in Didsbury phoned.

"Janette, you've just got to see this house. I walked in the front door, and I felt that Laura Ingalls Wilder must have just walked out the back," she raved. Since Janette loved old houses, she quickly agreed to see it.

One could see that the little farmhouse had been a beautiful place at one time. Now it stood deserted and empty, even though there were still reminders that it had been home to a family. The children had grown, and the elderly farmer had been stricken with cancer. The family had urged their parents to move to town where it would be more convenient for them. Reluctantly, they had agreed.

"But I don't even know how to pack for a move," the old man had objected.

"Then don't," the kids had answered. "We'll just take what you need as you need it." And so the house still held some furniture—even some medicine in the washroom cabinet. Garments hung on pegs in the closet, and old, worn neckties draped on a hanger beside them.

However, the house showed signs of wear and neglect. Janette knew that if something were not done soon, it would begin to crumble. "Someone should save it," she mused, feeling sad at the thought of it falling apart.

She and Edward had often talked of her having a place to go to do her writing, a quiet atmosphere with no interruptions. They looked at the property and saw the potential, and in the end purchased the quarter section of farmland along with the little broken-down house.

They didn't quite realize what a big job they had undertaken. Though it was obvious that the house had never had electricity, water, sewer, or natural gas connections, each step taken seemed to uncover additional work needed. They began renovations by moving the house off to the side, putting a full basement under it, gutting the interior, and basically starting over. Because Janette wanted to stay as close as possible to the original structure, they preserved all the heavy wood-work, numbering it and laying it aside. Then they started to rebuild.

Janette herself took on the job of general contractor and brought in the tradesmen as they were needed. It turned out to be a great deal of work, and she vowed never to take on such a task again.

In August of 1987, an extended family reunion was planned at the Mountain View campus. Since everyone was interested in "Janette's farmhouse," she led several little tours out to see the project. Already the place was beginning to take shape, but there was still a long way to go.

Ashley and Nate were eighteen months now and really enjoyed being together. At two months, Amanda was still too young to know what all the fussing was about, but she seemed to enjoy the attention. Even someone who was a stranger to her could coax her to smile or coo. The reunion over, the family hugged and laughed and said good-byes and returned to their homes.

On the morning of September 10, Edward answered the phone. Janette could tell by the look on his face that the news was not good. Setting the receiver back in its cradle, he was not even able to share with her concerning the call before the phone rang again. This call confirmed the tragic news. Edward hung up the receiver from the second call, turned to an anxious Janette, and pulled her close. "Amanda is gone," he said in a choked voice.

She would not believe him. She did not want to believe him. She could not possibly believe him. There had to be some mistake. They had seen Amanda such a short time ago, and she had been healthy and whole. She had not been sick. What could possibly have happened?

"Crib death. Barbara found her this morning."

The tears that followed were not for her own loss, but for Barbara. She could only imagine the horror of the scene, and she began to fervently pray for her grief-stricken daughter-in-law.

"God, wipe away the memory of what she found," she prayed over and over. "Leave her with beautiful memories of her precious baby girl."

"We've got to go," she declared with urgency.

It was a three-hour trip from Didsbury to Edmonton. Edward made a few brief phone calls to make some arrangements for his college responsibilities while Janette got ready to go.

What a long, long drive it was. They were so anxious to get to Terry and Barb; and try as she would, Janette could not make herself stop hoping that there had been a dreadful mistake and that they would find Amanda alive and well—not really *dead*.

But it was true. A tearful son and a distraught daughter-in-law met them at the door. Little Ashley had been taken to the neighbor's home earlier.

Terry had gone to work at the usual time, they explained through their tears. Barbara had gradually become aware that two-and-a-half-month-old Amanda was sleeping later than usual. She went to the bedroom and, sensing something terribly wrong, slipped her hand under the blanket to touch Amanda's little leg. She was horrified to find her baby cold and stiff.

Quickly she pulled her from the bassinet and ran to the phone to call Terry. "Come home," she cried, "I can't get Amanda to breathe!"

Terry tried to calm her enough to have her call 9-1-1. The person who took the call kept Barbara on the phone while the Emergency Unit sped to her aid. They took over immediately, calling both her doctor and the pastor after finding the telephone numbers in her purse. When they were able to convince Barbara that she should give them the baby, they diverted her attention by drawing her into the kitchen and asking her to make tea.

It was obvious that little Amanda was beyond help. The doctor later told Barbara that the wee baby must have passed away shortly after she was put to bed the night before. He had given Barbara medication, but she still seemed to be in shock when Edward and Janette arrived. She tried to be brave.

"We can't cry," she warned them all. "They're bringing Ashley home."

The funeral service was held in Calgary at the church where Terry and Barbara had stood to say their wedding vows. Terry read a poem that he had written the night after Amanda died as he looked at the empty cradle and then out at the star-strewn sky. Barbara sang to her baby one last time. And in answer to Terry and Barb's request, Janette wrote a tribute that was read by the pastor.

Amanda

So tiny! So fragile! And yet in two-and-a-half short months, you changed our world so much.

You responded to Mommy as soon as you were placed in her arms and learned over the weeks to enjoy the songs that she sang to you with love in her voice.

You made your daddy proud with your sturdy, fast-growing little body and your refusal to sit down when you could see so much more by standing on your strong little legs.

And you brought such pleasure and joy to your big sister Ashley as she shared her toys and pushed you in your Jolly-Jumper.

You learned to smile and make your baby sounds so early, your little face crinkling up so completely your eyes would be forced to shut. Your grandmothers loved it.

You endured, good-naturedly, the many impromptu hugs and kisses bestowed upon you by loving, yet sometimes not so gentle, big sister and cousin Nate.

You cooed and gurgled and smiled your way right into each one of our hearts.

Your grandparents proudly discussed you. Your gentle disposition. Your quick responsiveness. Your strong little body.

Such a beautiful baby!

Such a sweetly responsive little "punkin."

Such a treasure from heaven!

We are all so glad that God sent you to us. We were not prepared to return you to Him so soon. We wanted to keep you—to watch you grow and mature and become all that He wanted you to be.

But I guess He thought that you are perfect just the way you are—that you had, in such a short time, completed your mission here. You brought love and happiness and joy into our hearts and homes.

We love you. We miss you. But even your "going" accomplished much, for it has drawn us even closer to God and to one another.

It has reminded us again that life here on earth is so fragile—

so temporary, and that we should spend time building relationships, not empires, that we should learn to treasure moments and
memories, not things, that we should concern ourselves with at-
taining spiritual growth, not worldly gain.

And heaven? Heaven is a much dearer place—for among all of
its treasures, God has added another little jewel. You, our dear
little Amanda.

We know that you are not alone. We know that you will be
well cared for. Be patient, sweetheart. The days pass quickly. It will
not seem very long until your family, one by one, will join you in
a far better world than the one we leave behind.

It was so hard to say good-bye to one so small—so precious. And
then there was poor little Ashley. Over the weeks that followed she
nearly broke her grandma's heart. Being much too young to understand about death, she continued to ask for Manny over and over.
Then she began to have nightmares and could not sleep. There were
so many times when Janette would have given almost anything to be
able to place that little baby sister back into Ashley's arms.

"Remember how often you said that you felt God allowed you to
lose Brian so that you would understand and be able to comfort others," Lavon reminded Janette. "Well, I'm sure you never guessed it
would be someone in your own family."

It turned out that the work at the farmhouse was good for Janette,
though she often longed to just forget the whole project. But once
begun, the work had to go on. Workers were coming and going, and
she was needed to coordinate the action. The project was right in the
middle of the heavy tasks and had to be completed before winter set
in. And, too, Janette had another manuscript deadline coming very
close, and she really needed the little house for writing.

It was therapeutic for her to keep her mind active with something.
The last draft of the manuscript needed to be finished by the first part
of December, and she finally dismissed the last crew, deciding that the
remaining renovations of the house could wait. For the time being it
was usable. The manuscript was sent off to Bethany in time to meet
the proposed deadline, but it certainly had been a struggle.

Barbara had begun to pray that she would be expecting again by
Christmastime. The family was pleased for her when she made her
announcement. But things did not go well from the beginning.
Shortly after Christmas, she miscarried. How difficult it was for her to
lose two babies in such a short time.

The following January, Janette left for Indiana. Another grandchild had arrived. Jessica Brianne had chosen a Saturday to be born, conveniently scheduling her birth around her daddy's hectic class schedule. She was born in the evening, with Marvin's mother and sister waiting nearby and ready to hold her. Janette arrived late Sunday evening, with Jessica and her mommy already at home to greet her.

With the grandchildren growing, Janette began to treasure the little stories of their antics and accomplishments. This visit with Laurel and Marvin was her introduction to baby Jessica as well as a time of enjoying and discovering Nate. Although he was not yet two, Marvin had noticed one day that he could recognize all his letters and was remembering many words by sight. So when Janette arrived she came with a small set of homemade flash cards. She had included all the really important words, which he had soon mastered: Jesus, Grandma, Grandpa, Mommy, Daddy, Nate, Ashley, baby, and McDonalds. And one very special card said "Jessica"—the new little sister they were all just beginning to get to know.

In the summer of 1988, Edward, Janette, and their boys embarked on a business venture together known as *Oke Grove Publishing*. They had purchased a newspaper in the nearby town of Innisfail, with Terry to manage it on their behalf. Edward was also very involved, helping with the computer work with which he had become adept. Eventually Barbara became a full-time employee as well.

Ashley, being the only grandchild close enough to make frequent trips to see her grandparents, loved the opportunity of visiting on her own. She of course loved her own parents dearly and was always glad to see them after a few days at Grandpa and Grandma's, but after the initial welcoming, she was quite content to let them go and leave her again, should they be so inclined. She was a good girl for Grandpa and Grandma and a great source of enjoyment. She talked early and clearly and brought many chuckles.

Janette began a memory book in which she wrote many of the accomplishments and cute sayings of her grandchildren. Day by day the pages were filled with more and more little items of interest. Though she continued to be very busy with writing and other responsibilities, she took special delight in watching her grandchildren grow and change.

On one occasion Ashley and Grandma were just returning from a trip to the farm, one of Ashley's favorite outings, and as they wound their way through the streets to get to Grandma's house, the sun suddenly shone directly into the front seat and into Ashley's eyes.

"Gramma, will you make the sun go back?" she asked, turning to Janette.

She chuckled. "Do you think Grandma can make the sun go back?"

"Yeah."

Just then they rounded another corner and the sun was gone. Ashley turned again to her grandmother and said simply, "S'anks."

It was wonderful for Janette to be a grandmother. When little faces turned to her own, there was a particular glow in them. They seemed to say, "Grandma, you're special." And Janette was convinced that these little people believed there was nothing she could not do.

Someone once said, "If I'd known grandchildren would be this much fun . . . I'd have had them first." But there were also times when Janette was reminded of how wonderful motherhood had always been. And she often thought that she would love to have just one day with those little babies of her own—now grown.

During the fall when their men were busy with the paper, Janette and Barbara, as well as Ashley, Orville, and Jean, drove down to Indiana to visit Lorne, Lavon, Laurel, and their families.

The drive was a long one, especially for two-year-old Ashley. Her car seat was not comfortable for such long periods of time and was even more difficult to nap in. For most of the trip she did well, but once, totally out of sorts, she reached for the drink that Aunt Jean offered her; then looking directly into Aunt Jean's face, she deliberately turned the cup over and poured out the contents. Aunt Jean had to be quick not to have a lap full of juice—and Ashley required a reprimand.

When the carload arrived at the Logans' home, Nate and Ashley flew at each other, falling to the ground in their rough hug. It was strange how, even with the long months between visits, the pair seemed to remember each other and felt that they "belonged."

Laurel was especially glad to have Janette arrive. Only two days before, she had been in the hospital because of a miscarriage and appreciated the comfort of having her mother nearby. Her life wisdom and gentle words helped to ease the sting of losing this child.

The following December, just one week before Christmas, Lorne and Deb welcomed their first child. Kathryn Louise was born in Mishawaka, and not only did she have an anxious father in the delivery room, but an uncle pacing the nearby waiting room. After Katie made her appearance, the nurse bundled her up and passed her to her new daddy for inspection. When she turned back, she found that both father and newborn had disappeared.

Without a moment's thought, Lorne had taken his new daughter out to make acquaintance with her Uncle Lavon. The frantic nurse, eyes over her shoulder watching for a doctor, quickly shooed the new father and his daughter back where they belonged.

Since it was Christmas, Janette and Edward planned to arrive shortly after Debbie's baby was born. But Edward had been playing with Ashley, tossing her into the air as he loved to do, and unfortunately his back had gone out. This was just three days before they were due to fly, and the hours of sitting in an airplane were much more than he could have managed. So Janette came alone that Christmas.

On February 23, Courtney Elizabeth was welcomed as Ashley's new baby sister. Ashley, three years old, had just celebrated her own birthday. Now there were five little grandchildren, with an additional one already waiting safe in heaven.

With Terry and Barbara living so close, Janette baby-sat periodically and enjoyed the chance to have tea parties and dress dollies with Ashley. Another favorite activity was to play dress up, and once the three-year-old exclaimed, "I can get so pretty and so glamious!"

It was not as easy to get her to say good-bye. Little Ashley would plead, "I wanna stay here for a little couple whiles, Grandma."

In the spring of 1989, Marvin and Laurel decided to make their best effort to move closer to family and planned a job-hunting trip to Alberta. The last trip that Grandma had made had ended with such a tearful good-bye that it had raised questions in the couple's minds about why in the world they were living so far from family. When Marvin was given an opportunity for employment in Calgary, they chose to take it.

After officially accepting the offer, Marvin left with the understanding that they would begin their move as quickly as possible after the arrival of their expected third child. His new employer was not quite certain how to work this out in the written contract, but he seemed willing to oblige the unusual arrangement.

Both of Laurel's children had arrived before their due date, and she was convinced this one would follow suit. So Laurel convinced Janette to fly to Indiana two weeks short of her due date so they could "share" one of the deliveries.

Janette arrived on Wednesday evening, and Jacquelyn Leigh arrived just after noon on Thursday. So Janette was in the delivery room, making teasing bets with Marvin as to the time of birth, and was on hand when Jackie first appeared. Even there, Grandma had her camera clicking, though she followed strict discretionary guidelines.

The move to Canada followed when Jacquelyn was only two weeks old. Janette had suggested that she take Jessica back with her on the plane, and Laurel was grateful for her help. Jessica was a busy, energetic almost-two-year-old who did not like long car rides and was under the age limit for needing an airline ticket. The small family car would be crowded enough with four, along with the luggage needed for the trip.

Edward and Janette had spent days house-shopping for the couple, and they suggested a little house on Allen Street in the town of Airdrie. It was perfect, halfway between Marvin's work and Grandma's house.

There were regular trips to visit Grandma's house and sometimes even a visit to her farm. At this farm there were planned events, like picnics and Easter egg hunts, but mostly it was just a few hours here and there of relaxation shared with Grandma, listening to the wrens and the chickadees, or caring for the big country garden.

The grandkids loved the farm. They headed for the rows of carrots almost as soon as their feet touched the ground. When they had pulled themselves a carrot, almost as long as themselves from the tip of the root to the top of the feathery leaves, they scampered to the hose to wash off the dirt—or at least most of it. The rest of the day's activities were carried on while munching the carrot.

One summer the neighbor's cat gave them all a wonderful surprise by coming over to Grandma's farm to have her babies. It could not have been planned better. Six darling little kittens for six darling grandchildren. When Janette showed the cluster of preschoolers where the kittens were tucked away in her barn, they fondled and fussed over the new babies, especially Jessica who claimed the many-colored runt as her own right from the start. All summer long the kittens were a special treat at the farm. When winter neared, the neighbor girl came and collected her brood, taking them back to where they belonged.

For the children, the farm was also a nice place where they could run and shout, with no one telling them to settle down. Just what busy, happy preschoolers needed—and during this time, Grandma was given many new anecdotes for her memory book.

Nate loved the cows that fed in the adjoining pasture. One day he took Grandma's hand and led her to the fence. "Look, Grandma! All those cows are for sale."

"Why do you say that?" she asked, puzzled.

"They all have price tags in their ears." Janette laughed when she realized he was referring to their identification tags.

When evening fell at the farm, stars spread out across the enormous prairie sky and the moon hung low over the horizon.

"It's getting dark," Nate stated.

"Yes, it is."

"God sure is a tricky God."

Janette smiled. "He is?"

"Yeah. It's a little bit tricky to put the moon out now." Janette raised her eyes to the glowing orb, and she had to agree.

On another occasion when Ashley was having her turn at the farm, Janette saw a coyote and tried to point it out to the child. "Look, Ashley. There's a coyote."

"Uh-uh. That's not a coyote," she argued with a knowing look. "Coyotes are always on a hill by the moon."

The farmhouse/writing studio proved to be a good purchase. Once the renovations were complete and Janette had taken advantage of the few pieces of furniture left behind, the house took on a wonderful air of antiquity. Other antique pieces were added to complete the picture, and the result was homey and a good setting for her imagination. It was a small bit of solitude in a hurry-scurry world.

Both Janette and Edward enjoyed the quiet retreat—even the many hours of hard work that went with cleaning up the place—the house, the outbuildings, the yard and fields. And here Janette showed her farm girl upbringing, as well as her own tenacity to stick with a plan. For many hours of back-wrenching labor, she cleared bush, dug stones, and pulled weeds. By the time she and Edward were finished, the little farm was a model of beauty and neatness.

There were many others who helped as well. Lavon and Lorne came home in the summer and painted the barn and the pump house. It was a big task but they did a good job of it. And on a blustery, cold fall day, Terry helped shingle the double garage that Edward had built.

Orville and Jean spent countless hours helping clean up the yard, but it had all been worth it. Only bird songs and the lament of coyotes broke the stillness. And Janette had so faithfully and patiently fed the little birds that the chickadees would fly down and eat right out of her hand.

But even with everything that had already been done, there were always things to do at the farm. Edward built new doors for the barn and new steps for both the front and back porches. Janette added landscaping, decorated inside, and spent hours in the little office over the kitchen.

Sometimes, while the grandchildren were visiting, they would share in Grandma's activities. Sitting beside her in the kitchen was always a good time to chat.

"Grandma, can I have a peach?" Ashley asked, eyeing the fruit basket that usually sat on the kitchen table.

"Remember, I told you they aren't ripe yet," Janette reminded.

"Oh, yeah. I'll just sit here and wait," she decided.

Nate's strategy for appealing to Grandma was slightly different.

"Please," he asked on one occasion when he had already been given a "no."

"No," Grandma answered again, just as firmly.

"You're suppose to say 'yes' when someone says 'please.' That's how please works," he insisted.

CHAPTER THIRTY-SEVEN

Saying Good-bye to the Family Home

IN JUNE OF 1990, Amy Steeves was hospitalized. There was fear that she might slip away, but her condition gradually improved. For six years she had enjoyed her little house in Rimbey, entertaining scores of people as they came and went in spite of the fact that she had long been confined to her wheelchair.

But after this hospital stay, it was evident that she would not be able to return to living on her own. Amy requested one more summer in her house and signed up for the new long-term care unit that the Rimbey hospital was building. The sisters all took turns staying with her from June until October when the new hospital was ready.

It was not an easy move for any of the family. Amy began early to give away many of her treasures to family members and friends. When it came time for her to enter the new facility, they pushed her wheel-chair along the road the short distance from her house to the new unit. It was easier than making her climb in and out of a vehicle.

Her room had been fixed with the few things that she could fit in, along with a basket of fruit and a bouquet of flowers. But they knew these things did little to alleviate the pain. Amy had lost her home, and they had lost their "last post" of security and refuge. It would never be the same again.

Janette, Betty, Marge, Joyce, and Sharon gathered together to sort the remainder of her things. Jack and Ila came to help as well. Jean, always on hand to help when she was able, was sick at home. A family auction was held, each person writing a bid on the list of items to be sold. Many other items were given as gifts, and whatever remained was set aside for a garage sale. At last the task was completed, but it had been a painful process. Janette had not realized just how traumatic the change would be. It took a great deal of bravery for her mother to adjust to and accept the move to her new room.

But, all in all, Amy did well in the health care facility. Her attitude was good, and for that the family was thankful. When Amy was offered a chance to do some writing for the newspaper about the nursing home activities, she was excited. Here was something she had always enjoyed and could still do while living in the facility.

There was something else, too, that Amy could still do well where she was. When someone else was feeling down in spirit, she would wheel herself to the room for a visit, leaving behind some of her good-hearted outlook on life when she left.

Laurel was expecting again soon after Christmas, leaving Janette with the difficult decision of whether or not to travel to Winnipeg, Manitoba, as previously planned for a visit with Edward's sister and her family. In the end, they boarded the train and headed across the miles of prairie, but they left a key to their house with the Logans so it would be available to them when the "time" arrived. Laurel had chosen to use her family doctor from childhood and the Didsbury hospital for delivery.

On a snowy night just after Christmas had passed, Laurel convinced Marvin that if he would just drive the family to Didsbury, she would do her best to see that he had good reason for missing work in the morning.

He said, "Now, you promise?"

What could she say? No, she guessed she didn't quite promise. But she hoped good and hard.

Early in the morning on December 27, Alexander Nicolas arrived. He was quite different from any of her other babies. He was blond with a round face, but they were thrilled to bring him home to the other three who were waiting at Grandma's house, all ready to hold baby Alex. He was passed from one little lap to another faster than he could begin to focus on the grinning faces. Jackie was still only seventeen months old, but she seemed to think that this baby was her own for keeps. It was difficult to talk her into sharing.

In just a few short days, Janette and Edward returned from Winnipeg and were able to do some kissing and hugging of their own. They enjoyed the newest addition and the effect he had on the other three.

Janette caught Jessica kissing Alex gently on the head when he was crying. "You got a headache?" little Jessica asked her new baby brother.

In February, just short of two months later, Debbie gave birth to her second daughter and Edward feigned a moan. He tried very hard to sound disappointed at yet another Oke granddaughter. The ordered Oke grandson had yet to appear, and he teased that the little Logan boys did not truly count as "name-bearers."

But no one could resist little Kristalyn Lorene. She was bright and happy from the first. And as she grew, her sparkling eyes and comic stunts kept her parents busy and her grandmother writing quickly just to keep track of all the new stories. With six beautiful granddaughters and two fine grandsons, there was hardly a week without someone achieving a new accomplishment or another saying something terribly amusing.

Janette stopped by the Logan home one day on the way to do some shopping and took Jessica along for an outing. Edward drove them into Calgary and then let them out at the mall entrance, planning to pick them up later.

Jessica scrambled out of the car and hurried behind Grandma until the big glass doors swung shut behind them. Then she took a good look around, appearing troubled.

"What did we do with Grandpa?" she asked with big eyes.

After spending a while choosing some things for Jessica, Janette waited at the checkout counter as the cashier rang up her purchases and then presented her check and I.D. to the woman.

Jessica pointed at the picture license and explained to the clerk about the card, "It says 'Gramma'."

They decided to stop for a bite to eat before Grandpa returned, taking time to chat. Then Janette noticed that they had better hurry so he would not have to wait.

"Finish your ice cream, please, Jessica."

" 'Cause it might get cold?" she asked.

When Grandpa arrived to pick them up, Grandma was still smiling, ready to write the new comments into the grandmother's special memories book she kept.

Though she would have much preferred be able to spend equal time with the granddaughters still in Indiana, Janette had to be satisfied with writing down the cute comments that Lorne and Deb passed along.

Katie was a clever child and seemed to develop a quick wit early on. She loved to tease her parents by singing songs and deliberately slipping in the wrong words. Her favorite was to sing "Do, Lord, oh do, Lord, oh do remember me. Way beyond the YELLOW." Then she would giggle and start again.

One day Debbie caught her making grabbing motions into the air. "What are you doing?" she asked.

"I'm catching man cubs," she said.

CHAPTER THIRTY-EIGHT

Good-byes

AFTER ENJOYING THE PRESENCE of six of their eight grand-children close at hand, Edward and Janette found themselves suddenly faced with the prospect of having none of them nearby. In August 1991 Marvin and Laurel returned to Indiana, and soon afterward Terry and Barbara moved to Trail, British Columbia. It was a difficult adjustment, but they realized that all their children must make decisions as best suited their families. Saying good-bye to grandchildren was going to be especially difficult.

Little Courtney, then two and a half, confided to Janette one day, "Grandma, I don't wanna move to ABCD." Her version of "Trail, B.C."

Laurel did her best to prepare her own children for the day of their move, and had tears in her eyes when she heard three-year-old Jessica pray, "And, God, thank you for every single time we go to Grandma's house."

Ashley and Courtney returned for a visit. On a cozy evening at home, Courtney crawled up into Grandma's lap to read her a story. She began, "One on a time." Then she chattered for a while and finished with, "Amen." And Ashley presented her grandmother with her own homemade trophy for making "pretty well books."

In August word came that the Waldenbooks chain was to begin carrying Janette's novels. The stores were increasing the Christian stock on their shelves, and the wonderful news was greeted with gratitude.

In December Edward and Janette made a move of their own. Rocky Mountain College, the newly merged institute, had now progressed to the point where full-time employees were needed. A new president was named, and Edward was appointed academic dean. He and Janette decided it was time for them to move to Calgary. They put their house in town up for sale and, with great sadness, the little farmhouse as well.

The farmhouse had bids coming in on it even before the sale information was circulated. Everyone seemed to want it. There were offers and more offers, even above the asking price. It sold quickly. It was hard to let it go, but God had answered another of Janette's prayers. The new owners had been students at Mountain View, and Janette knew that the little place would be loved and cared for. In the summer following the sale, Janette drove by the farmhouse and found it as pretty as ever. The lawns were neatly trimmed, and the white fences gleamed in the bright afternoon sun.

When searching for a new home, Janette had three "wants": a mountain view, a dining room large enough to seat the family around the table and still have room to move, and guest bedrooms big enough to hold a queen-size bed comfortably.

She and Edward found a house on the outskirts of Calgary that met all her requirements. The mountain view was magnificent. The large dining room had a bay window and an opening through to the kitchen. The two main floor guest bedrooms were also large, and in the basement there were two more bedrooms along with a bath and family room.

Some things about the house did bother Janette, but she decided to either change them over time or learn to live with them. The purchase of the house was completed and possession set for mid-December 1991. Janette hurried to get everything moved and settled. The family—all seventeen—was planning to be home for Christmas. Janette unpacked boxes as quickly as possible and did some decorating and general quick fixing. In a week the family began to arrive. They were amazed at how settled she was.

The house worked nicely. All the adults were comfortably situated in bedrooms and the little ones were given hide-a-beds and cots. There was enough space that the family was easily able to keep from tripping over one another, while leaving Edward and Janette their own quiet spot upstairs to get away from the constant commotion. It was a good plan, though no one seemed to be able to control the midnight visits from small grandchildren wanting to sleep with Grandma and Grandpa.

After the family left, Edward and Janette began to talk about changes they wanted to make in the house. It took several weeks for the plans to be drawn up, and then work began.

For Janette, it seemed to take forever. They moved into the basement with a microwave and a Crockpot. The kitchen was entirely dismantled. The basement was the one livable spot in the house—and the workmen even invaded that, since they needed to remove part of the ceiling to get at the plumbing and heating.

Janette felt cold, caged, closed in. The workmen constantly left the door open, letting the cold Alberta winter air swish down the stairs into the basement where she huddled. So Janette decided on a project to alleviate the problem. She purchased some wool, deciding that working on an afghan might keep her sane and help the time pass more quickly, but it proved too uncomfortable to be bent over the project for such long periods of time.

Another manuscript was due at the publishers, and this time it was terribly difficult to accomplish. How she longed for her little farmhouse. She left, instead, for a few days at a Banff lodge, and the trip away helped tremendously with her writing project. She finished the first draft later in a Calgary hotel, and then started the laborious task of reviewing the work in the noise and confusion of her own home. As she usually worked through an entire manuscript four or five times, she was particularly relieved to bundle up the finished copy and mail it off to Bethany on schedule.

At long last the workmen were finished. The tiring ordeal was finally over, and Janette and Edward were thankful to be able to live in the entire house again.

In the spring of 1992 the final classroom was closed at Mountain View Bible College. It was difficult to say good-bye. Both had attended the school, met there, and grown together within its halls. Their sons had followed behind them, and Edward had spent many of his working years involved with the school in one way or another.

After the final celebration weekend, a large auction was held. All the antique furniture was sold, as well as other things that would not be needed in the new institution. While Edward chose not to go to the sale, Janette went.

One of the items on the auction block was a large oval mirror that had hung for years in the main hall. To Janette's way of thinking, it seemed to stand for the college. She made her first bid on the mirror and, after some rather vigorous counter-bids, came out the buyer. After the auctioneer declared it "sold" to Janette, a gentleman stepped over to her.

"Is that mirror special to you?" he asked.

"Yes," she admitted. "Yes, it is."

"I'm sorry. I wouldn't have bid against you had I known."

"That's what auctions are all about," she reminded him.

"No! I am truly sorry. I'm an antique dealer, and I wouldn't have bid. I stopped as soon as I realized that you really wanted it."

She was grateful that he had stopped. She had paid enough as it was and wondered if she had not acted a bit foolishly. But the antique dealer assured her the mirror was worth every penny she had paid.

When she got home, Edward was working in the yard. He walked over to ask how the day had gone. After commenting that the sale had gone well, Janette told him, "I bought two things." Along with the mirror she had purchased a piano stool she felt she could use.

"Come see," she offered, and raised the lid of the trunk.

"Oh! You bought the mirror!" he said, his voice a bit husky, and she knew she had done the right thing. She was glad she had found something that had been special to him as well. He never even asked her what she paid for it.

Rocky Mountain College opened its doors in Calgary for the first class on September 8, 1992. From the very beginning the interest was beyond expectations, and there was a great deal of excitement in discovering all the good things that God had in store.

With the family living in various parts of two countries, and the grandchildren growing rapidly, Janette and her family looked forward to any opportunity to be together, and Christmas became one of the focal points of each year. Many happy memories were tucked away during a week shared in a bed-and-breakfast in the mountains of Banff. Babies and young cousins played enthusiastically together, and the adults spent the days shopping or sightseeing. There was also a nighttime sleigh ride, and carols were sung as the horses pulled their load of tumbling passengers through the brisk night.

On another occasion, condominiums were shared with Edward's sister, Alta Mae, and her family. And the crowning moment came when Grandmother Oke treated her entire family to a lovely dinner at the famous Banff Springs Hotel. This imposing national landmark looms on the mountainside near the town of Banff. Constructed about one hundred years ago, the hotel's stone architecture gives it the air of a castle, and the dining was wonderful.

Oddly enough, the money for the meal had come to Grandmother in an unusual way. A gentleman from the town of Didsbury had contacted her and stated that he had an outstanding business debt he had owed Grandpa Oke before he passed away almost twenty years earlier. This man wanted to clear the debt, and Grandmother, somewhat surprised by the gesture, had decided to use the money to provide the family with an unforgettable evening of first-class dining at the Banff Springs. Course after course of fabulous food, and entertainment to match, were shared together during that unforgettable night.

CHAPTER THIRTY-NINE

Sharing Writing

IN 1992 BETHANY HOUSE PUBLISHERS contacted Janette and Laurel about the possibility of a biography. Laurel had previously written a fiction book for Bethany and, though her children were still small, was immediately interested in working on this project. One of the great benefits of the book was that Laurel and her four children were able to "come home" and spend a month with Grandma as the writing took shape. And delving into her mother's story proved to be a fascinating endeavor.

Teresa Budd, granddaughter of Jean and Orville, stayed at Janette's home to watch the children while Laurel worked at the computer, gathering together what Janette had written and poring over family histories and the many letters saved over the years. The result was the release of *Janette Oke: A Heart for the Prairie* in 1993.

Bethany House invited Laurel to accompany Janette on her usual trip to the Christian Booksellers Association convention, which was to be held in Atlanta, Georgia, that year. They signed books together, were interviewed for radio and television programs, met many interesting and exciting people, and attended the yearly Guideposts banquet. All of this was familiar ground for Janette, while Laurel was overwhelmed with her mother's fast-paced world.

Physical complaints continued to plague Janette, despite her best efforts to thrust them aside. There had been no satisfactory answers to the elusive list of her aches and pains. Then she began to hear of a new medical diagnosis called fibromyalgia. Finally, it seemed, there was a name for what she'd been experiencing: constantly sore muscles, throbbing headaches, breathless moments, and periodic clouded thought.

Unfortunately, the identity of the disease was so new and so poorly understood that even the medical community was uncertain how it should be treated. At least there were doctors who would acknowledge the legitimacy of what she'd been suffering. After a confirmed diagnosis and a trip to California, Janette began taking a concentrated nutritional supplement. This helped somewhat, but the wearying symptoms didn't entirely disappear. She hoped that medical science would soon be successful in finding answers. For the time being, she determined to restrict herself to natural remedies rather than become a "test tube" for chemical treatments.

Janette was gratefully aware at this time of God's provision for her. Had she been in almost any other occupation, one that required fixed hours or more physical demands, she might not have been able to continue. Writing was something she could do. And with the aid of a housekeeper, and a great deal of self-discipline, she felt she had some measure of control over the management of her condition.

Meanwhile, Lorne and Lavon were setting down roots in Mishawaka, Indiana, even sharing a house for a period of time. Lorne was teaching math and coaching volleyball, and Lavon taught music and periodically coached hockey. Then Lavon began working toward a master's degree in music at Indiana University, spending several summers there.

For Lorne, there was an offer from Bethel College to join their staff. He and his wife, Deb, also coached the Bethel volleyball team, and were successful at it for several years. Soon they decided to purchase a house next to the college campus. With students, family, and friends so close at hand, their home was immediately teeming with life, and Deb was busy entertaining great numbers of people.

She also put her skills in cooking and entertaining to good use when she began a project shared with Barbara Oke—compiling recipes for a family cookbook. Bethany House published *The Oke Family*

Cookbook in 1994, featuring family photos and anecdotes along with time-honored recipes passed down through the years.

Emily Marie Oke was born to Lorne and Deb, giving Janette and Edward their ninth granddaughter—not a single Oke grandson had been born. But Emily was irresistible. She was a rough-and-tumble, ready-for-anything sweetheart who quickly joined with the older cousins in whatever play they had concocted.

After a trip south to Indiana to visit with the whole family, and to celebrate Lavon's graduation, Janette and Edward returned to Calgary mulling over thoughts about a comfortable place for Janette to do her writing. Memories of tucking herself away at the farmhouse in peace and quiet to write made a special place seem a necessity again. Trying to write at home in Calgary was never without the ringing telephone and constant lure of housework and errands.

West of them in the mountain town of Canmore, they found a lovely little two-bedroom condominium with mountain views all around. It seemed perfect. Not too far from home, yet far enough to provide the necessary sense of seclusion. They decided to purchase it.

Unlike the farm, there was little upkeep to the place, and it was much more practical for this time in Janette's life. Though the writing studio wasn't nearly as "cute" as the farmhouse—no period antiques or pleasant sense of its previous occupants—after breaking it in with the next book due to the publisher, Janette decided she was pleased with the arrangement.

CHAPTER FORTY

The Farm

FOR SOME TIME, AMY'S HEALTH had been declining, and she had been audibly tiring of life at the long-term care unit at the Rimbey hospital. No one could blame her, though her children tried to cheer her with frequent visits and updates about all the family members. Then Sharon drew her into a project that she, as family "historian," had begun many years before and had continued to develop. The family history had been researched, but there were so many stories and people from the more recent generations that Sharon wanted to capture on paper for posterity. She and Amy set to work, and *Tide of the Years* was gradually compiled, edited, and then published. Pictures of family members were added and personal writings included. Many of the words were Amy's own, having been written throughout her days on the farm.

By the expected date of its release, many in the family and community had heard about the project and were anxious to congratulate the authors and acquire a copy of the book. So a book-signing party was arranged. Amy was suitably dressed and fussed over, and then guests began arriving at the Rimbey hospital. It was a gala event.

All too soon during the following summer Amy's health failed entirely, and she was taken to be with the Lord. She had touched many lives with her kindness and generosity. She had remained witty and charming, and ready to offer her words of testimony to anyone with whom she crossed paths. It was a difficult time for the entire family and brought an avalanche of decisions to be made.

The will stated that the farm property was to be equally divided among Fred and Amy's eight children. To properly accomplish this the farm would need to be sold and the funds apportioned. But the thought of giving up the homeplace, the meeting place, the foundation of so many memories, was painfully difficult to imagine. So much of life had been centered on the tiny home.

After prayer and discussion, it seemed that there might be a way to fulfill the demands of the will and yet manage to keep the home in the hands of family members. But it proved to be a difficult and time-consuming task. It would be "sold" to the family members most interested and able to buy it from all the others. Then it would be repaired and made available for all to use.

Many of the outbuildings on the farm were not salvageable, some already well on their way to collapse. Those that remained were in need of immediate attention if anything was to be saved at all. Surveying the weathered house, it was difficult to imagine the work that would be necessary to repair it.

Soon Joyce, Margie, Janette, and their spouses became heavily involved in the project. And other family members, too, helped as they were able—both in labor and in material ways. Betty contributed much in time and energy, and Jean, always a steady support, lent her hands as well. However, Jean had begun struggling again with cancer, and she was losing ground.

The farmstead was envisioned as a place for the family to claim its "roots." A place where future generations could gather and feel connected and welcome. It would serve not only as a reminder of Fred and Amy Steeves but also stand as a "living testimony" of God's provision for the family throughout the years. In a world that so often rends families apart, the team of sisters, who were now grandmothers too, sought to establish a tangible place where their families could come together—body and spirit.

The first major task was to move the creaking little house so that a solid foundation could be placed under it. It was stripped down to bare logs, both inside and out, in anticipation of the professional house movers hoisting it up and setting it aside while a proper concrete basement was constructed for it. Even this proved to be more difficult than anticipated. Dave Shaw and his work crew spent many hours crawling under the building, digging out enough room to work in, cutting out old floor logs, and putting in supports. Finally the machines were able to take over, coaxing the house slowly away from its old resting place, and the basement work could begin.

Though a full basement hadn't been part of the original home, it was felt that the additional storage would be practical. The home had rested directly on the ground, and every effort was made to keep it as close to ground level as possible when it was replaced in its original location.

Then the rebuilding could begin. Many family members pitched in for various tasks, with Joyce emerging as general contractor and her son-in-law, Berwyn Maconochie, serving as building project manager. These were not official titles, of course, but the roles were assumed nonetheless. Many hours of donated labor by those who could find the time to help saw the roof reshingled, the exterior resided, the interior walls reconstructed, doors rehung, and the wood floor re-laid. Each facet of the home required rebuilding of some kind.

The further the renovating progressed, the more interesting facts about the house emerged. From the time they moved in, the family had known something of the history of the house. It was one of the first to be built in the Hoadley/Haverigg area, and originally functioned as both a residence and the local store and post office. Opened in 1912 by John Hoggarth, the house had been changed several times, but traces of its previous use remained. For all the years that the Steeves family lived there, a letter drop remained in the front door.

During the renovating, other discoveries were made that confirmed the multipurpose origins of the building. A second entry door from the shed was uncovered that appeared to be used as the public entrance to the small post office and one-room store. Some of the family recalled a strange window through the pantry wall into the small hall of the bedroom. Piecing together the information as they worked, it seemed logical that this had been a service window—perhaps for handing out mail or speaking to customers.

The walls themselves were unusual. Roughhewn logs had been either hand cut or produced in a primitive mill. Many of the earliest settlers in the area were of Scandinavian descent, and were skilled in the use of building tools. The family presumed that the expertise displayed in the wall construction was a tribute to the hard work of these earliest residents. The logs were also without chinking, tightly fitted together instead, with one interlocking against another. Building paper was then applied directly over the flattened sides of the logs and was covered with wallpaper—sometimes several layers. It is interesting to note that through all the years of the house's "settling," there never seemed to be a problem with the paper cracking or buckling. Perhaps this was due to the fact that the floating floor had shifted, and not the walls of the structure itself. A smaller log, used for support beneath the floor, had twisted so dramatically over time that the kitchen floor had acquired marvelous hills and valleys, slants and ramp ways, perfect for rolling small cars or playing marbles.

The logs supporting the walls lay directly on the ground—yet only the very bottom ones showed signs of deterioration. Little had changed on the exterior. The small dormer window still peeked out from the large attic upstairs, and the rooms below were returned to what they had been when the family was growing up: two bedrooms, a kitchen, living room, and pantry. Of course, all indoor plumbing and kitchen cupboards were removed, sparing only the electric lights for convenience sake.

As the finishing stage approached, painting, staining, and wallpapering began in earnest until finally the house began to resemble, as closely as possible, what it had once been. Some minor changes were made. The trapdoor for the cellar was moved from the kitchen to the newly constructed shed. And the new shed was now one room, with the ceiling a bit higher than the original two parts. As much as possible, replacement materials closely matched their earlier counterparts. The home was nearly complete.

During the winter and spring of 1997–98, other additions were made to the property. First, a large garage was built to temporarily serve as a gathering room. Kitchen cupboards were placed in it, and tables for eating or playing games—there was even a foozball table donated for entertainment. It was a nice spot for the family workers to rest for a cup of tea before heading back to their physical labors. Wilf, Elmer, and Edward used it regularly as they continued to progress through the list of jobs needing to be completed, and Berwyn maintained a dizzying pace, juggling work on the house with the demands of his "regular job."

A teahouse/craft shop was added where the pump house had previously stood. Boards taken from the exterior of the original building were carefully added to the finishing work inside, and a wood-burning stove completed the ambiance. In the basement they created a Janette Oke writing museum, which displayed many of her original manuscripts, her awards, and a large aquarium filled to the brim with some of the reader mail that she had received over the years. Edward carefully built and added special display units to make the room complete.

Another building containing a kitchen, laundry, and public rest rooms, with showers, was constructed. This would be necessary whenever campers used the homesite, or the tearoom was open for customers. Finally, an expansive deck was built to connect the buildings and keep visitors out of the sticky mud of an Alberta spring.

On Mother's Day 1998, Edward took Janette out for supper to a restaurant where they had prearranged to meet Terry, Barbara, and their girls. Janette was entirely unaware of the fact that Lavon had flown to Canada with a surprise in store. He had brought Monica Galloway with him, a young woman to whom he had just proposed marriage.

Lorne and Deb's daughters had approved of Monica for some time. She had often been their baby-sitter while she attended Bethel College, and Katie and Kristie had already recommended her to "Uncle" as a good catch. After she returned from a one-year mission trip to Russia, Lavon found opportunity to spend more time with her and realized that his nieces were right. She was just the one he'd been waiting for.

The extra dinner guests came as a big shock to Janette, but an even happier surprise once she heard their announcement. The meal quickly became a party, with rollicking laughter, party hats, and a little joyous dancing (quite an unusual dinner date for the normally restrained parents).

As summer approached, the farm property was taking shape nicely, though not nearly as quickly as all had envisioned. It seemed that every task had become complicated along the way—typical of construction projects. At last, the time drew closer to the work being completed and the planned family reunion getting underway.

Just a couple of weeks before the celebration date, Laurel and her children arrived, ready to pitch in and join the workforce. They parked their camper next to Edward and Janette's, and began in earnest. Laurel took up a paintbrush, and the kids pitched in on such things as weeding the garden—that is, between bouncing on the trampoline with cousins, picking berries, building tree forts, and baking pies with Great-auntie.

There was a great deal being accomplished on the grounds, as well. In honor of Fred, who always loved his flower garden, a new one had been established with "descendants" of his original plants along with some new ones. The hummingbirds and the chickadees that he had taken such joy in feeding were once again cared for and loved. And a very special "memory garden" was created to remember family loved ones lost over the years.

Here an evergreen was planted for each of the eight family members who had already gone home to be with Jesus. Individual plaques bore their names: Fred Steeves, Amy Steeves, their infant son Kenneth, Janette's baby Brian, June's twenty-one-year-old daughter Karen, Terry's baby girl Amanda, Jean's granddaughter Angela, and Betty's infant grandson Christopher. Each one precious and dearly missed.

Mervin Steeves, Jack's son, dug the holes for the trees, and Joyce showed him where each was to be planted. As they talked, he asked her cautiously, but candidly, if they'd need to leave room for an extra one. Jean had been so ill that the family was forced to face the possibility that they might lose her in the next few weeks or even days.

"No," Joyce answered. "Not yet."

But before the date of the celebration, news came that Jean had passed away, and another tree was prepared for her. It brought a twinge to hearts, knowing how much Jean had given to her family through the years, and how much everyone had wanted her to share in the reunion at the homeplace.

Happier news soon followed. Lorne and Deb had delivered their fourth child. Finally there was an Oke grandson for Edward! The details that followed were even more unexpected. Deb had gotten up in the night and made her way to the bathroom. She became alarmed when she realized she was already in active labor, and called out for Lorne.

Immediately he dialed the prearranged baby-sitter for the girls, and then, at Deb's insistence, also placed a 9-1-1 call. The operator instructed him to have Deb lie on the bathroom floor so he could check on her progress. It was then that he discovered the head had already crowned.

He struggled for some minutes, trying to juggle the telephone, follow the instructions of the emergency operator, shoo the girls away from the scene, and calm Deb as best he could. The ambulance was on its way, but the baby had no intention of waiting. With no hands to spare, Lorne passed the telephone to Deb, and she relayed the instructions being given.

Connor Edward was born in his very own home, with his daddy serving as doctor and nurse. Lorne carefully followed each of the instructions that Deb passed along, catching his new baby in his hands and checking to be sure he was safe.

"Is he breathing?" the operator asked.

Deb affirmed that he was.

"Wrap him up," she instructed.

Lorne hastened to do this.

"How's the mother?" the woman questioned next.

Deb could only retort, "I *am* the mother."

Apparently her conversation was so controlled that the operator couldn't imagine that the woman to whom she was speaking was delivering and coaching *at the same time.* When the ambulance arrived, Connor was already cozy against his mommy.

In commemoration of the amazing event, the couple hung a framed copy of the front-page newspaper story on the wall above where the birth had occurred.

Of course, Janette breathed a heartfelt prayer of thanks that it had ended safely for all. And she joined in the laughter later when Marvin teased Lorne that he had taken his new "doctorate" education a little too literally, and suggested they name the baby "John."

Lavon and Monica arrived in time to spend a few days helping to paint the farmhouse. The weathered gray was covered over with a fresh coat of white, and the trim boasted its original dark green. At last the finishing touches were falling into place, and campers began to arrive for the reunion.

On the opening day, in July 1998, a ribbon-cutting ceremony was held to which the community was invited. Amy Loov, a local teenager who had been named after Amy Steeves, cut the ribbon. The simple ceremony included a prayer of dedication. The weekend that followed was the first of many family reunions. Over one hundred family members gathered to celebrate the occasion.

Today the little farmhouse rests contentedly, facing the road with a welcome expression. It will be maintained for many years to come. There are periodic guests, and, of course, family members drop by to check on it regularly. And the museum, tearoom, and craft shop are open during the summer.

Periodically through the year, the family descends en masse upon the property. And at Christmastime, those who live locally have a pre-Christmas family dinner. Throughout the year, any of the family who wishes a retreat can take full advantage of the site for camping. Their children can enjoy the playground equipment, the trampoline, and the playhouse.

Terry and Barbara have also returned to the Hoadley area and built their home on the adjoining wooded quarter of the Steeves' farm, overlooking its fields and farmland. Now Janette's grandchildren can share in the hopeful expectation of going to "Grandma Steeves' place" and seeing all their cousins (there is little distinction between the first cousins and the second cousins). In fact, Alex once commented, "You know that *other* grandma, Scott's grandma? She's really nice!" Even the grandmas are freely shared. There is still a heartfelt welcome for all, with many exciting activities to share, and even a Rook game at the ready for anyone who cares to pull up a chair.

The little house, the simple prairie homestead, and the family ties are still intact. The treasure of a homeplace has been preserved for the next generation. The family's goals for this have been accomplished. The heritage continues.

CHAPTER FORTY-ONE

Europe

IN THE SUMMER OF 2000, a wonderful family adventure was planned. Fred Steeves, a distant relative and professional travel tour director from Eastern Canada, had taken on the planning of a "Steeves Family Heritage Tour" to Europe—and, most notably, to the small town of Munsingen, Germany, from which Heinrich and Rachel Stief had originated. Janette became interested immediately, and forwarded the information to each of her children and their spouses. Her suggestion was that all ten adults make the trip together. The response was unanimous, and plans were put into action.

The tour would consist of two weeks in Europe aboard a bus filled with Steeves family relatives. Arrangements had been made to meet with the mayor of Munsingen, and to be shown the pertinent local sites by the town historian. In addition to this, there would also be sightseeing in other locations in Germany, Austria, and Switzerland.

The extended group left in mid-July from Halifax, Nova Scotia. Many of the Steeves family relatives were still living in the Maritime provinces, though included in the tour were members from across Canada and the United States, and from as far away as Australia. Janette, Edward, Terry, and Barbara flew ahead and were waiting in Frankfurt, Germany, for the rest of the family to arrive.

The first real stop would be in Munsingen for an official welcome by the city. Unfortunately, one of the first German words the group became familiar with was *Stau*, meaning "traffic jam." For all of its acclaimed speed, the Autobahn proved treacherously slow for the anxious tourists. Long after they were due in Munsingen, the Steeves' tour bus descended upon the town—to find that the welcoming ceremony had been cancelled. It was a truly disappointing turn of events.

But the lovely little village of Munsingen was just what they had hoped it would be. Their accommodations were in a charming bed-and-breakfast inn, the Gasthoff Herrman, whose owner-chef served marvelous gourmet meals. And immediately they felt welcomed by the townspeople.

In the evening, a service was held at the Martinskirche, the very church that the Stiefs would have attended. Janette read the Scripture, while Herbert Steves led in prayer as well as led the hymns that were sung together. Reverend Sigmund Fischer oversaw the service, and then gave a brief tour and history of the church building. Some of the family were brave enough to climb high into the bell tower for a bird's-eye view of the village.

It was an amazing thing to stand inside the ancient church and imagine the thousands of people who had stood in that very spot to pray and to worship through the hundreds of years of the church's existence. And to picture Heinrich and Rachel there was more amazing still.

Bright and early the next morning, Rolf Deigendesch, the town historian, met with them by an original fountain to introduce his wife, Heike, and his daughter who would conduct the group on a guided walking tour. With stilted English, she pointed out each site and gave a brief history of it. Through the narrow, stone-paved streets the family strolled, eyeing the well-kept buildings, amazed at the antiquity of it all. There was so much in the town that suggested medieval inhabitants, yet modern updates were blended alongside. She even pointed out the town lot where the Stief house had stood until recently when it had been demolished.

The tour ended at the museum, where they could observe a splendid collection of period pieces and be introduced to the general history of the area. Their guide had done a marvelous job of acquainting them with the hometown of Heinrich and Rachel Stief.

The days in Munsingen were far too brief to thoroughly explore the town. A family history presentation by Herb Steves, and a few more wonderful meals, and the visit to Munsingen was over. None felt they had *really* gotten to know the village. Janette was drawn to return someday when she might have more time to rest there and to properly acquaint herself with the area.

What followed was a whirlwind of sightseeing in the other locations in Germany, Austria, and Switzerland: exploring castles, taking in the splendid scenery, the ancient churches, and the breathtaking mountains. It was all very wonderful. But Janette and her family knew they were taking home with them far more than the memories of lovely sights. They were each just a little more grounded, a little more aware of their family roots. And they understood a little more of how God had guided the family so long ago, assuring them that He would continue to do so tomorrow and in all the days to come.

They had also been delighted to find that their traveling companions—many of whom they had not previously met—shared a spiritual commitment. Everyone took part in impromptu Sunday services aboard the bus, sharing in prayer, devotions, and song.

CHAPTER FORTY-TWO

Rewards of Faithfulness

AS I HAVE WRITTEN THE HISTORY of my mother, I have tried to give an overall picture, not focusing only on her life achievements, but also on how she came to be who she is. It has been my intention that her readers understand the ties that she shares with the lifestyle of her characters. Her own "story" has prompted so much of her ability to communicate not only the pioneer-type lifestyle but also the blessings, burdens, and emotions that go along with it. But there is more to Janette than this simple background. She has clearly excelled professionally, and I'd be overlooking so much if I didn't take the opportunity to share this side of her as well.

Some years ago, when she was very young, Ashley began to realize that Grandma not only wrote books but that she was also "famous." While dining out together, Ashley whispered tersely, "Grandma, I don't think those people over there know who you are. Let's tell them you're the Janette Oke who writes all those books."

After assuring her granddaughter that "those people" would probably not be interested, Mom couldn't help but be amused at the child's grappling with fame. It is a somewhat intangible idea, even for grown-ups.

In July 1992 my mother was surprised at the 15th Annual Gold Medallion Book Awards banquet by being given the Evangelical Christian Publishers Association's President's Award. It states:

In recognition of your contribution
to Christian writing
and leadership in creating Christian fiction,
and the outstanding achievement of
selling more than
TEN MILLION COPIES *of your books.*

When you began writing you set a goal:

". . . anything that happens in my
writing will be God's doing."
So much has happened, and we thank you
for your faithfulness to that goal
which has resulted in such wonderful accomplishment.

The plaque bears the names of Bruce Ryskamp, President, and Doug Ross, Executive Director, and is dated June 27, 1992.

The award came because Mom's books opened wide the Christian fiction market. She shares much credit with Carol Johnson, the Bethany House Publishers editor whose enthusiasm for Mom's first novel convinced the editorial board to publish it—this at a time when very little in fiction was being offered at Christian bookstores.

My mother has been granted many other awards as well. She received the Evangelical Christian Publishers Association's Gold Medallion Book Award for *Love's Long Journey* in 1983. In 1985 she won ECPA's Award of Merit for fiction for *Love's Unending Legacy*, and has been a finalist on six other occasions.

She has earned Gold Book Awards for selling over 500,000 copies of a single title for eight of her novels, in addition to a platinum award when *Love Comes Softly* passed one million. There have been eleven Angel Awards, and a Christian Booksellers Association Life Impact Award in 1999.

Bethel College, Mountain View Bible College, the Rocky Mountain College Alumni Association, and the city of Calgary have also honored her. And in 2000, she won the Christy Award for Best American Fiction, which she shared with coauthor T. Davis Bunn for *The Meeting Place*.

Mom has been featured in many magazines, spoken in many and varied settings, and had her books published in German, Norwegian, Dutch, Spanish, Finnish, French, Polish, Indonesian, Icelandic, Korean, Danish, and Portuguese. There's even been a musical produced of *When Calls the Heart*, with text by David Ludrum and music by Orpha Galloway.

I have always been proud of my mother. She has been to me an excellent partner for conversation (usually late into the night), an example of faithfulness, and the ultimate role model of self-discipline and hard work.

Her commonplace roles as daughter, sister, wife, mother, and grandmother are shared by thousands of women. But is she extraordinary? Of course. In the same way that all Christians are if we're willing to be everything that God intends us to be—whether or not it happens to be in the spotlight. We don't have to be a Janette Oke, a Joan of Arc, or a Billy Graham to be used of God.

I know my mother well enough to say that she takes no glory for her writing. In fact, she is almost embarrassed by "the fuss" made over her. When she showed me a beautiful plaque that was given to her, she sighed at how inadequate she felt for the honor.

I treasure her even more because she has come from "common folk" and was not branded throughout her life as "extraordinary." Talent does not make a great person. It is a gift—a responsibility—that God gives us, whether in writing or music or organization or hospitality or instruction—and the list goes on and on. The only way to greatness is complete surrender to the God who wants our devotion—this I have learned from my mother.

It's a paradox that the first step to God's type of "success" is to give up, and to realize that we on our own cannot accomplish anything that lasts through time. But it is not so incredible when we realize that our God accomplished one of His greatest works when He made Jesus vulnerable and helpless, an infant born to a poor family.

God uses best what He can use *completely*—no matter what the building material is.

Acknowledgments

THERE ARE SEVERAL SOURCES that have been used in the writing of this book. First of all, my mother has spent many hours putting her memories down on paper, and I know that this was at times enjoyable; at others, very difficult. It was her willingness to open up her heart and share what is inside that has allowed this book to be written.

Sharon Fehr, my mother's youngest sister, has spent many hours researching the family tree and compiling stories of past events in the family history. I have used as a reference much of what she has written, and have also appreciated her reading through the manuscript to check for accuracy.

Special mention needs to be made of the foresight of my grandmother Mabelle Oke who faithfully saved my mother's letters through the years and returned them to her just in time for me to use in writing this book. These letters have been a wonderful and cherished gift.

There were also several other family members who read through the manuscript for accuracy. I would like to thank Grandma Steeves (Amy) and those with her who helped to ensure a credible account of my mother's childhood.

Samphire Greens, by Esther Wright Clark, was written in 1961 after a great deal of work on its author's part compiling a much broader history of the Steeves family.